NARCISSISTIC ABUSE RECOVERY POWERPACK

---

3 Manuscripts

Fundamental Strategies for Handling Emotional Abuse and Toxic Relationships

---

PRISCILLA POSEY

Table of Contents

Part I: Dealing with a Narcissist

Understanding and Engaging the Narcissist in Your Life 1

    Introduction 3

  Section 1: The Narcissistic Mind 7

    Chapter 1: Narcissistic Personality Disorder 9

    Chapter 2: Everyday Narcissism 14

    Chapter 3: Secret Feelings 19

    Chapter 4: The Perfectionism Problem 23

  Section 2: Engaging the Narcissist 27

    Chapter 5: Therapeutic Approaches 29

    Chapter 6: Assessment & Identification 36

    Chapter 7: The Narcissist's Awareness 44

    Chapter 8: Maintaining Yourself 48

    Chapter 9: Different Contexts 53

  Section 3: Working with Others outside the Circle 59

    Chapter 10: Family and Triggers 61

    Chapter 11: Best Friends & Platonic Loves 64

    Chapter 12: Kids Involved 67

  Section 4: Bonus Chapters 73

    Chapter 13: Helpful Mobile Apps to Make Dealing with a Narcissist Bearable 75

    Chapter 14: 25 Helpful Affirmations for Dealing with a Narcissist 78

Conclusion 89

References, Resources, and Helpful Links 91

Part II: Recovering from Narcissistic Abuse

How to Heal from Toxic Relationships and Emotional Abuse **93**

Preface 95

Chapter 1: What is Narcissistic Personality Disorder? 99

Chapter 2: The Surprising Impact Narcissistic Abuse Has on Your Brain and
Reversing the Damage 109

Chapter 3: Coping With Narcissistic Abuse 123

Chapter 4: Common Questions Asked by People Recovering from Narcissistic Abuse 135

Chapter 5: Getting Back on Track with Trust 147

Chapter 6: Ultimate Strategies to Overcome Narcissistic Abuse 152

Chapter 7: Indications that you are Recovering from Narcissistic Trauma and Abuse 170

Conclusion 175

References 176

Part III: Gaslighting

How to Classify, Counter, and Conquer the Covert Control of Others **181**

Introduction 183

Chapter 1: Understanding the Ins and Outs of Gaslighting 190

Chapter 2: Illusion vs. Reality 198

Chapter 3: Manipulation Where it is Least Expected 211

Chapter 4: They're Not All the Same 220

Chapter 5: Victim vs. Manipulator 229

Chapter 6: Standing Up For Yourself 238

Chapter 7: Path to Recovery 252

Conclusion 263

Resources 266

PART I

DEALING WITH A NARCISSIST

Understanding and Engaging the Narcissist in Your Life

PRISCILLA POSEY

INTRODUCTION

I was just 19 when I had my first encounter with a narcissist. He was charming and handsome, and his smile alone could light up the entire room. When we locked eyes, it was like we had an instant connection. Despite meeting at a party in college, we spent the entire night outside, just talking with one another. We had similar hobbies, enjoyed the same movies, and we even both shared a love for the taco stand just off campus that most people never bothered giving the time of day.

I told him all about how I had deliberately chosen a college far away from home to escape from my parents who were far too overbearing for my taste, discussed my hopes and dreams for the future, and he told me a bit about himself as well. We immediately kicked off what I thought would be a lifelong friendship. Within two weeks, we were exclusively dating. After four months, he proposed and I said yes and moved in with him. One year later, we were married, and just two months later, I was pregnant with my daughter at the young age of 20.

Once the rings were on our fingers, his personality shifted completely, something I now understand as him finding the persona he used to attract me was no longer necessary. My husband, who I loved deeply, began to grow distant. He would criticize everything. Nothing I did was as good as him. If I scored less than 100% in a class, he would tell me I wasn't smart enough to be going to college, and it was a waste of money to keep paying for my tuition when I would be a stay at home parent anyway, something he decided with no input from me. If dinner wasn't perfect, he would throw it all in the garbage and order a pizza, but if he burnt something, I was not allowed to say a word about

3

it without enraging him. If his clothes were not perfectly ironed for work when he got up in the morning, he would wake me up and insist I do it for him because it was my job, even if that woke our daughter in the process. If I tried to protest at all, he would remind me that my job was to maintain our home, care for our daughter, and get perfect scores in the class. Anything less than that was absolutely unacceptable.

I was convinced I had to do what he asked. After all, he went to work for us, so his expectations weren't unreasonable. Of course, it would fall on me to take care of the home and our daughter. And it made sense that I had to score as highly as possible because I wanted the best bang for my tuition. He only wanted what was best for me because he loved me, so he held me to a higher standard than other people. That made sense to me.

Over time, his criticisms of me became more direct. He would call me fat if I ate something he didn't approve of, or tell me to change my clothes or makeup if he thought my shirt was too low-cut or my makeup was too provocative. If I protested, he accused me of cheating. Eventually, it got to the point where I felt like I could do nothing without running it by him first and confirming everything was to his impossible standards, and even that was not good enough. I couldn't do it anymore, and once I came to that revelation, I suddenly felt a little freer.

When I finally began to open up to others, one of my friends suggested I look into narcissism. Imagine my surprise as I read through the criteria for being diagnosed with narcissistic personality disorder and discovering that my husband met most of them. That began the start of a new journey, and I began delving into any material I could find on the subject. The more I read, the more it all made sense. Then began my journey of disentangling myself from my ex. I had to escape his grasp one claw at a time to disengage from the relationship, and I have never been happier now that I am free. My narcissistic ex was downright toxic, but yours may not be. You may be able to salvage your relationship with some of the techniques provided in this book if you think it is worthwhile.

I eventually managed to more or less recover from my period with my narcissistic ex, and now it is time to pass on my wisdom to those trying to escape or heal from their own narcissistic abuse. This book is my comprehensive guide to what narcissistic minds are, how to best engage a narcissist, how to interact with others in regards to supporting you in your journey, and some bonus chapters that I found might provide some useful content. Hopefully, you will find this book useful as you begin your journey to understanding the narcissistic mind, and you will find valuable insight into why narcissists do what they do.

WAIT!!!

READ THIS BEFORE GOING ANY FURTHER!

How would you like to get your next eBook **FREE** and get new books for **FREE** too before they are publicly released?

Join our Self Empowerment Team today and receive your next (and future) books for **FREE**! Signing up is easy and completely free!!

Check out this page for more info!

www.SelfEmpowermentTeam.com/SignUp

As A Token
of My Gratitude...

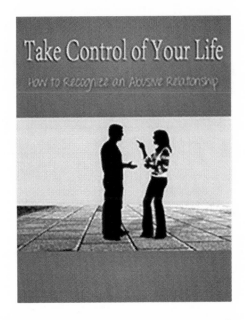

I'd like to offer you this amazing resource which my clients pay for. It is a report I written when I first began my journey.

Click on the picture above or navigate to the website below to join my exclusive email list. Upon joining, you will receive this incredible report on how to recognize an abusive relationship.

If you ask most people on the street what an abusive relationship is, chances are you'd get a description of physical abuse. And yes, that is most certainly an abusive relationship. However, abuse comes in many forms. The actual meaning of abuse is when someone exerts control over another person.

Find out more about recognizing an abusive relationship and learn how to take control over your life by clicking on the book above or by going to this link:

http://bit.ly/RecognizeAbusiveRelationship

SECTION 1

The Narcissistic Mind

CHAPTER 1

Narcissistic Personality Disorder

Narcissistic personality disorder: It sounds as intimidating as it is. This disorder is primarily characterized by grandiose or self-important behavior, a constant desire for attention, and a lack of empathy. This is behavior that is common and expected in children, but narcissists are adults that never outgrew this childish way of thinking. However, being diagnosed with narcissistic personality disorder (NPD) requires more than a childish way of thinking. The fifth edition of the Diagnostic and Statistical Manual of Mental Disorders (DSM-5) has identified nine specific behavioral patterns or traits that are relevant to NPD. If a person has at least five of the nine specified behaviors in a wide range of situations or circumstances, they qualify for a diagnosis. People with less than five are not diagnosed with NPD, but the narcissistic tendencies can still be particularly toxic or harmful for those the person targets.

A grandiose sense of self-importance

Perhaps one of the most recognizable traits of those with NPD is the grandiosity or superiority complexes narcissists possess. The narcissist believes that he is the most important person in the world, and is better than those around him. As far as he is concerned, he never has to prove this superiority; it just *is*. He automatically is more important than you just by virtue of being him. He may never have earned it, and you may actually have proven yourself to be the better athlete, employee, artist, or anything else, but he will absolutely assert that he is more important.

Along with this belief of superiority, grandiosity comes with a certain level of infallibility as well. The narcissist believes he cannot be at fault for anything, or that he is invincible. Even when his behavior is clearly in the wrong to everyone looking in at the situation, he refuses to admit or believe that he could be the problem. It always lies with someone else.

This behavior can be as seemingly innocent as denying blame in an argument, citing the other person's behavior as the real cause for everything, or as delusional as insisting that some outside source, such as a big patch of ice was the real reason he ran into a building and not the fact that he had chosen to have a few drinks before leaving. He insists that the problem was not with him and his choices or behaviors, but rather with the world around him or the people he interacted with.

A preoccupation with fantasies of unlimited success, power, brilliance, beauty, or love

Because the narcissist believes she is superior, she believes she is entitled to perfection, riches, or power and obsesses over these ideals. She dreams of a grand life, filled with fortune, beauty, the perfect romantic partner, and anything else she ever could desire. Despite her expectations being impossible for the average person, she wholeheartedly fixates on them. Anything that falls short of her expectations will either face her wrath or be discarded while she continues her conquest.

Unfortunately for the narcissist, nothing in this world is as perfect as she believes, and her grandiose beliefs and fantasies are perpetually challenged and proven false. Ultimately, the narcissist never feels satisfied, despite her best effort to attain everything she believes she deserves simply by virtue of being a perfect person.

This preoccupation with having something better at all times is why, in relationships, narcissists often begin demanding more and more from their partners, and nothing you ever do is good enough for them. They want more from you than you will ever be able to provide, and once you acknowledge that desire they possess is for an impossible standard, the weight of trying to be good enough for them begins to diminish.

A belief of uniqueness

The idea that he is superior in all ways also lends itself to many narcissists believing they are unique or special. This uniqueness comes with the added burden of being misunderstood by all the so-called commoners that surround him. His uniqueness comes with a higher social status than the people around him have attained, and those who have not reached his higher status cannot possibly understand how he thinks or why he does what he does.

To the narcissist, this uniqueness is the perfect excuse to disregard other people's dissent. Since those around him disagree, they are clearly not the same status as him, and therefore their opinions are unimportant. He has no reason to pay attention to the opinions of the uneducated. After all, a neurosurgeon would never take advice from a burger flipper on how to perform a surgery; the burger flipper almost definitely does not have years and years of experience in the medical field, and therefore, his opinion on a technique would be irrelevant and likely misguided.

Unwilling to admit mediocrity, the narcissist exhibiting this behavior oftentimes tells those around him that they do not know what they are talking about, or they do not understand genius. He likely refuses to associate with certain people or brands, worried about how it would reflect on him if he were ever caught inside a commoner's store like Walmart.

The narcissist believes his specialness qualifies him to be an expert in everything, and also as a weapon when he needs to be a victim. No one else has it as bad as he does, and if they do, then they obviously do not have the same problems he does for some other reason. If someone else's mother has passed away, the narcissist is quick to chime in that his entire family died in a car crash when he was young. If someone else is struggling with schoolwork, he had it worse because he had to work full time and study, and while he is doing this, he is attending a much more rigorous university. The uniqueness or specialness is not limited to superiority; the narcissist is just as quick to be the ultimate victim in the story as he is to be the ultimate protagonist protected by the shield of plot armor if that will feed his ego.

A need for excessive or constant admiration

Narcissists, in a sense, are addicted to admiration, or at the very least, attention. True to addict behavior, the narcissist often does anything to draw attention her way. If she can, she often prefers to get it positively, through seeking careers that lend themselves to attention and public spotlight, or are powerful, such as doctors, politicians, police officers, or teachers. Each of these offers a steady stream of *narcissistic supply*, which is the attention narcissists crave.

In the event that working for narcissistic supply is too difficult or impossible, narcissists will just as quickly turn to the victim role in order to garner sympathy. They will suddenly have a gravely ill family member, or may even claim to be terminally ill themselves, or they will create a situation that makes them vulnerable so others will rescue them, such as drinking too much, or even resorting to causing an injury that is not quite bad enough to be serious, but is enough to cause others to stop and help them.

The narcissist's insatiable craving for attention and admiration drives them to suddenly announce their own engagement at their best friend's bridal shower, or worse, their wedding reception. The attention must always somehow shift back to the narcissist any time it is not on her.

A sense of entitlement

Along with his delusion of grandeur, the narcissist believes that he deserves whatever he wants specifically because he wants it. Rather than having to earn affection, attention, money, power, or anything else in his life, he expects it to be handed to him on a silver platter. While the average person must earn respect, power, and money, and may feel entitled to them after going through the effort of earning them, the narcissist prefers to skip the earning stage. He demands it all with none of the effort.

For example, a narcissist may feel entitled to a perfect score on an exam even though he barely studied. When he gets his test results that reflect his effort accordingly, he may painstakingly go through and challenge every point his professor made, attempting to justify why his wrong answer could technically be right. Likewise, a boss may expect respect from his employees, even though he has done nothing to earn it other than wearing the title of boss. He feels entitled to it, even though he may actually treat his employees like garbage.

Exploitative or manipulative behavior

As people with unrealistic goals and expectations, it should be unsurprising that narcissists are also master manipulators. Even the person they present to everyone around them is a lie created through manipulative techniques such as mirroring and projecting. On top of lying about who they are at a fundamental level, narcissists also manipulate those around them to give them what they want, even if that manipulation comes at a serious cost. They often hide this manipulative behavior behind a veil of plausible deniability, enabling them to deny any time they are called out for manipulating.

Oftentimes, the narcissist will deny any claim of fault, such as denying he is cheating on his partner when he really is carrying on an affair. Immediately after, he attacks his partner, claiming that she is delusional and insecure because of previous relationship experience, and immediately after, reversing the claim, accusing her of being the one cheating and projecting onto him. This manipulative behavior puts his partner on the defensive, derailing her accusation and shifting the focus from his behavior to hers, and she now feels that the onus is on her to prove she is innocent.

A lack of empathy

Lacking empathy makes manipulating others much easier, so it is no surprise that a manipulative individual may also lack the capacity for empathy. Empathy has a key point in the survival of humanity; without being able to empathize, we would struggle to make sure our social group is cared for because we would have little reason or motivation to care about their wellbeing. Empathy helps us not only care for those around us but also shows us when not to cross boundaries and when to give each other space to defuse conflicts.

Without this empathetic connection to others, the narcissist does not care about their feelings. He understands how they feel on a superficial level, but seeing someone in pain does not make him feel bad or sympathetic for that person. Likewise, seeing the teenage cashier break down into tears at the store after he berates her does not make him feel guilt that cues him to stop. Instead, he sees an opportunity to feel powerful and in control of the situation, which feeds his ego, and he continues goading her.

Envious of others, or expectant that others are envious of him or her

Since the narcissist feels entitled to anything she desires, and also has an obsession with perfection, whenever she sees someone that has what she wants but does not have, she cannot help but feel envious. Someone who was chosen for a promotion she wanted will not be congratulated, and may even find their accomplishment minimized by the narcissist instead. She may even manage to spin the minimizing in such a way that she instead convinces herself that the other person should be envious of her instead. After all, that promotion came with such a small boost in pay but had so many more responsibilities. She convinces herself that she would have turned down the promotion if it had been offered to her because it was not the right fit at all.

Presents as arrogant or haughty

The last of the nine traits that present in NPD is a haughty or arrogant disposition. Since the narcissist believes he is superior, he often acts as such with little regard for the feelings of others. Those who are not his superior or equal are less than him and therefore do not deserve basic respect or human decency. After all, they are only there to serve him if they are beneath him, and it is not serving him if he is busy pandering to their delicate feelings. If they wanted to be treated better, he believes, they should have done more with themselves than work a job in a service profession.

The saying that you can tell a lot about a person by how he treats the waiter on a date rings true here; the narcissist will likely jump at the opportunity to belittle or upset the waiters, and then use the fact that the waiters are upset, to begin with, to negotiate some sort of discount or special treatment from management. If the waiter dares to say anything in defense of himself, the narcissist may snap back that he is paying the waiter's bills by virtue of being in the restaurant, and the waiter needs to learn his place and remember that the customer is always right.

CHAPTER 2

Everyday Narcissism

Oftentimes when people realize they are facing a narcissist, they feel the need to ask themselves why. Why do narcissists behave the way they do? What do they gain by doing so? Do they choose to be this way? The short answer is not usually: Narcissism as we know it is a personality disorder. It is caused by a series of disordered thoughts and irrational behaviors that affect the narcissist's ability to understand the world around her. Answering why the narcissist behaves the way she does requires a much longer answer, but at its simplest, there are three common reasons for narcissists to behave narcissistically: As a coping mechanism, as a reaction to a perceived threat, and due to cognitive distortions born from the previous two reasons.

Narcissism as a Coping Mechanism

Nobody likes to feel like they lack control over a situation. Being at the mercy of someone else, fate, or strangers with no connections to you is terrifying, even for those of us without distorted thinking or personality disorders. For the narcissist, that lack of control is absolutely devastating; he thrives on being in control and making sure his expectations are adhered to and meet his standards. This fear is so overwhelming that he feels the need to develop methods to avoid it at all costs. He needs to have control over himself or his situation, or he risks spiraling into a depression of negative feelings.

Oftentimes, for the narcissist, this fear of lack of control over his situation is due to some sort of trauma or neglect during childhood. He lacked the control to protect himself as a child, so he now seeks to seize control of everything within his reach, grasping at any opportunities to influence what happens around him in a sort of coping mechanism. It is his way to ensure that he is never at the mercy of someone else's control in order to protect himself. In his mind, by always being in control, no one is ever in a position to hurt him. After all, a position of power is one of the most dangerous to those beneath him.

The trauma we face as children never gets processed the way we process trauma as adults; children lack the skills we learn through growing up with someone there to help guide us through navigating through trauma and stress, and oftentimes, the trauma is repressed until later, when it eventually exhibits in different ways. The abused child may grow up to be fearful of all conflict, even if he does not remember the actual abuse. The sounds of even a polite argument could send him into a panic if that was a trigger from childhood. For the narcissist, the neglect or abuse was likely emotional; his caregivers were likely unavailable when he needed them, or may have belittled everything he did and made him feel unworthy and guilty about not being good enough. Because of this, he develops a fear of criticism and powerlessness at an early age. Despite his best efforts, he felt like he was never good enough to get his parents' attention and affection, and because of this, he quickly began to believe that he was not good enough. After all, if he were, then his parents would have been much more interested in interacting with him. Regardless of whether the abuse was through angry words spewed at him, degrading him and wearing away his self-esteem or through ignoring his emotional needs and being an absent parent, the result is the same: A child who has deeply internalized that he is not good enough and has built his entire personality and perceptions of the world atop that assumption. Just as a skyscraper built on a crooked, cracked foundation will never support the weight of the whole building, the narcissist's personality's foundation is incapable of bearing the weight of normal, day-to-day adult stressors

Over time, the child's mindset shifts to one more reminiscent of a narcissist than is typically expected of a child; he may become hyper-focused on perfection, or tell himself that he is better than everyone else as a way to cope with feeling inadequate. By maintaining a façade of perfection, he tries to avoid any sort of backlash. He feels as though he cannot be criticized if he manages to maintain a perfect image, protecting his fragile ego from further damage. The child grows up and never manages to get past that way of thinking. He is still obsessed with perfection or convincing himself that he is special in some way, shape, or form, except now he is an adult, and it is no longer within normal behavior standards. His coping mechanisms to deal with a lack of control are not considered normal behavior, and those around him may judge him harshly if they catch him in the act of such childish behavior, something he also desperately fears. Humiliation and degradation are the worst pain someone can inflict upon him, and because of this, he oftentimes hides his behaviors as best as he can. Ultimately, however, these behaviors are coping mechanisms, and under significant pressure or feeling as if he is spiraling out of control, he may snap and lash out, or even intentionally hurt whoever he deemed the cause of his powerlessness. By hurting the one without power, he has, in his own distorted way, asserted that he is, in fact, in control over the person who sought to steal his power. After all, if he were not in control, at least at some superficial level, he would not have been able to cause the person pain. Even only having power over someone's pain is enough for him to feel justified in his control over the situation, despite the cost of potentially ruining a relationship or severing a connection with someone who may have been useful to the narcissist in the future.

Narcissism as a Reaction to a Threat

The lack of control the narcissist has over the situation and world around her, being the narcissist's biggest fear, means that she is constantly in a state of reacting. Every time any control is perceived to be out of her hands is seen as a threat that needs to be neutralized. The narcissist seeks to gain that control back by any means necessary, even if that involves manipulation, coercion, or even abuse. Narcissists will rely on whatever tactics they have in their toolbox to get their control, even if it is morally wrong or causes pain. The narcissist does not empathize with others and has no reason to not manipulate her way into power if that is how she gets what she wants and protects her fragile ego from harm.

For some, this will be as simple as manipulating the situation and becoming the faultless victim. They make it so nothing negative is their own fault, which allows them to avoid whatever control they cannot have from hurting them. People will not usually harass or demean the victim, so if she cannot outwardly be in control and powerful, she will skillfully manipulate the situation. This is a sort of power in and of itself; even though she takes the role of the powerless, blameless victim, she is still in control by virtue of being able to skew the perceptions of everyone around her.

Sometimes, the narcissist seeks to gain outward control and puts on a façade of importance, confidence, and intelligence that allows her to gain a legitimate following. People naturally defer to the charismatic, intelligent leader that knows exactly what to do and always seems to present with an air of perfection. By creating this persona, the narcissist gains power in careers or communities, earning higher positions that fulfill her need for control and power. She cannot feel threatened when she is in a position of power, neutralizing the threats of powerlessness. By earning respect in the community, she is automatically regarded with the respect she desires, and by having manipulated herself to that position in the first place, she satisfies her desire for control.

Sometimes, narcissists use abusive, coercive tactics to exert control. They browbeat those around them into giving them whatever they want. They will demean, belittle, and manipulate if that is what it takes to get their control. They are so afraid of losing their position they perceive to be invulnerable that they will hurt those around them to maintain it. They are able to do this by first building rapport with another person and then systematically tearing them down, little by little until they leave behind someone so utterly broken and defeated that they are easily controlled. The narcissist's victim, in this case, is oftentimes someone close to her, either a romantic partner or a family member, and she will completely convince her victim that he or she is incapable of anything without her power or influence. Oftentimes, the threat perceived from family members is the threat that they will leave and therefore control the pace of the relationship. The narcissist cannot accept that someone other than she would be able to make decisions on if or when the relationship ends or what pace it will take and she seeks to destroy the other person's ability or desire to leave. This does not necessarily mean that she wants to maintain the relationship, however; she will have zero qualms overthrowing her victim to the side and never contacting him or her again if that is what she desires to do.

For the narcissist, so long as she perceives she is in control and unchallenged, she will likely be relatively harmless. However, challenging that control can have explosive results. Just as she reacted strongly to the perception of a threat of powerlessness, she will react strongly to any threat of her claim of power. She will feel like any criticism must immediately be crushed in order to discourage anyone from attempting it again, and will become belligerent if she feels that is the only way to protect herself. A challenged narcissist can be dangerous, as they will lash out with every ounce of vitriol in their body in order to beat everyone back into line and complacency, leaving her sitting atop her throne of manipulation rather than forcing her to face her shattered sense of self head-on.

Narcissistic Distortions

The lies that the narcissist tries to perpetuate are his own deeply-held beliefs. In order to cope with the traumas of childhood, he has literally rewritten the narrative on his life in order to benefit himself. The irony of the narcissist is that he is so afraid of losing control and exposure that he has even manipulated himself into believing the lies he spins. He has inadvertently given over control out of fear of acknowledging his lack of power by clouding his own judgment to the point that he is no longer able to see the world for what it is. He is so preoccupied with attempting to protect himself that he has lied to even himself about what has happened to him.

The narcissist has convinced himself wholeheartedly that the persona he projects and his revisionist history are accurate, which is part of the reason he gets so defensive when it is challenged. To challenge his control, his actions, or his legitimacy is to challenge his fragilely constructed persona and his deeply held beliefs of what is happening and what has happened in the past. Like a glass sculpture, it will only take one or two major cracks before the entire persona comes crashing down.

Just how you may have beliefs that you are devout about believing and learning that that belief was fault would leave you devastated, the narcissist would be utterly destroyed if he felt as if those beliefs were proven wrong. Those are fundamental parts of the personality he has tried to piece together with all of the broken shards of his ego, and cracking that would mean that he has to admit that he himself is a lie. The person he thought he was is a lie. That is a devastating realization to grapple with for those of us with healthy coping mechanisms. For the narcissist who lacks these healthy ways to deal with stress, it is far too excruciating to even acknowledge, so he lives firmly in denial. Rather than dealing with the lies he is weaving and correcting them while they are still small, he instead sits in the middle, continuing to weave the lies to sustain the original ones as he grows more and more entangled, insisting everything is fine. Eventually, all that remains is a knotted mess in the center of the web, unrecognizable as what the narcissist may have become, given a chance. The truth becomes so deeply buried that the narcissist would have no way to discover it without completely and utterly destroying the web that he has created and everything that has been built atop of it. This could be careers, marriages, wealth, and connections that he has only gotten out of his pretense of being the persona he created.

Instead of doing the morally right thing and being truthful, he continues to build delusions and narratives that support his own perception of the truth. He becomes so obsessed with justifying his own delusions to others that he sees no other option but to believe them. The truth is so convoluted and entangled at that point that it is impossible to see, so there is no going back. It is easier to move forward than it is to try to disentangle everything. Eventually, what is left is a persona built with lie upon lie on a fragile, cracking foundation. The narcissist does what he can to defend this distorted personality he has created, and it often means relying on narcissistic behavior to do so. He has to lie and manipulate others, so they believe his perspective. He has to control others, so he does not risk them going out of their way to prove him wrong and send the entire thing shattering. He has to project onto others as a distorted way of coping with his own complicated feelings of self-loathing and broken self-esteem. He feels the need to hurt others to feel as if he has gained control of a situation he deemed as spiraling out of control.

Each of these narcissistic behaviors is done in order to protect the persona he created at the center of it all and prevent it from shattering and leaving the real him standing in the middle of the wreckage, exposed for all to see. All of it is to protect that fragile self he has invented to shield himself from emotional harm as a child. The delusional self he created as a child feels like the only thing between himself and the constant threats of the outside world, and the only thing holding that persona together is an ever-growing web of lies and manipulations he spins. Ultimately, his intense drive for self-preservation is more powerful than his drive for anything else, so he will say anything necessary to maintain his delusions.

CHAPTER 3

Secret Feelings

Despite how narcissists tend to present themselves, full of charisma and confidence, on the inside is typically a broken, wounded individual with no true sense of self. The narcissist never had the chance to develop a normal, healthy. While some narcissists' lack of sense of self is turned into a true, deeply held belief of superiority, many others are much more vulnerable. This is even a recognized kind of narcissism: Vulnerable narcissism, in which the narcissist feels inadequate and insecure and overcompensates with the grandiosity, tendency to manipulate, and creating a persona of the perfect victim that is never to blame for anything. These narcissists are overwhelmed with all sorts of secret feelings they aim to hide from public view at all costs, though their mask will fall under extreme stress or emotion.

Identity Crisis

Insecurity and vulnerability are at the foundation of many narcissists. Whether due to abuse during childhood or some other trauma, the narcissist has internalized that insecurity. Where most people have a voice that regulates their sense of self-worth, telling them that they are good enough and keeping them comfortable in their own skin, the narcissist hears a voice telling her she is inadequate. Nothing she ever does is good enough for her, and she constantly hears her inner voice putting her down. She constantly feels insecure in her own skin and humiliated that she feels the way she does. The idea that other people can see how insecure she really is horrifies the narcissist because she feels as if that admission of insecurity is an admission of weakness and that the voices that shaped her own poor sense of self-worth were correct. Other people acknowledging her insecurity makes her vulnerable, as that would be the easiest target to further humiliate and degrade her the first time she makes a mistake.

That inner voice we all hear is created by our parents or primary caregivers; the way our caregivers speak to us becomes the way we speak to ourselves. When our caregivers are overly critical, harsh, or cruel, their disapproval and loathing become internalized. We believe their word because, as children, we are hardwired to defer to our caregivers. We instinctively trust their judgments as correct because it is their jobs to help us learn to navigate through the world. The parent's role in a child's life is to teach the child how to be successful, well-adjusted, and all the skills he or she will need in order to cope with all of the turmoil that comes with being an adult. Some parents fail miserably, sometimes due to their own abuse or just through lacking the empathy and parental instincts required to be a successful parent. When parents constantly criticize or put down their child, their words become the child's frame for seeing the world around her.

When the child hears nothing but negativity and sees the world in that negative mindset, her entire way of thinking changes. She becomes insecure about everything, constantly feeling incompetent and vulnerable. Her entire sense of self is shameful, negative, and self-loathing. With that loathing sense of self, she feels the need to overcompensate, and her behaviors become standoffish. She creates a persona focused on herself, pretending to be perfect, faultless, and likable in order to combat these feelings of worthlessness. By presenting as confident and perfect, and convincing others that this is who she is, she is able to protect herself from the scathing words she has come to expect from herself and others. She is even able to sometimes convince herself that she is as confident and fantastic as she presents to those around her, though she frequently swings right back to feeling insecure and vulnerable a short time later. Living in this nearly permanent state of insecurity leaves the narcissist constantly feeling defensive and on edge, unable to relax for fear of someone around her taking advantage of her vulnerability and using it to climb the social hierarchy.

Issues with Intimacy

The intense levels of shame these narcissists feel act as deterrents from any real intimacy or relationships. Intimacy requires vulnerability that the narcissist seeks to avoid at all costs, and therefore, it is avoided. The narcissist refuses to become vulnerable others, seeking instead to protect her fragile ego from harm. She recognizes that being vulnerable means risking her ego being harmed, and that is not a risk she is willing to take. Vulnerability requires trust, and the narcissist will not trust anyone but herself. She knows that as soon as she makes herself vulnerable, she risks having the shame and self-loathing she feels confirmed and validated by the person she emotionally exposed herself to, and she refuses to risk that. Her fragile ego would not be able to take any sort of criticism from someone she trusted, so instead, she decides to avoid trusting anyone at all.

Despite the fact that narcissists are emotionally stunted, they are typically quite intelligent and do recognize that there is a relationship between trust and vulnerability. Recognizing that trust and vulnerability are required for an intimate relationship, the narcissist instead decides not to commit. The relationship does not seem worthwhile enough, and the promise of intimacy is not enough for the narcissist to intentionally render herself vulnerable to someone else. Remember, her narcissistic behaviors are a coping mechanism to make herself invulnerable to harm; it would be counterproductive to go out of her way to become vulnerable, regardless of the reason. At the root of refusing to become vulnerable is the shame and self-loathing that underlies all of her behaviors. She fears being humiliated, berated, or harmed again, and that fear makes a connection with others quite difficult. True intimacy is never achieved with the narcissist because of her narcissistic nature's existence as a coping mechanism, although she will pretend and go through the motions of being in a relationship if she sees the benefit of doing so. It is important to remember, though, that she will never truly trust her partner and will never really make herself emotionally available or exposed.

Self-Direction and Deflection

While nobody enjoys being humiliated or embarrassed, narcissists fear humiliation more than anything else. Because narcissists already have impossible standards set for themselves and they already see themselves as broken and fragile, to have someone else make them feel that way feels like salt in the wound. Knowing how fragile they really are and fearing that fragility being exposed, narcissists seek to avoid humiliation at all costs.

Because the narcissist fears humiliation, she instead resorts to humiliating others around her. Rather than attempt to address any humiliation on herself, she prefers to insult others, shifting negative attention away from her in ways that leave her blameless, but leave someone else being humiliated. This is another misguided coping mechanism; the narcissist feels too fragile, too self-conscious, and too vulnerable to survive humiliation, so she seeks to instead deflect it to others, even if they were just as undeserving and innocent as the narcissist. This also serves to allow the narcissist to look better in comparison, providing an ego boost where there could have potentially been ego injury.

The narcissist may point out a mistake someone else made, even if it was previously undetected, or even make up a mistake and blame it on someone else in order to keep potential negative attention away from her, even if there was little chance of negative attention being on her in the first place. Oftentimes, she fears humiliation from imagined sources, and that is enough to send her on the defense. The easiest defense to make while maintaining an image of innocence is to force others to be defensive as well. After all, when everyone is behaving defensively, no one is lashing out, and she remains unchallenged.

Undeserving of Empathy

One of the basic tenets of narcissism is the lack of, or diminished capacity for, feeling empathy. This lack of empathy makes it difficult for the narcissist to imagine feeling deserving of empathy. Since empathy is almost foreign to the narcissist after a childhood of never having it emulated for her, she does not consider herself worthy of it, and if she is not worthy, others must not be worthy either. This leaves her thinking the worst of those around her at all times, rather than seeing that many humans are kindhearted and will go out of their way to help due to their empathetic natures. Despite knowing the concept of empathy, it remains utterly foreign to her, and unless she is pretending for a good cause, it will never cross her mind to legitimately be empathetic with someone. Likewise, it would never cross her mind that anyone else would ever treat her with empathy, as even her parents, the two people in the world who are biologically supposed to treat her with empathy and respect, never gave her that courtesy. She must be undeserving if even her parents could not manage to muster up enough care about her to treat her as a human with feelings that deserve to be recognized.

Because of this belief of being unworthy of empathy or kindness, the narcissist views everything as suspicious. Nothing is to be trusted, and every action has an ulterior motive simply because the narcissist always has an ulterior motive. She refuses to see the best in others, and cannot recognize that sometimes people do something out of the kindness of their hearts to selflessly help others because the concept of selflessness is entirely foreign to her. Those behaviors were not modeled for her when they mattered, and she no longer considers them options.

This lack of deserving empathy paired with feelings of worthlessness creates even more feelings of inferiority, as the narcissist does not believe that making a mistake will be treated gracefully or kindly. She is certain that making a mistake is one of the worst-case scenarios, and that it will reflect much worse on her than it actually will. Because of that, she will go to great lengths to hide any mistakes she may make, or push the blame away from herself, using any possible plausible deniability, no matter how realistic or ridiculous her excuse sounds.

Since she is unworthy of that kindness and believes that others will treat her poorly, it becomes easier for her to treat others unkindly instead of empathetically. It is a negative cycle of believing others will treat her poorly because she is unworthy, and therefore, she will treat others that way preemptively to avoid being in a situation of vulnerability. She falls into this habit in order to protect herself and avoid from exerting any energy she could potentially put to better use caring for herself. Since others will not treat her with kindness or help her meet her needs without prompting, she feels driven to force the point and manipulate those around her to get what she feels like she needs or deserves.

CHAPTER 4

The Perfectionism Problem

Narcissists are known perfectionists. They have impossible standards, both for themselves and for others around them. Of course, this creates plenty of opportunities for problems to arise. These perfectionism problems create multiple challenges for the narcissist, who frequently face these expectations of perfection falling short and feeding their feelings of unworthiness or inferiority. When they feel as if they are falling short or feel as if their delusion of perfectionism is teetering on the edge of being shattered, narcissists often react strongly due to their own fragile senses of identity and insecurity that they are hiding behind the perfectionism. When that delusion of perfection is threatened in any way, narcissistic behaviors are more likely to occur for a variety of reasons.

Stress Management

As has been established, narcissism tends to be a coping mechanism. In this context, narcissistic behavior is a way to cope with stress as opposed to a lack of control or insecurity. As people with very rigid expectations of perfection and fragile senses of self, these people struggle with any sort of stress. The narcissist presents himself as perfect and infallible to those around him, and when stressed, he struggles to respond appropriately or on the fly. Stress occurring is typically a major emotional trigger, and his behavior may become volatile and unpredictable. Stress was likely a common theme throughout his childhood, and his ability to deal with stress in a healthy manner never fully developed without proper guidance.

While we know narcissists present themselves as confident, that confidence is a façade. A truly confident person is able to work through stress, even though it is uncomfortable and unpleasant. The narcissist, particularly the vulnerable one, feels an amplified level of stress compared to non-narcissists. A study completed by the University of Michigan psychologist Robin Edelstein[1] measured and tested for stress responses of undergraduate students, and supported that assertion.

During this study, students were told to prepare a presentation to be delivered in front of an audience composed of people who, unknowingly to the presenters, were told not to respond in any way. They were told not to smile, nod, shake their heads, or do anything else acknowledging or reacting to the students. The students were told that the audience was made up of experts of human behavior, though they were random observers. Right before giving the presentations, the researchers took away the presenters' notes and forced them to present from memory to a completely unresponsive audience. The researchers then measured levels of cortisol, the stress hormone, and compared results.

Despite the confidence narcissists present, they showed increased responses to stress, with men rated as more narcissistic displaying higher levels of cortisol, along with worse mood. This result shows narcissists as having much more sensitive negative stress responses compared to non-narcissists, and these results have been replicated in other similar studies as well. The narcissists' fragile egos and true vulnerability they have kept hidden away from everyone betray the persona of confidence they present, and every time something stressful happens, that persona is threatened, or sometimes even shattered.

The narcissist, depending on whether grandiose or vulnerable, will either roll with the stressor or struggle to function. The higher the narcissist's self-esteem, the better he will be able to cope with stress, and grandiose narcissists typically have plenty of self-esteem, as opposed to the vulnerable narcissists, who lack it.

Change Aversion

Similar to expecting perfection, narcissists often feel an intense aversion to change of any kind. Change implies surprises, which typically cause more stress. Their aversion to change only makes them more stressed when change inevitably occurs. The rigidity becomes yet another shortcoming for the narcissist. Oftentimes, this change aversion can actually be used to identify whether someone is a narcissist or not.

When faced with challenges that people can typically take in stride, the narcissist may become triggered and lash out. Something as simple as the store being sold out of an item needed for dinner can cause a meltdown of screaming profanities at the employee that told him she was sorry, but they are sold out at the moment. The stress of being told he has to choose something else is too overwhelming, and he is not afraid of lashing out at other people he sees as at fault.

The narcissist believes he is entitled to exactly what he asked for, and because he is entitled, being told no is a shock. Imagine going to a bank to withdraw some of your money and being told, "No, you can't do that today. The sky is the wrong color, and the wind is blowing the wrong direction, so I'm not giving you your money. Oh, and your cards have been disabled. You'll be able to use it eventually." You would be outraged, and for a good reason. Your money is your own and you bank it with the expectation you are entitled to use it or move it at any time you please; if your bank told you that you were being denied access for an inane reason, you would probably be changing banks at the first opportunity, and most reasonable people would agree.

For the narcissist, anything not going according to plan causes the same level of outraged disbelief, and he reacts as such. The narcissist, with his entitlement combined with his penchant for perfectionism, believes that things will always go his way, even when it is unrealistic. He expects certain things to happen in a certain order, and he feels threatened when that does not happen. Things not going his way is essentially the world challenging his distorted perceptions of the world around him, chipping away bit by bit at his perfect persona. That challenge forces him to come to terms with everything he has worked so hard to bury behind his mask, leaving him once again feeling self-loathing.

In order to cope with those feelings of loathing, he feels the need to redirect that loathing to whoever or whatever is the perceived reason for exploding in the first place. As you may have noticed by now, redirection is one of the narcissist's favorite tactics to avoid blame and explain away any discrepancies in his distorted world. Redirection shifts fault from him, but also allows him to cope with his negative feelings. It becomes a sort of outlet for his frustration; instead of sitting on his frustration and letting it fester, he lets it explode and affect others as well. Misery loves company, and this way, at least he is not the only one miserable, stressed, and frustrated. This allows him to soothe his own fragile ego a little more, reminding himself that the other people around him are equally as outraged, even though the other people are more frustrated about the narcissist's behavior than whatever happened.

Falling Short

Another common problem also entails from this misguided perfectionism: Constantly failing to meet expectations. While those around him see the narcissist as harsh, unrealistic, and overly demanding, he is even harder on himself. He knows that the people around him are not perfect; that is part of how he justifies his own superiority. He expects himself to be perfect and presents himself as such to hide his fragile self-worth in a misguided attempt to push those feelings of insufficiency away.

Unfortunately, perfection is something that only exists in theory. Humans are perfectly imperfect, and that imperfection that so many of us embrace as the beauty of humanity is seen as nothing more than a flaw that ruins the image for the narcissist. If it is not flawless, it is not valuable or worthwhile, and he holds himself to that standard as well. Flaws and weaknesses do not develop character; they are hindrances. Hindrances cause us to make mistakes, which cause blame, which lead to humiliation and shame.

This perceived spiral into shame is something the narcissist seeks to desperately avoid. With humiliation being feared more than anything else, the narcissist instead attempts to create perfection to create something invulnerable to criticism. Unfortunately, this is counterproductive, as the narcissist has now created an unattainable goal, which will inevitably lead to the humiliation of falling short that he so desperately sought to avoid.

When failing, narcissists are prone to spirals into either rage or depression, and at that moment, *narcissistic injury* occurs. Narcissistic injury refers to threats to the narcissist's self-esteem or that challenge the narcissist's delusional perception of reality. The narcissist's reaction to narcissistic injury is visceral; the narcissist responds in such a way that those around him may think he is fighting for his life as he flies into a narcissistic rage, and in some ways, he is. He is fighting to protect that carefully constructed persona that has become his life. He cannot let that mask slip without admitting that he has been fake the entire time. The narcissist's reaction to other people's failure is often disproportionate to the perceived crime, ranging from a silent treatment to screaming, or even hurting the source of injury in an attempt to make it disappear.

The reason for this visceral reaction is a way to shift from feeling like the victim to being in control of the situation. It is a method of self-soothing, albeit a poor one. By reestablishing himself as dominant by inflicting pain on others, he is able to feel as if he is in control and like the world is in line with his perceptions once again. If he cannot be in control of his own perfection because that is an impossible idealistic standard to achieve, he can at least be in control of those around him who fail.

SECTION 2

Engaging the Narcissist

CHAPTER 5

Therapeutic Approaches

Approaching correcting narcissistic personality disorder or narcissistic tendencies can be quite daunting; after all, narcissists' façade of perfection means they can never admit fault with their behavior. Even if they do, their proclivity to rage when they feel challenged or threatened in any way makes it difficult to work with narcissists that are willing to begin the process of developing a whole, healthy self that they currently lack. Narcissists tend to react poorly to change, being challenged, and failure, all of which are present during therapy to correct narcissistic behaviors. Between their inability to admit fault and their tendency to avoid change, treating narcissists becomes incredibly difficult, and narcissists that are willing to go through that ordeal are quite rare. However, when a narcissist or someone exhibiting narcissistic behaviors is ready to begin changing or admits that different behaviors would be more beneficial, schema-focused therapy is one of the most effective methods of treatment.

What are Schema-Focused Approaches?

Schema-focused therapy is a type of psychotherapy, or talk therapy, that combines some of the key features of cognitive behavioral therapy, experiential therapy, and interpersonal therapy together to create an entirely new approach in order to treat various personality disorders. This therapy is based on identifying which schemas, or patterns of negative behaviors that a person repeats. Schema-focused therapy has been found to be beneficial for those with self-defeating schemas that do not respond well to other kinds of psychotherapy, making it sound quite promising for narcissists.

In this therapy, it is believed that negative schemas cause destructive thinking and that those destructive schemas are developed during adolescence through experience and treatment by family. As you will recall, narcissists tend to internalize criticism they heard growing up, and therefore, they should be a good fit for schema-focused therapy when they are willing to cooperate. Schema-focused therapy occurs in three steps: The therapist identifying schemas, the client discovering his or her own schemas, and correcting the schemas as they are relevant in real life situations.

The first step involves the therapist identifying whatever schemas the narcissist is trapped in. This involves conversations with the narcissist to delve into the narcissist's past and plenty of discussions on motivations. The therapist may listen to what the narcissist has to say and ask guiding or clarifying questions in order to begin to develop an idea of the narcissist's personality and why he behaves the way he does. Through training, the therapist learns to identify which aspects of the conversation may be relevant to the narcissist's behavior, even if what is being discussed at the moment and the narcissist's behavior seem entirely unrelated.

The second step involves the therapist helping the narcissist begin to identify her schemas. By learning what they are, they are then prepared to begin identifying when they occur in everyday life. The purpose of this is that being aware of the schemas and being able to identify them in real time allows for the narcissist to correct the behaviors in real time. This is achieved through various forms of role-playing, imagery, and any other techniques the therapist may find useful for that particular client. At this point, the therapist is guiding the narcissist to come to the conclusion of why they act the way they do, with the hopes of understanding their behaviors more in-depth and recognizing why they are harmful.

The third step involves improving thinking patterns in the real world in real time and replacing negative, distorted, or unhealthy thoughts with healthy, productive, and positive ones for positive results. This is a key facet of cognitive behavioral therapy, in which by recognizing the relationship between thoughts, feelings, and actions, you seek to alter your actions by changing your thoughts. If you change a negative thought into a positive one, your feelings on the subject will also become more positive as well. When you are in a positive mindset, you are more likely to behave positively in return.

Maladaptive Schemas

One of the most fundamental concepts in schema therapy is maladaptive schemas. By understanding a schema as a pervasive pattern of behavior, we can then identify a maladaptive schema as a negative pattern of behavior, oftentimes developed some time during childhood. Maladaptive schemas are the results of an upbringing that made developing a normal, healthy sense of self and behavior difficult or impossible. By not having basic emotional needs met by the parent or caregiver, the child compensates by falling into these schemas in order to meet the need the best he or she can. They are deemed maladaptive coping mechanisms to the many stressors the world throws at us.

Since we learn these schemas early in life, they are all we know. For the narcissist, or for others with maladaptive schemas, these thoughts have been present for as long as they can remember, and therefore are familiar. As creatures of habits, we automatically seek out the familiar and comfortable, no matter how dangerous it may be. This is why we often see people who grew up with dysfunctional families falling victim to dysfunctional relationships in adulthood. It becomes a cycle of the person not knowing any different, and seeking it out for themselves in adulthood. To the one with the maladaptive schemas, this is the way of life, and that is accepted.

The problem with this, however, is that the narcissist begins to distort his perceptions of reality in order to force them to fit into the schemas he has developed. If the narcissist expects the square to fit in the circle spot in a puzzle, it is easier for him to cut off the corners and edges to force it into place than it is for him to accept the truth. If the narcissist develops a pattern of thought in which he is always the victim, he will always twist situations around to make himself the victim even when he is the true antagonizer. This can make things especially difficult when dealing with a narcissist, because he may truly believe that he is the victim when he has been calling you names all day, or blame you for his bad behavior, citing that he would never have done what he did if you had never upset him.

These schemas may remain hidden away the majority of the time, only triggered by certain experiences or situations. This can make discovering which maladaptive schemas a narcissist has difficult, as it can be hard to unbury them all if nothing relevant to the hidden schemas comes up during the identifying stage of therapy. Luckily, this therapy is a longer-term intervention, sometimes lasting upwards of three years, so there will be plenty of time to identify even the most hidden of schemas.

Informing Patterns of Thinking

Ultimately, the core intervention in schema therapy aims to reduce the prevalence of the maladaptive schemas and behaviors associated with them in order to reduce the problem behaviors. It does this by focusing on the origin of the maladaptive schemas. By knowing where they came from, the therapist can help the narcissist begin to correct the behavior. Knowing that the schemas were developed due to unmet needs, the therapist seeks to help the patient navigate through his thoughts on those unmet needs and begin to remove the negative connotations and try to meet them now as an adult. The idea is to help the patient create a healthy adult mindset that is prepared and capable of handling stress without falling into old habits of maladaptive schemas and behaviors.

The therapist will try to guide the narcissist through his childhood, typically first starting by asking how his childhood was and how his relationships with his parents were before delving into anything that may be relevant to the behaviors. For example, if the narcissist tends to be hyper-focused on perfection at all times, the therapist may search for signs of his parents being controlling or completely disengaged from their child's life. It is possible that the narcissist is so perfectionistic because his parents were strict to the point that he would be punished for anything less than perfection, or that his parents were so uninterested in him that he overcompensated by trying to be perfect in order to earn their attention.

Neither overly controlling nor negligent and uninterested are healthy parenting styles that meet a child's emotional needs, so it would be no surprise that a child who grew up with a helicopter parent or with little supervision would have some emotional scars. Unable to learn how to cope properly with stress or failure, the narcissist instead lashes out at the possibility of failure, no matter how small. Even something as innocuous as spilling some milk when pouring it into a bowl of cereal could set the narcissist off.

Once the trigger for the schema has been identified, the therapist seeks to identify the cause. Through asking questions and guiding the conversation, it may come to light that the narcissist's own parents were harsh whenever he made normal messes that would be expected from children, and they would punish him for spilling his milk or leaving crumbs on the table. Over time, the child would develop an aversion to anything short of perfection and would get to the point of reacting strongly when not living up to those standards.

By understanding that the narcissist's parents were the cause of the behavior of obsessive perfectionism, the therapist would seek to heal the intensity of emotions associated with that particular instance. By slowly changing how the narcissist feels about the incident, the narcissist's own reaction should change as well, which should begin to correct and replace maladaptive schemas with adaptive, healthy behaviors. This change in feelings associated with the memory is done with three types of techniques: cognitive, experiential, and behavioral, as well as with what is known in schema therapy as limited reparenting. Each of these serves a different purpose and has a different use in healing from schemas.

Cognitive strategies take parts of cognitive behavioral therapy and apply them to the narcissist's schema. They may take the form of pros and cons lists, in which the narcissist is asked to make a list of pros and cons of his behaviors in hopes of seeing that there are far more cons than pros. This also may involve testing the validity of a schema, which requires the narcissist to reflect on it and identify how true it really is, or if it is distorted or negative. By identifying it as distorted or negative, it is flagged as needing to be repaired.

Experiential strategies draw from Gestalt psychodrama and imagery techniques. Psychodrama is a form of roleplaying where the patient dramatizes his own life and behavior in order to gain insight about their behaviors and thoughts. It requires a protagonist that is facing a certain problem, such as when the narcissist spilled milk as a child. The narcissist is then asked to reenact the scene of spilling the milk. The reenactment may include soliloquies, where the acting client is told to speak his thoughts as they are happening in character, in order to gain insight into his mental state. This allows for the narcissist to deepen his emotional development and understanding of his own behaviors that have been largely unconscious until that point.

Behavioral strategies draw from traditional behavior therapy such as roleplaying an interaction during therapy, then being expected to execute that interaction in real life in real time before the next meeting. This seeks to teach the narcissist how the proper interaction should go between two healthy individuals, then expects the narcissist to execute it himself. This provides the tools necessary without hand-holding.

Limited reparenting is one of the core features of schema therapy. Knowing that schema therapy assumes that a child with unmet emotional needs develops maladaptive schemas, it seems intuitive to believe that by meeting those needs now, the maladaptive behavior can be corrected. Limited reparenting involves establishing a secure attachment to the therapist, with clear boundaries to keep the relationship appropriate between professional and patient. The therapist does what he or she can in order to meet the needs of the client that went unmet through childhood. This secure attachment allows the client to begin learning to function in a healthy way.

WAIT!!!

READ THIS BEFORE GOING ANY FURTHER!

How would you like to get your next eBook **FREE** <u>and</u> get new books for **FREE** too before they are publicly released?

Join our Self Empowerment Team today and receive your next (and future) books for **FREE**! Signing up is easy and completely free!!

Check out this page for more info!

www.SelfEmpowermentTeam.com/SignUp

Just a Friendly Reminder...

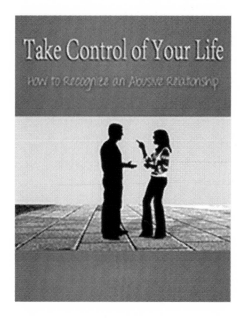

I'd like to offer you this amazing resource which my clients pay for. It is a report I written when I first began my journey.

Click on the picture above or navigate to the website below to join my exclusive email list. Upon joining, you will receive this incredible report on how to recognize an abusive relationship.

If you ask most people on the street what an abusive relationship is, chances are you'd get a description of physical abuse. And yes, that is most certainly an abusive relationship. However, abuse comes in many forms. The actual meaning of abuse is when someone exerts control over another person.

Find out more about recognizing an abusive relationship and learn how to take control over your life by clicking on the book above or by going to this link:

http://bit.ly/RecognizeAbusiveRelationship

CHAPTER 6

Assessment & Identification

Throughout the course of schema therapy, Dr. Jeff Young, the creator of schema therapy, identified eighteen common maladaptive schemas[2] that may be encountered. Any combination of any number of these can be present at any given time in an individual, and any number of them can influence behavior in negative ways. Understanding these maladaptive schemas will help you recognize that the narcissist may not mean to cause the toxic behavior she exhibits and will give you ideas on how to better deal with the narcissist in a way that defuses the situation instead of causing it to explode.

Recognizing Schemas

The eighteen schemas can be easily divided into five categories for ease of organization and understanding. These categories are disconnection or rejection, impaired autonomy or performance, impaired limits, other-directedness, and over-vigilance or inhibition. Each of these can be recognized as traits of narcissist personality disorder: Narcissists fear rejection and humiliation, they believe they are entitled, they often play the victim, they are impulsive, and they often obsess over other people, whether for their attention or to control them. Understanding the various schemas behind each of these behaviors can help you not only empathize with the narcissist but also help you learn how to interact with her in the healthiest way possible. Particularly when you want to maintain a relationship with a narcissist at any level, understanding these schemas and using your knowledge of the schemas to guide your own behaviors will help you begin to interact with the narcissist in a much more productive, healthy way.

Disconnection/Rejection

Abandonment

Those who have developed a schema of abandonment fear the end of relationships. Oftentimes, they feel disposable and that their partners are likely to toss them aside, whether due to conflict or disagreeing on something mundane, such as what shows to watch before bed or what their favorite restaurants are. Sometimes, they also fear that death, divorce, affairs, or fights, are all inevitably there to end the relationship because of past experiences. While death will eventually take us all, they worry that it will come too soon, or if they let themselves get attached. They assume that they are unworthy of relationships and that anyone who does want them must have some sort of issue or they would go out of their way to choose a more suitable partner.

Mistrust

People who find themselves stuck in the mistrust schema fear being hurt by others, either physically or emotionally. They fear being lied to or betrayed and worry about those around them being out to get them. Ultimately, the fear of being betrayed or hurt leaves them constantly doubting the people around them and latching onto any signs that their friends or loved ones are out to get them. Even an innocent mistake, such as forgetting that the mistrustful individual absolutely despises tomatoes and serving spaghetti, and a garden salad with grape tomatoes mixed in at a large dinner party would be deemed an attack on the person with the end goal being to tell the mistrustful one that her friend hates her and wants her to feel unwelcome and uncomfortable at group events. Accidents are deemed passive aggressive and intentional, and ultimately, the person's ability to form meaningful relationships is degraded by the constant mistrust.

Social isolation and alienation

People who develop the social isolation schema develop the belief that they are different from everyone else. This can be for positive reasons, such as because they are smarter than everyone else, or for negative reasons, such as they are worth less than everyone else. Because of this belief, they begin to think that they cannot ever fit in or identify with others, or that they should not associate with others due to their uniqueness. Because they are so different, they believe there are no other people they can really connect with, even though in reality, someone else has likely had similar experiences, interests, and thoughts. This makes it difficult for them to find friends because they are constantly inundated with people they feel cannot relate to them. Oftentimes, for narcissists, this schema either feeds into their delusions of grandeur or their feeling of worthlessness. Their inability to connect with others is seen as either proof that they are unique and more important or as proof of their worthlessness.

Emotional Deprivation

People with this schema have come to believe that they will never find someone else that will give them the emotional attention and care they need to feel supported. They constantly feel deprived of support they need, and because of this, they find that they have a hard time leaning on others. They constantly expect to be denied or let down, so they oftentimes stop trying. By no longer really trying to seek out that emotional support they crave, however, they only solidify that thought in their mind as they continue to be unsupported due to not letting anyone know they need it. This self-affirming cycle perpetuates itself indefinitely until someone or something snaps them out of it.

Defectiveness and shame

When falling victim to the defectiveness and shame schema, the person believes that she is defective in some way. Whether physically unattractive or incapable of meeting a certain goal, emotionally needy or unstable, or less intelligent than those around him, these people always find faults with themselves. Oftentimes, they believe that their defects or shortcomings make them undesirable as friends or romantic partners, and their undesirability makes them unworthy of love from others. They become ashamed of their assumed shortcomings or perceived defects and struggle to believe that anyone could possibly care for them as their true selves, using this as further justification for needing to present themselves as their personas.

Impaired Limits

Entitlement and Grandiosity

This schema involves the person to feel that they are worth more than those around him. This is one of the key features of the narcissist, as he believes he is automatically more important than everyone else for no reason other than he is. These people feel like they deserve better treatment and privileges than everyone around them and that everyone should automatically recognize and respect his natural authority. These people oftentimes seek to control others and seek fame and power, even if it has to come at the expense of the needs of others. Ultimately, to this person, only his needs are important because of his superior status, and he will have no qualms with letting other people's needs go unmet if that means that his every whim has been satisfied.

Poor self-discipline

This schema causes individuals to lack tolerance for discomfort or setbacks. Due to not being able to handle setbacks or difficult situations, they instead give up to save themselves the trouble. The success is not worth the effort for these people, and they fail simply by not bothering to complete the work in the first place. Likewise, these people often struggle with controlling impulses or outbursts when emotions are high, causing issues with staying on task or when handling a difficult situation. Their emotions become overwhelming, and they end up failing due to their lack of discipline or ability to control themselves.

Impaired Autonomy and performance

Failure

People with this particular schema have a strong belief that they have never managed to succeed. Even past successes are seen as failures, with some sort of flaw being the reason it was a failure. For example, not getting a perfect score on a test may be deemed a failure because questions were missed. Because of their belief, they have always failed in the past; these people often feel as if they will always fail in the future as well, regardless of what the task is. Even something that they are good at or have done well at in the past will be seen as an impossibility.

Vulnerability to harm

This schema convinces people that they are at a higher risk of injury or illness. Even though there may be no basis for this thought, they constantly fear to get hurt or sick. This leads to fear and distrust, constantly thinking that those around are out to hurt the person with this schema, and the constant fear of getting hurt or ill may hold the person back from normal living. For example, if someone fears getting hurt, they may choose to avoid driving or walking along busy roads out of fear of being hit by a car. Someone who is sick may avoid crowds or doctors' offices when they need to see a doctor out of fear of contracting a serious illness in the waiting room.

Enmeshment

People with an enmeshment schema feel as if they cannot live without support from a specific person. They usually latch onto a major relationship in their lives, such as with a spouse or parent, and feel incapable without constant support. They develop a serious dependency on the other person, whether it is as an emotional crutch or to get them out of trouble when they are struggling, and have a strong aversion to being away from whoever they have attached to. Without the presence of the chosen person, they feel empty and incomplete, and they often become increasingly more demanding on the person's time and energy.

Dependence and incompetence

People falling victim to this schema feel incapable and incompetent. They feel as if they are unable to do anything on their own, and feel reliant on significant amounts of assistance from others. They may be unable to work without the support off the other person, whether through driving the person to and from work, or feel as if they cannot stay on task on their own. They find themselves afraid to try without someone else's support, and their reservations keep them from flourishing or proving themselves wrong and showing that they can actually be independent and competent if they try and apply themselves. They may even unconsciously sabotage their own attempts, believing they are unable to succeed on their own.

Overvigilance or Inhibition

Emotional inhibition

This schema gets people stopping or censoring themselves in fear of other people's reactions. They essentially force themselves to bottle up all of their thoughts and feelings rather than potentially inconveniencing someone else. They put themselves last and hide their true feelings in hopes of keeping the people around them satisfied. Oftentimes, these people will go along with anything, even if it means doing something they hate because they would rather suffer in silence than lose a relationship with someone they deem important.

Unrelenting standards

When people have unrelenting standards, they often set goals that are excessive or unattainable, even though failing will cause damage to their lives. They constantly set impossible expectations and try to meet them, even when a reasonable person may recognize that they are impossible. They also frequently aim for perfection and believe anything short of that perfection they aspire to achieve is a failure. This black-and-white thinking leaves them in a constant state of failure as they fail to meet their impossible, unreasonable standards.

Negativity and pessimism

This schema paints the world grey and has the people with this mindset, only seeing the bad parts of life. They focus in on the negative, such as sad or difficult times, and ignore the positive aspects. While they may have had a perfectly good day, they may define the day as bad due to one small incident, such as spilling a drink or getting the wrong order at lunch. The tiniest inconvenience could be enough for a person stuck in a negativity schema to say the entire day was horrible, even if she had spent the day at an amusement park with her loved ones, doing everything she wanted. She would focus instead on the fact that she got a sunburn, spent too much time waiting in line for one ride, and that time she got splashed by a water ride was horrible. They always find something to complain about and never acknowledge the good parts.

Punitiveness

People that fall into the habit of the punitiveness schema believe that any error, no matter how serious or harmless, deserves to be criticized and punished. They are often just as harsh on themselves as others, and are quick to angrily correct people around them that misstep or make a mistake, even if it was a harmless misunderstanding. These people fail to acknowledge that we all make mistakes at some point in life, and also refuse to consider that sometimes, circumstances could reasonably explain the error as a mistake that anyone would make as opposed to it being from negligence or incompetence.

Other-directedness

Self-sacrifice

This schema makes people willingly forego their needs so they can ensure that someone else's are met. They frequently feel guilty about their own needs or wants, and worry that if they fail to make sure the other person is cared for, that the other person will be unable to meet those needs or will suffer somehow. While some level of putting other people's needs first is normal in certain contexts, such as a mother making sure her children are fed and cared for before herself, selflessness to the extent that your own needs are met is dysfunctional and can be harmful. These people neglect themselves to care for others, and this sacrifice only hurts themselves.

Approval seeking

People with the approval seeking schema require validation from others. They will seek it out relentlessly, and try to do things they think will gain appreciation from others, such as buying their friends drinks, or agreeing to go to a restaurant they hate or a to a concert they have no interest in. These people focus so much on getting approval from other people that they never get a chance to develop a healthy sense of self-worth. Their entire existence and value become dependent on other people's opinions; this leaves them constantly seeking to please those around them, regardless of the cost to themselves.

Subjugation

People who find themselves stuck in the subjugation schema feel as if they are pressured or forced into giving up their needs or wants by other people. They believe that these other people will threaten them if they refuse to comply. These threats can be anything from physical harm to withholding affection or attention. This keeps the people with the schema stuck feeling as if they have to give up their needs willingly or they will be taken anyway.

Testing Schemas

During the course of treating maladaptive schemas, rules for each schema are defined. Each schema has rules that keep the schema valid and prove it true. This works because they help the individual with the schema avoid catastrophic or triggering situations related to the schema. An example of this is someone with the self-sacrifice schema saying that he should never take care of himself because in taking care of himself, he is selfishly ignoring the needs of his loved ones and letting them down. In order to not feel as if he is selfish, he then makes it a point to avoid selfishly meeting his own needs. He dutifully puts his needs last and makes sure those around him are happy, even though this may be at a detriment to him. This is because he cannot cope with the guilt that comes with putting himself first. Since he feels like he cannot cope, he instead creates a rule of never putting himself first to ensure that he never ends up feeling intense guilt in the first place.

Once these rules are identified, they must be tested or challenged. Often, this is done with the therapist's guidance in a controlled situation, so they are able to slowly realize that their rules were flawed from the beginning. These rules are tested systematically with three main steps. First, the person needs to pick a situation related to the schema that will cause a small amount of fear or discomfort. They then plan out a reaction that will contradict the schema's rules. This reaction is healthier and productive, and the fact that it contradicts the schema's rules makes it a valid way to begin to disprove the schema. Lastly, the person needs to identify whether the predicted catastrophe or triggering event happened, and if the catastrophe was avoided, he must record what actually happened instead.

For example, a man with an abandonment schema may frequently find himself skirting around issues with his girlfriend, avoiding any heavy discussions and always deferring to her on any serious decisions. He fears that telling her his true opinions will make her think less of him, and once she thinks less of him, she will abandon him and find someone she deems more compatible or better than him. Once this abandonment schema is identified, he will then be asked to imagine a situation where he tells her his true thoughts. He may decide on telling her what he wants for dinner that night when she suggests dinner at the Thai restaurant he hates for their weekly date night. Then, with the help of his therapist, he role-plays how the conversation would go. He tells her nicely that he does not like Thai food, and really only went for her in the past. He imagines her laughing it off and telling him to be honest with her in the future, so he is not miserable. He identifies that the catastrophe he imagined, her abandoning him for having bad taste or disagreeing with her, did not occur, and feels a little more comfortable truly confronting her in person rather than role-playing it. Over time, with real-life experience, the schema's rule is slowly contradicted and loses power, and the test reveals that the schema's rule was false.

As the schema is disproved, it is important to begin establishing healthier thoughts as well. The man with an abandonment schema may tell himself that his loved ones will accept him for who he is, even if they have some disagreements between the two of them, or if they have conflicting interests. He will then begin creating healthier rules that affirm his belief in himself, with his daily interactions with those around him affirming it. As people do not decide they hate him for having his own taste in food, style, or music, he begins to discover that the people who really value him will stick around, even if they disagree with his taste.

Coping

Coping with these schemas can be incredibly testing when you are on the receiving end of the behaviors. It is important to remember that these schemas are coping mechanisms in their own rights. Even though you may see them as unhealthy or disordered, it is important to recognize them for what they are. They are the results of a person who has been broken down or neglected, attempting to manage overwhelming feelings of insecurity. They are not necessarily meant to hurt those around the narcissist.

By remembering that the narcissist is doing the best he can to navigate through the world with a broken sense of self and lacking healthy coping mechanisms, it may be easier to accept the behavior. Just as you would not be offended when a child throws a temper tantrum over not going her way because she has not learned better yet, it may help to remember that the narcissist also lacks these fundamental skills. Skills that you may take for granted, such as being able to cope with disappointment or conflict, are actually the result of years of experiences and guidance through difficult situations when you were younger. Through understanding what may motivate the narcissist to behave the way he does, it becomes easier to react productively to the behaviors.

CHAPTER 7

The Narcissist's Awareness

Narcissists are notoriously stubborn and difficult to get through to. Their lack of empathy and grandiose behaviors can make it hard for them to really understand the wider impact of their behaviors beyond just getting what they want when they want it. Sometimes, through raising the narcissist's awareness of what she is doing and how it is causing problems, you can begin to improve their behaviors. Rarely, they will be willing to improve themselves, especially if they are relatively low in narcissistic traits, or they are borderline narcissistic but do not have a diagnosis. Those who are more narcissistic by nature will likely be much more disagreeable about the process and less willing to even entertain the idea that they are not perfect exactly the way they are. Remember, narcissists typically lack normal self-awareness and see the world through a distorted lens. It will take plenty of patience to raise the narcissist's awareness, and if you feel like it is too much for you, there is no shame in saying you cannot handle it.

Willing Interactions

For those few narcissists who are willing to improve themselves or recognize their shortcomings, discussions of problematic behavior can be quite useful. Just as you would take a child aside to discuss why it is not okay to behave a certain way, you can also tactfully discuss why something the narcissist is doing is more hurtful. Remember, narcissists have fragile egos, so tact is of the utmost importance.

For example, if the narcissist has a tendency to seek perfection and you suspect a schema of unrelenting standards, you may look for ways that you notice the narcissist succeeding and comment on them. When you notice the narcissist begin to nitpick at himself or other people, pointing out flaws, it could be acceptable to gently remind the narcissist that small flaws will not be a problem. Point out that perfection, while a fantastic concept, is rarely ever a goal that is productive, and comment on how you have noticed how harsh he is on himself and others. Identify that no one is really comfortable with the insistence of flawless and that his expectations make it difficult to work. By identifying the problem you and your coworkers may have, you have provided some awareness to the narcissist, so he recognizes that part of his behavior is problematic. By providing him with praise, you may challenge one of his schema's rules. This sort of conversations repeated over time can be beneficial to the narcissist, and may even ultimately challenge the schema enough for him to relent, even if only a little.

By pointing out his unwarranted harshness toward himself, you begin to plant the seed of the idea that perfection is not necessary. He may have developed these unrelenting standards due to a childhood of strict adherence to perfection and could have been punished unfairly when they were not met. It is important to remember to treat the narcissist with the same grace you would use for a child still learning how to interact with the world. Do not feel discouraged or irritated if you have to continue to gently guide the narcissist toward the idea that less than perfect can still be successful.

It can also be useful to discuss with the narcissist that his actions can make him come across as harsh, or make people prefer to avoid him. This hangs another carrot in front of the narcissist: Attention. Narcissists crave positive attention and admiration, so the idea that being a little less unrelenting may bring more of that attention could be a fantastic motivator.

Unknowing Interactions

More often than not, the narcissist is not open to consciously correcting her behavior. True to her diagnosis, she is unwilling or unable to acknowledge that she may be any sort of a problem. If you were to approach her and say that something she is doing is a problem, she would likely explode at you, unleashing her narcissistic rage at you because you have just become a challenge to her distorted worldview. It is easier to chase you away than to accept that her view is flawed. With these people, much more tact is necessary.

Much like how you noticed the narcissist's unrelenting standards in the previous section, you should also look for the unwilling narcissist's schemas. Perhaps she has a tendency to distrust others, and because of that distrust, she is quick to accuse others around her as the problem and constantly sabotaging relationships because she would rather be alone than vulnerable to others. This makes her especially difficult to work with, and you often find yourself unhappy when work requires you to interact with her.

Rather than accepting the narcissist's haughty attitude, you can use her distrustful nature to your advantage; always follow through with what you offer to do, even if it is met with ungratefulness. If you offer to bring her a coffee, follow through with it, even if she accuses you of doing it to get her to do more of the work. She is distrustful of you because you have not given her a reason to trust you. If you offer to go over her paperwork to check for errors before submitting a group project for work, do it and make sure to sandwich any criticism between praises of things that are working well in the project. This not only lessens the blow to her ego but makes her feel less like you are intentionally trying to hurt her when you have more compliments than criticisms.

No matter what, you need to avoid affirming her rule of avoiding trusting people. Even when it is difficult, it is imperative that you try your hardest to follow through with everything you say you will do. Even if you have been making good progress, a single slip up could send all of that progress down the drain.

Over time, through plenty of diligence and working with the narcissist's traits instead of being offended and affirming the maladaptive schemas, you will begin to tear the schemas down. Eventually, she may recognize that you are not out to get her and are genuinely trying to help. When the narcissist is unwilling to admit fault, it is important to let the narcissist arrive at that conclusion without you saying it, making it their decision rather than them feeling as if they are bowing down to someone else.

Care and Practice

Ultimately, when trying to raise a narcissist's awareness of his disordered behavior, you must learn their schemas to the best of your ability and take special care to control the triggers that make the narcissist feel a need to act upon their schemas. Their schemas are poor attempts at coping with stress and discomfort, and remembering that can help you remember to have the compassion and understanding that the narcissist is not necessarily trying to hurt you, but is acting true to his nature. Understanding the narcissist's core self and recognizing it as his attempt to control the world to protect himself can help you remember that it is important to avoid known triggers if it is practical or reasonable. Think of this as knowing not to poke the sleeping bear, no matter how tempting it may be.

While you should never goad the narcissist into known behaviors by using their known triggers, you should also never force yourself to walk on eggshells around him. If the only reasonable answer to a situation is something that may trigger the narcissist, then that is understandable. Do your best to control the triggers, but do not dedicate your life to constantly placating the narcissist, as this will only feed into his sense of entitlement.

While taking care to avoid triggers when possible, you should also practice techniques that help establish a healthy relationship and create positive interactions between yourself and the narcissist. As discussed earlier, remember that working with the narcissist's schemas can help you begin to develop a more meaningful relationship built upon trust that you will not hurt them the way they have been hurt in the past. He may begin to recognize that you are there as support rather than as another adversary wanting to tear him down, and you may find his behaviors becoming healthier and more productive as he has less and less reason to use his maladaptive schemas to cope with stress.

CHAPTER 8

Maintaining Yourself

When dealing with a narcissist, you find yourself having to make plenty of concessions to avoid meltdowns or outrages. With narcissists, you often feel as if you have to make a choice between pleasing yourself or the narcissist, and it's frequently easier to forego what you want than it is to deal with the backlash from the narcissist. It is important to make sure you maintain your own sense of self during the process of dealing with a narcissist, and you need to be able to understand what the appropriate steps are to maintaining yourself. You need to know when flexibility is useful or if setting boundaries will be a better course of action. You also need to understand when enough is enough so you can take a step back from the situation and disengage from the narcissist for your own physical and emotional safety. Learning these skills will give you a much better grasp of how to interact with a narcissist while minimizing damage for everyone involved.

Bending, Not Breaking

Just as the tree bends to the wind to keep from breaking, sometimes being flexible with your own expectations is the best choice when it comes to dealing with a narcissist. Narcissists are stubborn by nature; they want everything to go their way and struggle to cope when things do not play out as they expect. The average person is much better at coping with small missteps in their plans without being tripped up, and sometimes, the easiest way to maintain yourself and your sanity is to remain flexible. If the concession is something you truly do not care about, it is likely not worth the battle of remaining firm. Pick your battles and let the narcissist have her way if you are indifferent.

Your own self-awareness and self-restraint will be two of your greatest defenses against falling victim to narcissistic behaviors. Unlike the narcissist, you can recognize when you are wrong without sending your world shattering around you, and you can also restrain yourself when something does go wrong. You have developed proper coping mechanisms and have learned to handle stress in healthy, productive ways that do not worsen your problems. Remembering to utilize your self-awareness will keep you aware that you are angry or frustrated with the narcissist. This recognition allows you to be aware that you may be more prone to lashing out at the narcissist at that moment, which also allows you to utilize your self-restraint. You can remind yourself to stop, take a deep breath, and count to four before reacting to keep from impulsively lashing out.

For example, imagine your husband is a narcissist: He is very resistant to change in plans and finds himself unable to cope with the stress that comes with the unexpected. Perhaps you two had been planning a two-day trip, in which one day you go see a play you were kind of interested in seeing, and the next day you go to an event your husband is excited to go to. When you arrive at your trip destination, you realize that the play and the event your husband really wanted to go to overlap and notice that you had written the date wrong when you were planning. Despite some mild disappointment, you realize that you are still mostly indifferent about the play in the first place. Instead of insisting on going, you tell your husband that you will skip it and the two of you will go to his event instead, so you do not miss it. This means your husband is not facing a change in schedule that will leave him stressed and possibly trigger a negative behavior, and the two of you still go on to enjoy your trip. Ultimately, your self-awareness allows you to recognize that you had only planned on going because there was nothing else interesting enough during that time, and you had little interest in it beyond filling the empty time. Your flexibility kept your vacation lighthearted, and your husband remained happy. This is an example of an appropriate time to be flexible.

Remember, by remaining flexible when applicable, you keep yourself from breaking. Your flexibility keeps you strong and able to withstand the difficult behaviors that come from the narcissist. Your patience will keep you firm as you encounter the same issues over and over, and your self-awareness will help you acknowledge your feelings so you can cope with them in a healthy, productive way.

Setting Boundaries

Now, if the play was actually something you were really interested in, and you realized that there would be a second day your husband's event was happening that would not conflict with the play's actual date, you would require less flexibility. In this case, you would be better off setting a boundary. You have strong feelings about something, and you should not have to give in to the narcissist's demands just because he struggles to cope sometimes.

Setting boundaries involves you standing firm on an issue. This can be anything you feel strongly about. Oftentimes, boundaries involve respect and an expectation to be treated with basic human decency. People want to live without being harassed or hurt, and they expect to be given that opportunity. When they fight to get that treatment, they have set a boundary that they will not tolerate being crossed. Oftentimes, there is some sort of consequence for crossing the boundary, such as damaging the friendship or causing the wronged party to take a step back and disengage from the relationship altogether.

Even though some flexibility is necessary when dealing with a narcissist, setting boundaries is still important as well. You must be able to balance when flexibility is important, and when it is something that you must be firm on. Oftentimes, these boundaries need to be set if it will cause you physical or emotional harm. A reasonable boundary is telling your narcissistic spouse to respect your decision on something you feel strongly about without lashing out when he disagrees. Being firm that you are entitled to your own opinion, even if he does not like it, is normal and healthy. Telling him that you insist on going to the play you really want to see because you and he can go to his event the next day as well is reasonable. It is also reasonable for you to tell him that you will not accept him angrily lashing out at you when plans change.

When you do set a boundary with a narcissist, it is important that you follow through with whatever consequence you have set. If you tell your narcissistic husband that you will disengage from the conversation altogether if he cannot use respectful language or a respectful tone with you, you need to do so if he continues to say cruel things. If you do not follow through with enforcing your boundary, you are telling the narcissist that they are negotiable and that in the right situations at the right time, those boundaries can be crossed with no consequence. This gives the narcissist what he wants without working on getting it, and teaches the narcissist that his techniques work. He will continue to use name-calling and belittling to get his way, and you will have less of a standing to demand what you want after you have given in.

Think of the narcissist's reaction to your boundaries as a temper tantrum. You would not give in to a toddler's demands for a cookie at bedtime just because he is pouting, screaming, crying, and hitting because you would teach him that pouting, screaming, crying, and hitting is a valid way to get what he wants. Any time someone tells him no, he will scream and cry, fully expecting to get what he wants because it worked with the cookie. The narcissist will learn in the same way, so it is easier to remain firm, even if you ultimately decide after the fact that it is not as important to you as you initially thought. By keeping these boundaries firm and enforcing consequences when they are ignored, you protect yourself from much of the narcissistic abuse that is common in relationships or friendships with narcissists.

Drawing Lines in the Sand

Sometimes, despite your best efforts, a relationship becomes toxic and unbearable. No matter how hard you try or what you do, the narcissist continuously hurts you emotionally, and you are feeling less and less like yourself. In these cases, it is time to draw a line in the sand and walk away. Walking away is not the easy way out, despite what those around you might say; it will require immense self-discipline and willpower to walk away from someone you may deeply love, and it is okay to do so when you are being hurt.

Abuse is always a reason to end a relationship, even if it is caused by a mental illness or disorder. While you may have sworn in sickness and in health in wedding vows, that did not include a risk to your own health. You must take care of yourself before you are able to help anyone else, and if you feel as if you are being abused or mistreated, leaving is totally acceptable. Think of this as the ultimate boundary: You expect to not be on the receiving end of intentional harm, physical or emotional, from the other person. When that person intentionally harms you, that line has been irrevocably crossed, and the thought of the other person doing that again will always loom in the background, coloring your relationship. You do not have to live like that. You are entitled to live a life free of pain, and with respect every person deserves.

Even when a relationship does not involve physically harming you, sometimes the emotional toll it takes is too much. You find yourself constantly drained and like you can no longer enjoy the things that used to bring you pleasure. People may be telling you that you seem depressed, but in reality, you are drained by a relationship. Perhaps your parent is always downplaying every achievement you have, to the point that you believe that you are worthless and incapable of success. Maybe your best friend is constantly one-upping you, so you feel like you are wrong to feel proud of whatever accomplishments you achieve because she is always better. It could be a coworker who belittles and berates you every time you make a mistake, no matter how small.

Regardless of what the nature of the relationship is, taking a step back and cutting the narcissist off is almost always an option. When an entire cut-off is not possible due to sharing minor children, or because you live in such close proximity to the other person, you can take a huge step back and keep the relationship and interactions with the person as minimal as possible to avoid further exposure to their toxicity. It may not be easy, but just as you would not willingly spend time around a rattlesnake just because you have plenty of antivenin readily available, you should not spend time around toxic people. Their toxicity will eat away at you as time goes by, rendering you a husk of your former self.

After cutting off or limiting contact with the narcissist, you will begin to feel more like your old self, and you may realize just how much of a toll that relationship had taken. In hindsight, you may suddenly see all of the red flags and wonder how you managed to get yourself ensnared in such a big mess in the first place. Remember, narcissists, are typically masters at manipulating people around them, feeling it is necessary to their survival and mental health to do so. You are not the first, and you will not be the last, person to get ensnared in a toxic narcissist's web of lies, and you should not beat yourself up over it after deciding to break free.

CHAPTER 9

Different Contexts

While narcissists typically share similar traits with one another, challenges and conflicts with a narcissist can vary greatly based on the type of relationship you have with him. A workplace relationship with a narcissist often looks vastly different than a familial or romantic relationship with a narcissist, which will be different from a platonic friendship with a narcissist. Understanding how these different relationships present will help you to identify when you are interacting with a narcissist as opposed to someone who is just naturally abrasive or withdrawn. Of course, understanding when you are interacting with a narcissist will help you know how to interact with that particular person.

Workplace

Workplace relationships with narcissists can be particularly difficult. You go into work expecting a degree of professionalism but are met instead with the narcissist. They are scathing, desire perfection at all times, and are not above demeaning or belittling those who never meet their unrealistic, impossible standards. Oftentimes, a narcissistic boss will claim credit for anything her team produces, as the team is seen as little more than an extension of the boss, and therefore their work is her work by default. She will favor certain people that are useful for her, and those who are not are typically ignored when they are not being hassled about something.

Expect your narcissistic boss or coworker to be completely insensitive and blind to your needs. Unless you are providing her with premium work and are turning it in, she does not want to deal with you. Problems will be ignored or brushed off, and you will be used as little more than a tool to keep her well-oiled machine running perfectly. You are expected to play that role without complaint.

Keeping in mind that narcissists have sensitive egos, you should use tact whenever you have to interact. Pointing out mistakes or contradicting the narcissist typically only causes more trouble than it solves, and if you dare injure her ego, she will likely explode on you. She will either deny any blame, redirecting it onto other people, or she will lash out at others. Remembering the narcissist's penchant for perfection and lack of ability to cope with criticism, you would be best advised to avoid angering the narcissist and sticking to getting your work done whenever possible if the narcissist is not abusive or toxic.

Platonic

People often don't think narcissists are capable of friendships, and while narcissists do lack an ability to create healthy relationships, some do seek to make friendships. Often, these friendships are developed because you have something that the narcissist admires or envies, and she has gravitated toward you to either learn to emulate you or to get access to what she wanted.

In the beginning, she will do what she can to impress you to gain your attention. She will claim to share hobbies with you, even if she knows next to nothing about whatever interest you have. She will agree with you constantly and maybe make comments about how you two are so compatible. She shows you the best side of her, and once she is convinced that your friendship is securely developed, she begins to aim for what she wants. If she wants someone to compare herself to in order to make herself feel better, she may poke at anything you are self-conscious about to remind you that ultimately, she is superior. She also may suddenly have emergencies any time you needed her help, using this excuse to avoid doing anything remotely supportive for you. You may think nothing of it until you notice the pattern of her never being available.

Even worse, sometimes, she demands to be the center of attention. She will aim to one-up the guest of honor at a celebration. If you are having a baby shower, she may announce that she is pregnant as well, with twins, while you are opening presents. At your wedding reception, she may announce she is engaged during her speech. If you get a new-to-you car, she will suddenly have the same one, but in the newest model with a higher trim. She seeks to better you in every situation, possible with no regard for how this makes you feel.

Ultimately, you end up stuck, deciding between ending the friendship or continuing to accept her behaviors. She will likely never be reliable for emotional support and will likely always try to be better than you in all situations. Oftentimes, however, she makes the decision for you, and as soon as she gets bored, she will vanish from your life as quickly as she had appeared.

If you do wish to salvage the friendship, it can be useful for you to remind yourself what about your friend interested you in the first place. By keeping your focus on the positive aspects your friend brings to your life, you may find yourself slowly becoming more accepting of her shortcomings as you recognize them as a part of her as opposed to an intentional dig at you. Keeping your friend's narcissistic personality in mind and recognizing that she will always have those tendencies can help remind you to remain patient, while also reminding you to keep your expectations for her realistic and reasonable. Do not expect her to be emotionally supportive when you know that is something she cannot easily provide, as that would only set her up for failure. Instead, focus on what you enjoy about her and keep your interactions with her as positive as possible.

Romantic

Romantic relationships with narcissists often start out like fairytales. Everything seems perfect, and the narcissist is exactly your type. He displays all the traits you find especially attractive, such as being an attentive listener, intelligent, or interested in the same obscure sub-genre of movies as you. You feel as if you two have so much in common, and think it must be fate. Love, at first sight, is often used to describe these interactions.

However, his attentiveness is frequently more manipulative than kind; he uses it to learn all about how your mind works. He will learn what makes you feel loved and what your insecurities are. At first, he will use this insight to make you feel loved. His goal is to make you as attached to him as possible in as short of a period of time as possible, knowing that the relationship will not work if he shows his true self before you have fallen in love. He does not want to show his manipulative side to you until he knows you will not leave him at his first major transgression.

He will push for the relationship to progress quicker than normal, always wanting more. He wants to spend more and more time with you, asking you to go on dates more. He seeks to consume your valuable time, edging out competition from friends or family. You are quickly becoming his primary source of narcissistic supply, and he wants to make sure he has you all to himself. He may ask you to marry him or move in with him far sooner than is reasonable to most people, and as soon as he feels like you are well attached, he drops his act. He becomes demeaning and cruel, using all of the insecurities he has learned to manipulate you and keep you subdued and complacent. Over time, this behavior escalates, slowly acclimating you to the narcissist's true self. You find yourself soon accepting behaviors that would have been immediate deal-breakers during the first stages of a relationship.

Co-parent

Sometimes, you find yourself in the situation of having children with a narcissist, but you have chosen to end any romantic relationship with him. Co-parenting is difficult on its own, but adding in a narcissist to the equation is asking for trouble. Because you and the narcissist share children, you are likely legally obligated to foster some semblance of a relationship between the narcissist and his children. No matter how much you may wish to completely cut off contact, you will be required to maintain some level of contact for your children's best interest.

Narcissists typically struggle to parent. Lacking empathy, they struggle to really understand their children's emotional needs. They may make sure the child's physical needs are met but do not nurture their children. Despite knowing this, if you have a court order, you are required to offer your children to their other parent. You should be prepared for your narcissistic ex to manipulate the children in order to get back at you or use them as a way to get a response when you are ignoring him. He will be quick to utilize his own rights to the children when it is an inconvenience for you, but when it is inconvenient for him, he will not bother exercising his time with the children.

Ultimately, what he wants is control over your life, and being in control of a portion of his children's time gives him this over you by default. He knows that a good parent will not leave their children stranded or home alone, so he may call in the middle of the night to have you come and get them, especially if he knows it will interfere with other plans you had. He will lie to your children about why they cannot do things they want, returning the blame to you in hopes of hurting you by ruining your relationship with your child. He will call incessantly during times people are typically unavailable, such as during dinner or during your children's extracurricular activities, and if you dare suggest that the children are unavailable, he will say you are alienating the children and impeding on his relationship with them.

Ultimately, when co-parenting with a narcissist, you have to recognize that the narcissist does not have his children's best interest at heart. He will do things that work for him, even if it is harmful to the shared children, and he will not think twice about hurting them emotionally. He may draw the line at physically abusing them, but his emotional unavailability and lack of nurturing is still a form of emotional abuse.

Children Exhibiting Narcissistic Traits and Charges

With both children and adult charges, you are in control of everything. You control the environment, the scheduling, exposure to media and people, and just about every other aspect of life. This puts you in a great position to begin alleviating narcissistic tendencies or behaviors. Dealing with both children and charges have a lot of similarities: You influence their behaviors by influencing and controlling the environment and potential triggers for maladaptive behavior. They also differ greatly in that children are children while charges could be adults. However, despite the age difference, the advice for handling children often also carries over to adult charges, though the execution should be altered to reflect the proper audience.

It is important to note that children are not yet old enough to be diagnosed as narcissists, but they do often exhibit narcissistic traits. Narcissists never developed proper coping methods for stress, so it should be no surprise that children often behave similarly to narcissists. The good news is that children often outgrow these behaviors, though that does not mean you should not try to correct them.

One of the upsides of having minor children with narcissistic traits is that you can control their environment with hopes of influencing their behaviors while their minds are still developing. You can begin your intervention early before it evolves into a full-blown narcissistic personality disorder, and hopefully, teach your children to develop a healthy sense of self and proper coping methods. With adult charges, you have missed the window for shaping the developing brain, but you can still influence patterns of thinking and seek to begin testing and disproving plenty of the charge's maladaptive schemas.

Since you now understand that narcissistic personality disorder often consists of a lack of a healthy sense of self, low self-esteem, and a lack of empathy, you should be able to see those as areas your child needs extra support in developing, or that your charge needs help in learning. Create situations that encourage and reward your child, while fostering a sense of empathy for those around him. For your charges, make sure you create interactions that allow you to model empathy so they can begin to learn how to interact with a healthy level of empathizing with others. You can also make it a point to empathize with the narcissistic charge, verbally discussing it in the most tactful way possible. For example, saying to your angry charge, "Wow, I can see that you are really angry right now. I would be too if I were losing the game. You look like you need some time to cool off. Come over when you calm down, and we can continue this game then." Keep it calm, direct, and do not back down from requiring the narcissist to be calm before continuing. You have acknowledged his feelings, validated them, provided a getaway from the stressful situation, and created an incentive for the narcissist to calm down rather than blow up.

You can cultivate empathy by empathizing with your child and modeling empathy for others. While it may seem childish, you can talk through this process as you do it, so your child really gets the idea. For example, if your child has been disappointed and is crying while teetering toward throwing a temper tantrum, you should stop, get down on your child's level, and place a hand on his shoulder. Tell him that it is okay to be disappointed, and it is okay to cry, but a tantrum and not listening is unacceptable. Get him to take a few deep breaths to calm down, and ask if he wants a hug. By identifying and validating his feelings before giving him a technique to cope with them, he feels acknowledged and may begin to follow your instructions and calm down, especially if you tell him about a time you were disappointed and sad once too. You can further model empathy by empathizing for others. Imagine that you are at the store with your child, and you see a busy mother with two young children in the cart. She accidentally drops her eggs, shattering them and making a mess all over the tile. You can tell your child that that is too bad; she looks sad and overwhelmed. Then ask him what you should do to help. If he does not come to the conclusion of helping her clean the mess, or seeking out an employee to get help, you can suggest doing so to the child. If age appropriate, allow him to go through the effort of helping, and praise him when he has finished. Remind him that he helped her during a tough time, that it was a very nice thing to do, and then ask him if he feels good after being such a big helper to someone in need. Try not to buy him a treat or reward at the store, as he may associate doing good deeds as being done solely for rewards.

In order to cultivate self-esteem, remember to never be critical of your child or your charge. It is good to correct behavior, but there is a fine line between productive corrections and harsh criticisms. Knowing to toe the line will help you avoid accidentally crushing any developing self-esteem, your child or charge may have. Remember to praise your child or charge's successes when appropriate and give him plenty of opportunities to succeed at tasks. Rather than seeing this as coddling or babying, think of it as no different than him spraining an ankle and needing a crutch. The crutch is necessary to help keep weight off of the ankle so it can heal, and your praise and avoidance of criticism will help your child or charge to develop a healthy self-esteem that will carry him far.

SECTION 3

Working with Others outside the Circle

CHAPTER 10

Family and Triggers

When we are stressed, afraid, or in need of support, one of the first sources we often turn to is family. These people have supported us in our lives up until this point, and we often see our family, especially those older than us, as a valuable source of sage advice and wisdom. However, when dealing with a narcissist or narcissistic abuse, family may not really understand. They may not understand what you are going through and may not even know what narcissistic personality disorder is. Though they mean well, you will have to educate them, strategically teaching them about the disorder in a way that will help them support you in the way you need. Do not be afraid to tell them exactly what you need for them, or even to hand over a copy of this book to read in order to help them understand what you are going through. Family typically will go out of their way to help family members in need, if they know their help is needed. Just as you likely would not hesitate if a family member turned to you for support, many members of your family will also gladly help you if you reach out.

Mental Health

Mental health is something that many people are ignorant of. As our mental state is largely invisible to those around us, it is something that many do not understand. You need to be prepared to have a discussion about this with your family if they prove to be ignorant of the seriousness of mental health issues. You should be able to discuss that mental health is just as important as physical health and that it is not always as easy to recognize a mental health issue as opposed to a personality flaw. Especially if they know the narcissist, they likely see the narcissist as successful, confident, and essentially perfect, only seeing his mask as opposed to who he really is.

You should gently breach the subject, mentioning that while you love your narcissistic partner, the behaviors are beginning to wear down on you. Emphasize that the narcissist is not necessarily trying to hurt you, but his personality disorder is making your relationship increasingly more difficult. It may feel strange to be on the lecturing side of the relationship, especially if you are primarily speaking with parents or grandparents. They also may struggle to take what you are saying as worth accepting if they are accustomed to being the ones in leadership positions. Ultimately, it will be up to you to help them navigate the muddy water that is understanding a narcissist, and showing them how to best support you during your journey.

Ultimately, you need to show your family that you are trying to protect or prioritize your own satisfaction in life. Life is far too short to waste tiptoeing around issues, and you are making an effort to either help the narcissist improve his behavior, or you are working toward cutting off the narcissist, both of which will improve your quality of life. You should be firm that this is what is best for you, and that you would like their support in that matter. They may react generally positively to this, telling you that they will support you however you need, or they may react negatively, accusing him of hiding behind a pretend disorder to get away with unacceptable behavior.

 It is important for you to remind your family that stigmatizing the narcissist's personality disorder is unproductive or counterproductive. Just as you would not shame someone for being ill or developing cancer, you should not shame those who struggle with mental illness. Remind your family that only a trained medical professional can really diagnose the behaviors and that they should not use a personality disorder to begin patronizing or belittling the narcissist.

Antagonizers in the Family

When members of your family insist on antagonizing you or the narcissist, offering none of the support you need, sometimes you need to reevaluate the relationship. Obviously, you do not want to spend time with people that will bring you down and make the already-difficult process of dealing with a narcissist even harder. When you find that you have family members that are particularly antagonistic, you may be better off making changes to how often you see them, if you choose to continue seeing them at all.

While family is important, and should absolutely be treated as such, the same rule applies here as does with narcissists: If the family is causing you pain or making your life unreasonably more stressful or difficult, it is acceptable to end the relationship, or even just put it on pause until you feel better equipped to deal with any negativity.

Think of support systems as large circles with rings inside. At the centermost ring is the person needing support, which is you in this case. Each ring that gets further away from the center is a degree further from the support. So, you are at the center, and your parents may be the second circle, as they are the closest to you. From there, your friends might be the third circle, and coworkers in the fourth, with everything outside of that circle being strangers or acquaintances. Support should only move inward. People in the second circle should only pour support to the person needing it, and they should only seek support from those further removed from the center of the circle. When people start pushing from support from or making things difficult for the inner circle, you begin to see a problem.

Luckily, there are multiple ways to limit the relationship with whoever is unsupportive of your journey through dealing with a narcissist. You can choose to avoid that person altogether, ending the relationship in its entirety. This keeps you from having to face the person at all during your stressful time. You can choose to take a step back from the relationship temporarily, which is essentially cutting off the person but only for a short period of time. This gives you time to cool off and get your thoughts straightened out while trying to deal with yourself. During this period, you will be focused on maintaining yourself, and you do not need any other adversaries to that sense of self while simultaneously dealing with a narcissist. You can also choose to moderately limit contact with this adversarial family, such as limiting interactions to amounts you can tolerate without feeling like it is detrimental to your wellbeing. You could choose to visit one day every month for dinner at a restaurant, rather than going to that person's house every weekend. This allows you to maintain a relationship with the people who are hindering you during your time trying to cope with a narcissist, while also taking enough of a step back that you no longer feel hindered.

Ultimately, any of these methods could aid in coping with unsupportive or antagonistic family members. It is up to you to decide how much exposure you want to their negativity or antagonism. It is reasonable for you to want to step back from a relationship, and being family is not a free pass to treat other family members poorly. If anything, you should hold your family members to higher standards than you would hold those around you, as you should expect those closest to you to treat you with more care and respect than perfect strangers do. Do not let family make your life difficult just because you share DNA. Family is not determined only by blood, and you are well within your rights to take a step back from people who are blood-related to you but only add strife to your life.

CHAPTER 11

Best Friends & Platonic Loves

While friends mean well and only want what is best for you, they may not be well informed, especially on the subject of mental health disorders, which are rarely well understood by those who have never had to deal with them. Your friends also may struggle to remain objective enough to understand that the narcissist likely does not mean to treat you the way he does. They may struggle to stay neutral enough to give you the support you need when they see you in pain, and they may struggle to not villainize the narcissist for behaving in such a way that causes you pain, whether it is intentional or not. They care about you enough that seeing you in pain can cloud their judgment.

Knowing that your friends may react in ways that they hope are beneficial, but do not help, informing them of what they can do is the best way to avoid disaster. While you do want your friends to understand your struggles, you do not want them doing something rash or detrimental to your attempts at dealing with a narcissist. For example, if you are working with a narcissistic spouse to get through therapy and try to better his behavior, you do not want to risk your friends saying something to the narcissist that immediately puts him on the defensive and leaves him lashing out in order to gain more control.

Just as with your family, you should be clear to your friends that this is a challenging endeavor, but one you want to attempt nonetheless. Despite the challenges, you want to remain committed to the narcissist, and you need their support as you work on how to do that. Tell your friends that you are trusting them to be there for you when you need them most, just as you would be there for them if they needed you, and the best way they can support you is by being there to listen to you when you need someone to talk to. Again, you may find it useful to recommend that your friends also look into what to expect with narcissists, and even sharing this book with them could provide valuable insight, so they learn how best to support someone suffering through a narcissistic relationship.

Triggering Friends

Ultimately, knowing that your friends may become upset, listening to your discussions, you must make decisions on how to balance everyone's needs. You likely do not want to push away people you value as friends, but you also do not want to upset them with details that present problems for them. Particularly with more emotional friends that are easily upset, you may find yourself better off avoiding situations that involve high tensions or emotions. You may turn to that friend for entertainment or for a good time, but not for highly sensitive conversations. This is not the same as walking on eggshells around the narcissist; you are still able to have a genuine relationship with these more emotionally sensitive friends, but you are also mindful of their needs as well. They may need to not hear about your difficulties for a variety of reasons, including that they may feel upset or emotionally triggered at the discussion, and as a good friend, mindful of what your friend needs, you oblige.

You also may limit situations in which these more sensitive friends have to interact with the narcissist. They may be more inclined to snapping at the narcissist than you would like, or they may feel intense negative emotions if they have escaped a relationship with a narcissist before. You can specifically look to spend time with your sensitive friends in calmer, more neutral settings, and turn to your more levelheaded friends when you need a shoulder to cry on or someone to vent to. This keeps tensions from getting too high, and you avoid setting both your friend and the narcissist up for failure. Especially when you know that your friends and the narcissist being in the same area would cause problems, it is better for everyone involved to keep them separate.

If your friends are wholly unsupportive of your choices, you may have to reevaluate your friendships, just as you reevaluate your relationships with family members. Ultimately, you need to make sure that your inner circles are supportive of you and your choices. You do not need the added stress of worrying about letting your friends or family down by making the choices you feel are the right ones.

Council from Friends

Most people go to their friends to vent their frustrations, and many friends also return those rants with suggestions on how to better the situation. Oftentimes, these suggestions are based on the other people's own life experiences. However, oftentimes, these experiences are based on normal interactions with people who are not narcissists. These suggestions oftentimes also may be counterproductive to your goal of maintaining a relationship with a narcissist. Many of your friends may tell you to break up with him or end the relationship because the behaviors are unacceptable. They also may offer suggestions to you that will only irritate or trigger the narcissist into his maladaptive behaviors, which will escalate the situation, and potentially escalate any abuse.

You will have to find a balance between trusting your friends' opinions and your desires. If your friends are demanding you cut off the narcissist and your desire is to maintain, or even further, a relationship with a narcissist, you will need to take their advice and suggestions with a grain of salt. Ultimately, your choices must work for you, with everyone else as an afterthought, so you should not feel obligated to bend to their whims just to appease them. This will take plenty of self-reflection and attempting to identify your values, as well as your goals in your relationships.

When figuring out your priorities, you will have to ask yourself what the most important thing you want is. If the most important thing is maintaining a relationship with the narcissist, then that should tip the scales in his favor when considering who to side with. Especially in cases where you are already married and have children, you may want to focus on preserving and bettering your relationship with the narcissist instead of heeding your friends' warnings of ending it before it gets worse.

On the other end of the spectrum, some of your friends' advice could be downright dangerous. If the narcissist is known to be particularly aggressive when provoked, confronting him and telling him you refuse to take this behavior, as advised by your friend, may just be adding fuel to the fire. Along with weighing your own goals, you need to maintain your own safety, and sometimes, your friends' advice would do more harm than good. What will work in ordinary relationships will not work with narcissists, and your friends might not know this.

CHAPTER 12

Kids Involved

When children are involved, navigating the waters of a narcissistic relationship become infinitely rougher. A relationship with a narcissist already involves a major juggling act as you try to balance challenging his maladaptive schemas through your own behavior, keeping from triggering him into acting on his schemas, and making sure your own needs are met, and as soon as children come into the picture, all of the pins you have been so precariously juggling are suddenly on fire. Everything has to be far more precise, and you have to take special care to not drop the pins, but also to avoid burning yourself or those you love.

You may worry that your child's own self-esteem will be damaged by the narcissist's fragile ego if the narcissist lashes out, or that your child will be on the receiving end of manipulative tactics. You also may worry that your child will learn the narcissist's behaviors through exposure and try to emulate them, or will internalize that that is the normal way to treat people within the relationship you share with the narcissist. They may think that manipulation is normal in a romantic relationship, or that it is normal to seek attention and admiration when they are a parent or grandparent if the narcissist is your mother or father. All of these are legitimate, valid fears, and unfortunately, those are very real possibilities.

Despite these possibilities, there are ways to mitigate damage while you maintain your relationship with the narcissist, or if they are forced to maintain a relationship with the narcissist due to a court order in the event of custody or grandparent rights dictating that the narcissist is to have some degree of visitation. You will have to work hard with your children to explain what narcissism is and foster the skills your children will need to become healthy, productive adults without maladaptive schemas. You also have to know that sometimes, cutting off the relationship is in the best interest of your children in order to minimize contact with the narcissist in the event that your children are being impacted so negatively that you cannot assuage the damage. When trying to help children navigate the madhouse that is narcissism, there are three key points to remember.

Articulation is Key

Ultimately, the most important thing for children navigating narcissism is giving them an age-appropriate understanding of what is happening. Knowledge is power, and the more the children understand, the more able they will be to avoid falling into the narcissist's traps. Even if you have chosen to split apart from the narcissist, having an age-appropriate conversation about why you have made that decision will help the child. Honesty is the best policy when dealing with children, and the sooner they learn why certain people behave the way they do, the sooner they will be able to deal with it their own way.

Imagine your child has a narcissistic father. He has the tendency to be harshly critical of the child if he feels his child is not behaving the way he expects.

Even the smallest of missteps are treated like grievous mistakes, and he has a tendency to say, "You never do anything right," every time it happens. Even spilling a few drops of milk is regarded as disastrous to the narcissist. Explaining to your child that daddy has a hard time when things go wrong, and that is why he reacts that way may help your child understand. This helps your child to develop empathy and compassion for the narcissist without affirming that the narcissist's behaviors are acceptable. Remind your child that he or she is safe with you and that daddy just needs a few minutes to calm down and deal with his big feelings, just as you would likely tell your own child if she were in need of a few minutes to compose herself.

Older children may be prepared to have more in-depth conversations about what a personality disorder is and what that entails. Explaining to your children that the narcissist cannot see things around him for what they really are may aid them in learning that the narcissist's sharp words should not be given much of an afterthought. Teach them that it is not much different than a younger child calling them a meanie-head or saying that the child hates them. In a sense, this is true- the narcissist never developed relationship skills past a child's level, and therefore, a lot of his behavior is quite childish and selfish.

When having a conversation about cutting off another person, it is important to discuss with the child that sometimes, people are not safe people and it is better to stay away from them than it is to try to continue a relationship. Explain to the child that it is your job as the parent to keep them safe, and if it comes down to it, taking the children away from that person, even if it is a beloved relative, is better for everyone. Tell your children that even though they love candy, your job as a parent is to not let them have so much candy that they get sick, develop health issues, or rot their teeth. Likewise, it is your job to keep them away from people who are not safe or who make bad choices.

No matter what your end goal is with your relationship with the narcissist, remember that keeping your children informed with age-appropriate information is a key step to keeping them from being physically or emotionally harmed. Children are far smarter than most adults give them credit for, and they see more than most people expect. They will see your struggles with a narcissist, and it is better to explain it than for them to think that is just a normal interaction in a relationship. They will take your words at face value most of the time, so explain it as thoroughly as you think is appropriate. Most importantly, answer any questions they may have honestly in an age-appropriate manner. Remember that your articulation will set the stage for what your children are absorbing.

No Apologies

While you should explain the narcissist's behaviors to your children, you should never offer apologies for the narcissist. Offering apologies that the narcissist has not expressed only makes the child think that things will be different in the future, and sets up expectations that will likely not be met. Apologies imply feeling bad or recognizing the behavior is wrong, but the narcissist does not feel bad for his behaviors and does not see them as wrong.

Rather than apologizing for negative behaviors, you should instead take the option of explaining the reasoning for them. Do not think of this as excusing the behavior, or telling your children that it is acceptable to act any way they please so long as they can explain it away. This instead allows your child to begin to understand the narcissist's perspective, which is yet another exercise in empathy. The child begins to see the narcissist's side of things without learning to do the behaviors because the child learns it is essentially an illness that is causing it.

By treating the behaviors as a symptom of a mental health issue and emphasizing that keeping themselves mentally healthy is important, you teach your children to have compassion. Just as they would not judge someone in their class who is in a wheelchair and needs extra accommodations, they learn not to judge the narcissist for needing extra emotional support. They will be able to recognize his behaviors as symptoms of a problem that needs treatment rather than the narcissist being truly evil.

Perhaps your children have a narcissistic grandfather. He has a tendency to favor one and treat the other as an afterthought, and because of this, you have chosen to limit contact between your children and their grandfather. Rather than apologizing to your child who has been scapegoated, you should explain the behavior. You can tell your child that grandpa does not understand how his treatment makes her feel bad. Justify your daughter's feelings and let her know it is right to feel wronged and that it is not okay to hurt other people. You can further explain that because grandpa does not understand that hurting other people's feelings is why you are taking some time away from him.

During this explanation, do not make your children feel like they are in the wrong for feeling how they do. They will get plenty of gaslighting or thinking that they are wrong about how they understand the world around them, from the narcissist without you defending the narcissist's behaviors. Ultimately, your children need honesty at an age-appropriate level and general explanations of why the narcissist behaves how he does. They will eventually come to learn that the narcissist's behaviors are the opposite of what they want to do if you are thorough about your explanations and emulate and guide your children through learning to act with empathy and compassion.

Freedom to Express

The best thing you can do for your children that are exposed to narcissism is to foster empathy in them. By teaching your children empathy, you will foster an understanding of what behaviors are reasonable, and why some people sometimes react inappropriately. In seeing you try to work with the narcissist and help the narcissist learn adaptive behavior, your children will see that you value your relationships and will try to do what you can to understand and work around problems. They will see your caring, nurturing side that made you attractive to the narcissist in the first place, and they will learn to try their hardest to salvage a relationship before abandoning it when it is safe to do so.

Likewise, they will see what an inappropriate reaction to stress looks like, and you will teach them to have the compassion to help guide the stressed person through their inappropriate reaction. This conversation about inappropriate reactions also opens the door to explaining healthier coping mechanisms to your children. Guiding them through how to properly deal with stress in a way that will not have negative impacts on other people and will allow them to cope in a healthy manner is a life skill all people need. These conversations become learning opportunities that begin even more conversations, especially when the narcissist's behaviors can be so confusing to children. So long as you are honest about your explanations and objective about what you consider proper or improper reactions, your children will follow your lead, and if they are at an age where they are choosing their own actions, you will give them the knowledge and skills they will need to make informed choices about the narcissist on their own.

By validating your children's feelings when they discuss the narcissist, you are letting them know that they are entitled to how they feel, no matter how it is. Your empathy and compassion for your children will teach them that they can come to you if they need to, and give them the proof they need to be less vulnerable to the narcissist's behaviors. Even though you will be there, it is inevitable that they will not be exposed to some of the narcissist's maladaptive behaviors at some point, and it is best for your children to be well-prepared when that day comes.

SECTION 4

Bonus Chapters

CHAPTER 13

Helpful Mobile Apps to Make Dealing with a Narcissist Bearable

Communication with a narcissist can be especially difficult if you have ended your relationship with him or her but are required to maintain contact. Most often, the reason for required contact is when you share children. Communicating can become messy if the narcissist decides to direct his attention or rage at you. You may find him calling all hours of the night, asking inane things for the umpteenth time, like what time does Johnny have to be at soccer, or when is Kate's parent-teacher conference. He may call you incessantly to get information or switch to messaging you on social media or via texts. This can make it difficult to track all communication, as it is constantly changing from form to form, and in many states, you cannot record another person without his or her consent. Luckily, there are a handful of apps that can be used to record and document everything from shared calendars, messages, child support, and anything else you and your narcissistic co-parent would ever need to communicate about with one another.

OurFamilyWizard

The most commonly recommended app is OurFamilyWizard[3]. This app is comprehensive and is frequently ordered in court orders for families where abuse, either verbal or physical, has occurred. Communication with this app is court-approved, and according to their website, is recommended by courts in all 50 states of America to be used to manage co-parenting communication. This app allows for calendars to be shared, expenses to be tracked, files shared, and allows for the parents to share messages back and forth with one another.

This site also includes access for professionals to communicate with both parents. Doctors, lawyers, counselors, mediators, and other professionals will be able to communicate and view communication between the parents, so there is no denying what the narcissist said. Everything is documented in black and white for professionals involved in your custody case to see.

One unique feature of OurFamilyWizard includes is its ToneMeter. This is essentially a grammar checker, but it gauges tone instead of grammar. This flags when a sentence written has been emotionally charged, allowing the writer to see the tone of what is being written so it can be corrected and written in a way that may be more productive or better received. Since oftentimes, the tone is lost in translation with written correspondence, this can help both you and the narcissist word things in a way that are less inflammatory.

Overall, this app is great if you are in a high conflict shared parenting relationship. This will allow you to limit in-person or verbal communication, and will also allow for easier documentation.

Coparently

Coparently[4] is quite similar to OurFamilyWizard. It allows for parents to digitally share information pertaining to their children quickly in one place for easy tracking and documenting. This app keeps everything you could possibly need together and allows you and your co-parent to share calendars, messages to each other, manage expenses, and a list of contacts that are relevant to your children, such as their doctors, schools, extracurricular activities, daycares, or friends' parents. All of that communication and information in one place means you have to contact your ex significantly less, and when you do contact one another, it is all in one place and easily tracked and documented.

This app works on virtually any electronic device, with versions available for Android, iPhone, BlackBerry, Windows Phones, and Kindle Fire Devices. There are also desktop versions for all major operating systems and modern browsers. With such a wide range of ways to contact one another, you never have to worry about cross-compatibility again. You can also give guest access to your account, allowing professionals to see and monitor communication methods. There is also a special children's mode that allows kids to see the calendars, keeping them informed on what will be happening with them when.

This allows for all of the communication that is necessary to be passed back and forth for co-parenting effectively, while still maintaining some semblance of distance. Since all communication can be monitored, the narcissist will likely be on his best behavior to avoid being painted as the bad guy in the divorce. Pricing is available on their website, and at the time of writing this book, they were offering a free 30-day trial to decide if it is right for you.

2houses

2houses[5] is yet another mobile app that seeks to consolidate all of the information coparents need to be successful. This app is compatible with Android, iOS, and internet browsers, and offers a 14-day free trial at the time of this book's writing. They include access to a messenger, calendar, financial tracker, an info-bank where you can store all of your children's pertinent information, photo albums that allow for photos and memories to be shared, and a journal where you can record funny, cute, or interesting information about what has happened on your custody time to document your child's growth.

This site allows parents to grant access to other users as well and can specify how much or how little the others are able to see. This app also allows for you to set up multiple profiles under the same email address so if you require more than one family account, you are able to have them all created for the same email address.

Ultimately, this is yet another app meant to share information between co-parents without having actual physical or verbal contact with one another. The added features of being able to easily document a journal and share media files with one another is a welcome addition. With the added areas of contact with this form of communication such as the journal, it may be best to be used with exes lower on the narcissistic spectrum that would not be seeking to wreak as much havoc on your life as others.

Overcome Narcissism Self & Ego by Angie Atkinson

This app is different in that it is about overcoming narcissism instead of creating ways to communicate that mitigate abuse. Overcome Narcissism Self & Ego by Angie Atkinson[6] includes audio content about surviving narcissistic abuse, techniques to alleviate anxiety, and meditations and affirmations created by Angie Atkinson, a life coach. She regularly adds new content to the site on a multitude of topics that will help you navigate through healing from narcissistic abuse.

With this free mobile app, you will have access to certain content right from downloading, and you can purchase more. The content will give you ways to identify narcissistic behavior, resources for recovering, basic guides to what to expect, and more. If you feel lost and unsure where to go from here in your journey to healing or you would like some more content to listen to daily, this app will be beneficial to you.

CHAPTER 14

25 Helpful Affirmations
for Dealing with a Narcissist

Affirmations are fantastic tools to keep yourself level-headed. Often used paired with mindfulness or during various therapies, affirmations are short, simple phrases for you to repeat to yourself during times of stress to ground yourself and keep from letting your emotions or bad habits get the best of you. Affirmations can be anything, though they have three basic rules. The first rule is that they must be about yourself. This is because you are only able to control yourself. You cannot dictate how other people perceive or interact with the world, but you can control your own thoughts or actions. The second rule is that it must be positive. By focusing on positive language, you put yourself into a positive mindset. Think of the difference between, "I will not fall into my old habits," versus "I am taking steps to change my behavior to get the results I want." Between the two, the second is more inspiring. The third rule is that the affirmation must be worded in a way that is in the present tense. This way, you remind yourself that it is true at that particular moment because that is what you are experiencing. With these three rules, you can create any sort of affirmations you think will be useful to you and your situation.

Affirmations can come in many different forms, and having an arsenal of affirmations about a broad range of struggles can help you in almost any situation. Do you have a hard time trusting yourself? Repeat some mental clarity affirmations. Are you struggling to do what you need for yourself? Remind yourself of your self-worth with affirmations. This chapter will provide you with affirmations for clarity, compassion, patience, self-worth, and healing to help you on your journey. Remember to repeat these to yourself as you need them, and you will be able to keep yourself grounded, even in times of high emotion.

Affirmations of Mental Clarity

My perceptions of reality are accurate, and I will trust them to guide me through making decisions.

Narcissists are masters at manipulating others. They love to gaslight, convincing you that what you believe happened did not occur the way you think, or that it did not happen at all. Narcissists have a tendency to say things to get you to doubt yourself and believe their side of the story. This could be especially unsettling if you were already struggling with trusting yourself before, as you now have someone you likely respect a great deal telling you that you are wrong about what you think happened. You begin to feel like you are going crazy. This is what the narcissist wants, as it makes you easier to control. By repeating this affirmation to yourself, you are able to remind yourself that your own judgments are worthy of trust. Any time you are feeling doubtful about how you perceive something, you can remind yourself that you are trustworthy and your perceptions are accurate. Trust your judgment and follow your gut reactions, even if the narcissist tries to convince you to do otherwise.

I have the experience to see through attempts to manipulate me, and the strength to make sure I can stand firm against them. I have withstood the storm once, and I will do it this time as well.

This affirmation reminds you to use your experiences of being manipulated in the past to key into whether you are being manipulated in the present. If you are interacting with the narcissist in your life and begin to doubt yourself, reminding yourself that you can see through the manipulation. You also remind yourself that you were strong enough to get through the manipulation in the past, and you are even stronger now that you are standing up to it. Your strength will help you avoid being manipulated in the future.

I am grateful that I can see things for what they are, and that I know I can trust my judgment.

Reminding yourself that you are grateful for your clarity reminds you to never take that clarity for granted- it was earned through hard work and struggles. Your mental clarity came through adversity, and you have learned to see through the manipulative tactics that the narcissist employs through the first-hand experience. Reminding yourself that you are grateful for your clarity reminds you once again that it is valuable and trustworthy. When you begin to doubt yourself, reminding that you value your perceptions reminds you to rely on them rather than believing anyone who convinces you to doubt them.

I can clearly see my goals for this relationship in my mind, and I am actively taking steps toward that goal.

Reminding yourself that you know exactly what you hope to achieve reminds yourself that you know what you need best. If someone tries to make you doubt you know what is best, or tries to convince you to do something you are unsure of or disagree with, you can remind yourself that your own clarity is ultimately what you need to rely on, not what other people think you need or want. You also remind yourself that you are working on your goals any time you feel doubtful you are on track or like you are doing the wrong things for the wrong reasons.

My mental clarity brings me the strength I need to overcome any challenges or obstacles that get in the way of completing my goals and the wisdom to know when it is time to change my goas.

This affirmation reminds you that your clarity is your strength. Knowing you can trust yourself to see the world around you clearly will enable you to get past any manipulative or degrading behavior the narcissist may subject you to. Your goals are clear in your mind and you know exactly what you want. Your clarity also lets you see things for what they are so you can recognize when your goals are no longer viable, so you do not find yourself stuck in a sunk cost fallacy, believing that you have to keep going toward something that does not make sense because you have already put in a lot of energy toward it. Sometimes, knowing when to quit is important and practical.

Affirmations of Compassion

I have the compassion, patience and grace to get through this difficult time.

Reminding yourself that you have compassion and patience can be the difference between snapping and saying something in anger. That moment to take a deep breath and recite your affirmation will help if you ever feel like you are losing your patience. We all have moments when our patience is tested, and we have to remind ourselves to stay calm and collected. When the narcissist begins pushing your buttons, what he is seeking is a reaction to affirm a maladaptive schema. You reacting in anger would likely reaffirm the schema, so reminding yourself of your immense compassion and patience will keep you calm enough to avoid reactive behavior.

Any mistakes I or others make are simple missteps and they deserve to be treated with compassion and understanding.

Sometimes it can be hard to remain calm and react in a productive manner when someone messes up, even if the mistake is harmless. It is still an inconvenience to fix the mistake, no matter how small. Oftentimes, people are compassionate with other people who make mistakes and understand how it could have happened, but they are harsh on themselves. You are just as deserving as compassion after making a mistake as anyone else. After all, you are only human, and humans are not perfect. Making mistakes is a normal part of life, and by treating yourself kindly through the mistakes, no matter how big or small, you will help yourself become stronger and learn from what happened. This also reminds you to be gentle with the narcissist when he or she does something that is unkind or unexpected. Your understanding of narcissistic personality disorder will help you remain compassionate and firm in your goals of either maintaining a relationship or ending one.

I recognize that my compassion lets me see the best in others and gives me insight to be my best self.

When you realize that, despite the fact that the narcissist used it to his advantage, your compassion is a strength, you begin to embrace it. Being able to see the best in others is a blessing; you can see potential where work in progress is standing, and you can provide those around you with the support they will need in order to become that potential. This will also allow you to see the best in the narcissist, which may be buried under scars and maladaptive behavior, but you will be able to acknowledge the parts of the narcissist that you truly enjoy and embrace. These will be your reminders of why you want to maintain your relationship, as you see the narcissist beyond his flaws.

My respect and compassion for others reflect on my true character.

Remember, you cannot control how other people use your help, but not helping at all out of fear that your aid would be misused would ultimately reflect your character. Your compassionate nature is who you are, and recognizing that compassion as who you are can remind you to remain compassionate, even when it is the harder choice. Sometimes, it is harder to maintain contact with someone than it is to walk away, but maintaining that contact is the right choice. When maintaining contact with the narcissist, although difficult, is right for you even though walking away would be easier, reminding yourself that you are the kind of person that stays and aids others, even when it is tough, will keep your resolve strong.

I choose to treat everyone with compassion and respect because treating them with respect makes my world a more compassionate place.

Ultimately, you cannot control other people. Even the narcissist, the master manipulator, cannot fully control those around him. What you can control, however, is you. By treating others with compassion, you make your world a slightly more compassionate place. Your compassion creates a ripple effect that will hopefully do some good outside of your initial actions. Perhaps it inspires someone else to do a good deed. Maybe it helps the narcissist challenge one of his maladaptive schemas. Either way, your compassion is never wasted, even on someone who misuses the grace you give, because you are being true to yourself, even when you know it might be wasted.

Affirmations of Self-worth

My empathy and compassion are my greatest strengths, and despite the narcissist taking advantage of them, I am proud to be myself.

This affirmation reasserts that your empathy and compassion are strengths and not weaknesses, even though they were what the narcissist used to get what was wanted from you in the first place. The vast majority of the world sees your convictions and sees a wonderful, kindhearted person who is understanding and caring. You should always remember that you are valuable, and your strengths define who you are. That strength will take you far in life, and you should be proud to be you, even when you are beginning to doubt yourself.

Humans deserve to be treated with basic care and respect, and I deserve this too.

Narcissists often degrade your sense of duty to yourself. You spend so long worrying about the narcissist and catering to the narcissist's needs that you forget that you deserve it as well. After so long of being discarded as an afterthought, even you may begin to regard yourself as one. Reminding yourself that you are just as deserving as everyone else of basic care and respect will keep you taking care of yourself as well. After all, no one is ever as invested in caring for you than yourself! You would not let your phone or laptop battery die if it can be helped, and you should treat your own emotional battery the same. Recharge when you need it, even if you do not feel as if you deserve it, because you do deserve it, just like everyone else deserves to recharge.

I am deserving of love, kindness, and compassion, just like everyone else in the world.

The narcissist may have repeatedly told you that no one could ever love you as you are, or that everyone is only using you. The irony here is that he was only deflecting his own feelings onto you. He feels as if he is unlovable, so he lashes out at others. Just as you feel compassionate and kind toward others, you need to reflect some of that kindness toward yourself as well. Loving yourself is one of the first steps toward healing and having a healthy sense of self. Even in moments where you doubt yourself and wonder if the narcissist is right, remind yourself that you, like everyone else, are worthy of love.

I deserve the kind of healthy, stable relationships I crave, and I am taking steps to make them.

Another part of loving or respecting your self is making sure the relationships you surround yourself with are healthy. You deserve healthy relationships; no one deserves abuse or torment, and especially not from the person they have chosen to devote themselves to. Reminding yourself that you are taking steps toward healthy relationships can help you avoid situations that may become toxic, and recognize that sometimes, the only right answer is to leave a relationship to protect yourself, and you deserve to do that for yourself if it is the only solution.

I am worthy of loving myself and recognizing my strengths and the value I bring to other people.

This affirmation reminds you to never devalue yourself. Narcissists oftentimes purposefully put you down and tell you that you are worth less than you actually are. They want you to feel worthless so you feel trapped. By reminding yourself of how valuable you actually are to those you love and who love you, you remind yourself to treat yourself better. You have already spent time being belittled and demeaned, and there is no reason for you to perpetuate the narcissist's abuse to yourself.

Affirmations of Patience

I have the patience to get through these tests and the mental clarity to understand that I cannot control others.

Reminding yourself that you are patient enough to handle difficult situations helps you remain calm during even the most testing situations. Keep in mind that oftentimes, when dealing with a narcissist, he wants you to react negatively as that reaffirms everything he believes is true. By also acknowledging that you cannot control the narcissist, no matter how much easier that would make life, you remind yourself to keep your patience when things do not go as you were hoping them to. The narcissist will rarely react the way you would expect or hope, so recognizing that you cannot control him is a big step toward maintaining your composure.

I am flexible and I can roll with anything life throws at me with patience and perseverance.

Along with the previous affirmation, acknowledging that you cannot control the world around you, but you can control your own reaction will give you a sense of control over the situation. Knowing you can control your reactions and reminding yourself of this will help you to consciously make decisions that you are sure will be beneficial and productive as opposed to acting in inflammatory ways that only make the situation worse.

I have plenty of patience to care for myself and those I love.

Sometimes, the narcissist or other people we love are draining on our patience and good will. We feel as if our patience is a finite resource, and it is quickly running empty. This affirmation reminds you that you do have the patience you need, and that you are enough for yourself and others. Sometimes, what you need is a little reminder that you do have enough patience for everyone to be able to get through whatever trying event is happening.

My patience and my understanding nature will guide me through even the toughest times with those I love.

When things are going rough, it can be hard to remember that you need to remain calm. Especially when someone you love is doing something that hurts you or makes you unhappy, you may find yourself reacting rather than acting calmly. The narcissist will test and push you, looking for ways to prove he is right and you are reactionary. You need to remind yourself that your patience will help you remain calm, even when things get bad.

I stay calm even under stress.

Sometimes, the simplest affirmations are the most helpful in stressful situations. When you are beginning to feel overwhelmed, take a deep breath and repeat this affirmation to yourself before exhaling. After a couple of repetitions, you should be in a calmer mindset and able to take on whatever is stressing you at that moment.

Affirmations of Healing

I am healing, and every day, I get a little bit closer to finishing that process.

Healing is a difficult process, even in the best of situations. We often take one step forward and feel like we immediately fall back two steps as well. The grief and pain often feel like it ebbs and flows, and on the days when the pain is overwhelming, you may feel like you are failing. Remember, the pain means you are healing, and every day, you get one step closer to the wounds inflicted by the narcissist healing. Even when you feel like you are failing and the pain is worse, you are still moving closer to becoming whole once more. Take a moment to remind yourself of this when you feel at your lowest.

I am taking care of myself to promote healing and good health.

Sometimes, the effort of caring for yourself can feel impossible after the devastating effects of the narcissist on your life. The narcissist's influence over you can feel so overwhelming that you feel as though caring for yourself is undeserved and unnecessary. Remind yourself that the effort you are exerting to care for yourself is absolutely necessary when you are healing. Just as you would protect a broken leg and avoid bearing weight while it heals, you should care for yourself as well. You need extra attention and care during that time.

I am leaving my past behind me in order to make the future what I want it to be.

Oftentimes, we have a tendency to focus on the past. We get preoccupied with our struggles, and the pain from the past follows us, making it feel like it is happening in present time all over again. Reminding yourself that the past is over and cannot be changed can help you turn your focus from ruminating to working toward bettering yourself for the future to avoid that pain. While it is unhealthy to dwell on the past, it is healthy to learn from it so you can do better in the future. That reminder is sometimes necessary, especially on days when you find yourself missing the early stages of your relationship with the narcissist.

I know my future will be worth any troubles I am facing now, and I am keeping my mind focused on my goals.

Sometimes, when things get hard, we think it might be easier to go back to the way things used to be. At the very least, that pain is familiar, while the healing process may be entirely foreign to you. You may be missing the narcissist, or feeling lonely and worthless. No matter what the reason, reminding yourself that the troubles are temporary and are a necessary evil to get to the future that you desire will help keep you on track. You can use this to remind yourself to not give in to temptation of returning your old way of life. Remember, even though it is familiar, that life was not easy, or you would not have been seeking to change it in the first place.

It is my duty to protect myself and I owe it to myself to make sure I am taken care of and safe, even if I have to do things that are difficult to ensure it.

Ultimately, you are responsible for yourself. You owe it to yourself to take care of yourself, even if doing so is difficult or requires you to make sacrifices. If the only way to feel like you are healthy or whole is to give up on a relationship that brings you pain, no matter how hard it is, you owe it to yourself to do it. You must not sacrifice yourself for others, especially if they will not appreciate the effort or will only hurt you in return. If the narcissist is toxic, you have no business remaining in that relationship.

WAIT!!!

READ THIS BEFORE GOING ANY FURTHER!

How would you like to get your next eBook **FREE** and get new books for **FREE** too before they are publicly released?

Join our Self Empowerment Team today and receive your next (and future) books for **FREE**! Signing up is easy and completely free!!

Check out this page for more info!

www.SelfEmpowermentTeam.com/SignUp

Thank you for reading my book...

Don't forget to leave an honest review...

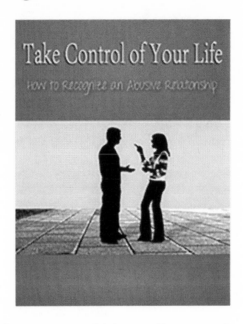

I'd like to offer you this amazing resource which my clients pay for. It is a report I written when I first began my journey.

Click on the picture above or navigate to the website below to join my exclusive email list. Upon joining, you will receive this incredible report on how to recognize an abusive relationship.

If you ask most people on the street what an abusive relationship is, chances are you'd get a description of physical abuse. And yes, that is most certainly an abusive relationship. However, abuse comes in many forms. The actual meaning of abuse is when someone exerts control over another person.

Find out more about recognizing an abusive relationship and learn how to take control over your life by clicking on the book above or by going to this link:

http://bit.ly/RecognizeAbusiveRelationship

CONCLUSION

Congratulations! You have made it to the end of the book. One of the hardest steps is acknowledging that you have a problem that needs to be fixed, and in seeking out this book, you likely have, at least to some degree. You may be suspecting that something is wrong in one of your relationships and are exploring options. Or perhaps someone you know is a narcissist and you wanted to know whether the relationship was worth attempting to salvage. Whatever your reason for picking up this book, you have been provided with valuable information about how to navigate the world of narcissism.

Through this book, you were given insight into what narcissistic personality disorder is, as well as how to treat it through schema therapy. Understanding that narcissism is caused as reactive, maladaptive coping mechanisms against stress will help you empathize and understand why the narcissist behaves how he or she does. It also provides insight into how to interact with the narcissist, through identifying certain schemas you suspect the narcissist has developed and interacting in ways that contradict the schemas. These skills are valuable assets when you either desire to maintain a relationship with a narcissist, or you have no choice but to continue contact. You were provided with suggestions for how to interact with others around you that do not understand what a relationship with a narcissist entails, and how to weigh suggestions from the uninformed with those you care about's feelings on the matter, and your own goals. With these skills, as well as some helpful apps and affirmations, you are a little more prepared to hold your own with a narcissist than you were before.

Ultimately, this is a long, arduous journey. Even cutting the narcissist off does not end the journey, as you will still have a long road to trek as you heal. However, you can do this. As difficult as it may be, you can learn to interact with a narcissist and you can mitigate damage and how often you fall for the narcissist's tactics. Trust yourself on this journey and follow your own pace. Regardless of whether you choose to maintain a relationship beyond a superficial level or if you desire to cut off the narcissist for good, find a support group. Do not be afraid to reach out to others who understand what you are going through. That support is essential to you, and you may find it is a valuable resource you never knew you needed.

Keep moving forward and keep your head up! Even if you feel hopeless or as if you cannot get through this, remember, that you can, and you will. Even setbacks, small or large, do not mean you are destined for failure, and you do not have to live your life unhappily. Choose what you truly want as your goal, and work toward it. Think of things one day, one hour, or one minute at a time if that is all you can get through at the moment, and keep putting your feet one step in front of the other. You will make it to the other side if you keep moving toward it.

References,
Resources, and Helpful Links

1. Edelstein, R. S., Yim, I. S., & Quas, J. A. (2010, June 25). Narcissism predicts heightened cortisol reactivity to a psychosocial stressor in men. Retrieved from https://www.sciencedirect.com/science/article/abs/pii/S0092656610000917

2. What is Schema-Focused Therapy? (2017, August 23). Retrieved from https://www.pasadenavilla.com/2017/04/05/what-is-schema-focused-therapy/

3. OurFamilyWizard. Retrieved from https://www.ourfamilywizard.com/

4. Coparently. Retrieved from http://coparently.com/

5. 2houses. Retrieved from https://www.2houses.com/en/

6. Atkinson, A. Overcome Narcissism Self & Ego by Angie Atkinson - Apps on Google Play. Retrieved from https://play.google.com/store/apps/details?id=com.pitashi.audiojoy.angieatkinson&hl=en_US

PART II

RECOVERING FROM NARCISSISTIC ABUSE

How to Heal from Toxic Relationships and Emotional Abuse

PRISCILLA POSEY

PREFACE

Welcome to the beginning of *Recovering from Narcissistic Abuse: How to Heal from Toxic Relationships*. In this book, you will find out what a narcissist is but mainly focus on the ways you can heal from being involved with a narcissist. This book solely focuses on the many benefits of what you will get when you decide to start moving on from a narcissistic relationship. This book is extremely good for you to read because you will learn many techniques that maybe you haven't tried yet. It is a literal step-by-step guide on how to move on with your life. The goal or feeling you should have once you have completed this book (exercises, and reading) is that you feel fulfilled, and successful. You will feel empowered and in control for potentially the first time ever. The things you will start to experience reading this book could potentially be life-changing. If you miss out on this opportunity, you will regret it to great depths. Say you put this book down now, and you don't buy it. You will go home and be thinking about your relationship; you will go in cycles over what happened, and why. You will be stuck in a cycle of overload, and then feel the urge to call your ex. But stop, if you buy this book right now, you can finally get out of this mind trap, and learn to fix these urges, and understand why this happens.

Do you fear that you will end up in another abusive relationship? Are you the person you want to be right now? Can you honestly say that you are living the life you have wanted to live? Don't live in fear any longer; don't feel powerless to the control of others; don't allow yourself to be the victim. It is time to stand up and make real change for yourself. Because this is what matters the most.

YOU. Your pride, your self-worth, your dignity, your mind, your body, your love, your decisions, your boundaries, your recovery. If your day-to-day is as devastating as when you ended the relationship months, weeks, or even days ago, then this book is the right pick for you. You will start to get out of this shell that you are in and dive into the mind of the narcissist and learn how to fight back. How to gain your control and be strong enough to walk away, but for good this time. Together, we can focus on loving yourself and understanding what it means to be powerful.

If you have self-esteem issues, due to the abuse, I can promise you that by the end of this book, you will be thankful for everything you learned. You will use the methods implemented in this book to help you start right now! This book will be with you every day of your life and is the smartest, perhaps the best decision you can make for yourself right this very moment. Do you want to get out of the slump of feeling so worthless? Do you wonder how long it will take to move on? Do you wish you could literally snap your fingers, and your trauma could just go away? Have you longed for the traumatic memories to disappear? Do you wish that your next relationship will be a good one? Well, this book will help you feel inspired and motivated to be better. It will teach you skills on how to let go of the trauma and find inner prosperity and peace. It will give you the peace of mind you have been searching for. Most of all, it will give you the strength to realize only you are in control.

So, if you want that control back, if you want to feel inspired, if you want to learn how to truly love yourself, and re-open your heart to others... Buy this book and love every moment of the opportunities inside. Remember, if you want to change, don't just wait for something to happen, make a choice to change for yourself. The next step is to read this book.

Good Luck!

WAIT!!!

READ THIS BEFORE GOING ANY FURTHER!

How would you like to get your next eBook **FREE** <u>and</u> get new books for **FREE** too before they are publicly released?

Join our Self Empowerment Team today and receive your next (and future) books for **FREE**! Signing up is easy and completely free!!

Check out this page for more info!

www.SelfEmpowermentTeam.com/SignUp

As A Token
of My Gratitude...

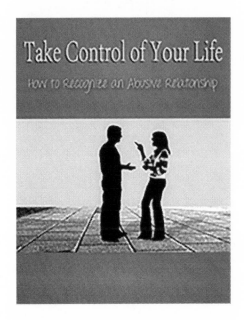

I'd like to offer you this amazing resource which my clients pay for. It is a report I written when I first began my journey.

Click on the picture above or navigate to the website below to join my exclusive email list. Upon joining, you will receive this incredible report on how to recognize an abusive relationship.

If you ask most people on the street what an abusive relationship is, chances are you'd get a description of physical abuse. And yes, that is most certainly an abusive relationship. However, abuse comes in many forms. The actual meaning of abuse is when someone exerts control over another person.

Find out more about recognizing an abusive relationship and learn how to take control over your life by clicking on the book above or by going to this link:

https://tinyurl.com/RecognizeAbusiveRelationship

CHAPTER 1

What is Narcissistic Personality Disorder?

Along with the many different personalities and traits of individuals in the world, there are also dangerous and dark personalities. One dark personality you need to look out for is narcissism. In truth, we all have narcissistic traits and may ask ourselves from time to time if we could be a narcissist; however, most of the time, we are actually trapped in a narcissistic relationship. This could be our parents, our spouse, co-workers, employers, and even our children. If you have asked yourself (especially recently) if you possess narcissistic traits or could be one, then you actually might be involved with this type of person - this is their trap to make you think you are the problem.

So, what exactly is a narcissist? It's a personality disorder (NPD), where the individual expects constant attention, becomes jealous if you don't give them what they need or want, feel superior to everyone else, and does not like or take criticism. Although, they sure like to dish it out, pointing out your flaws and everything that may be wrong with you, while they can do no wrong. They lack empathy and are the most selfish and self-centered people about. What can be confusing about narcissists or having narcissistic traits is that someone who suffers from this dark personality disorder, usually doesn't feel, think, or believe they are narcissists. This is mostly because, they don't see themselves ever doing anything wrong, and everything is someone else's fault. They hate taking responsibility, or rather, don't take responsibility for their actions because they see themselves as admirable. Although they can be charming, they show patterns of arrogant behavior, extreme need for appreciation, self-centered attitudes. They can come off as cocky, or demanding, seductive, or mysterious.

Everyone, at times in their lives, will be self-centered, demanding, charming, etc. however, if you notice it implement every aspect of their lives (with their work, family, and close relationships) you could be involved with a narcissist. So, what may cause someone to fall under the description of

NPD? It is unknown like most disorders. However, some theories could be genetic, childhood nurturing, and psychological indifferences (chemical imbalances).

- Some early development risk factors include:

- "Too strict" parenting.

- Lack of sympathy throughout childhood.

- Excessive, or overpraise - spoiled rotten.

- Unpredictable schedules, with neglectful care.

- Feelings of abandonment throughout childhood.

- Constant criticism. Child feeling like they can never do anything correctly.

- Abuse

- Trauma or repeated trauma

- Development of becoming really sensitive to small things.

So, how do you know if you under the influence of this type of character? Narcissists have low self-esteem and internal problems they struggle with on a daily basis. Even though they don't show it, or may not know, they portray their attitudes and point the blame on someone else as a way to cope with their inner demons. So, narcissistic abuse is common, and also, not your fault. It's like a bully in senior high - they pick on you because they feel superior, and haven't learned how to address their problems, so they point out your flaws to make themselves feel better. Although this was a high school example, some people never grow out of this stage, and things just become uglier and worse as they get older.

Narcissistic abuse relates to any type of abuse coming from a narcissist. This can include parent-child, child-parent, and adult-to-adult relationships. Parental narcissistic abuse is when the parent expects too high or too much of their child, always asking them to give things up for their own needs, and never giving their children credit for all the good they actually do. On the other hand, Parental narcissistic abuse can be excessive praise over everything they do, not implementing enough or the right kind of discipline. This can lead to unpredictable schedules, and neglectful behavior, which then can lead to bigger problems - the child becoming a narcissist. Adult-to-adult narcissistic abuse will be discussed throughout this book, and there will be ways on how to manage and deal with a narcissist.

While a narcissist may seem tough, intellectual (for their own needs), manipulative, and sometimes scary, they are hiding something underneath the facade. NPD sufferers have problems with their confidence, and are very sensitive to criticism, leading them to be vulnerable in almost every situation they are in. It may be fair to say that the reason they become manipulative and deceiving is to cope or deal with these inner feelings of negativity. However, the things that narcissists do, say, or implement into the world is not okay and should be addressed. Although there are different types of narcissistic personalities, they all share a few things in common.

Some of these traits are as follows:

- Very self-centered. Feel more superior to others - like they are better than everyone else.

- They require excessive admiration and like to take authority above others.

- Have high expectations to be recognized or appreciated for everything they do - or don't do.

- Exaggeration of their talents and successes to make themselves look good.

- Often fantasize about the perfect relationship, success, power, intelligence, and when they fail at certain attempts to have it, they can become violent or angry.

- Manipulative behaviors to get what they want and only for their benefit

- Lack of empathy

- Belittle others they perceive as less than or not enough.

- Hold too high expectations of others.

- Unable to accept responsibility or take the blame for anything.

- Can come off as cocky, boastful, or conceited.

Symptoms or traits of the narcissist may vary depending on which kind you may be dealing with or abused by. However, in most cases, narcissists who are criticized or feel judged by others may become angry when they don't get their expected result. They can react with rage to certain circumstances due to their inability to control or manage their emotions and behaviors. Almost every narcissist has a hard time with change, or adapting to new situations, which can make them moody or depressed if anything is "out of line." It's much like a perfectionist behavior, but to extreme lengths, showing these signs in everything they do with everyone around them. A narcissist is also very good at isolating their victim - lover, children, friends, etc. for manipulation and control tactics.

Types of Narcissists

Yes, there are different types of narcissism - as every personality is different, every narcissist has their own ways to manipulate, control, and abuse you. The importance of knowing if you are dealing with narcissists can benefit you greatly to escape from their power, control, and hold over you. Almost always, when involved with a narcissist, you are being manipulated, which is abusive. Although your partner, friend, co-worker, boss, etc. may not know they are abusive, if they show any of the signs above, you are trapped in an abusive situation. So, fighting back is your only way out. The first step is to detect which narcissist you are dealing with. When you are recovering from this type of abuse, you will forever thank yourself for gaining this information as you will be able to understand and avoid falling into the same acquaintance again.

If you feel you are in a relationship with an NPD sufferer, then these signs will sound familiar to you:

- They do not give you the same attention you give them.

- It doesn't feel like a 50/50 relationship

- You feel very low, then extremely high throughout your intimate relationship.

- They can be demanding of you asking for more than you can give.

- When you don't comply, they lash out and belittle you.

- Every argument gets turned around on you as if they have done nothing wrong.

- They apologize a lot, then do it again.

- They spend your money how they want. Then get upset when you do the same.

- They take up everyone's attention over you and may publicly humiliate you.

Sound familiar? You are being abused by a narcissist. There is also narcissistic abuse in the workplace. Does one of your co-workers, or employers, bully you as if you were back in senior high. Do you dread going to work to have to deal with this person? Well, here are some telltale signs you may be abused by a narcissist in your workplace.

- They try to impress people by chatting a fair amount instead of focusing on work.

- Make promises they don't intend to keep.

- Often take credit for yours or someone else's work due to jealous feelings of you.

- They may criticize you or knock you down verbally alone, or in front of people

- May make threats while you are alone.

- They talk negatively about others behind their backs but suck up in front of them (two-faced).

- Act superior, even when they are at the bottom.

In a relationship, it is important to understand that you **cannot change your partner,** and **you cannot change enough for your partner.** No matter what you do, it's as if their behavior or problems tend to repeat themselves. So as hard as you may try to please them, and ask for things in return, the highs in your relationship are only a facade to the lows of the type of person they are.

The WEB Method

Before we dive into identifying which *type* of narcissist you are dealing with, it is important to understand the WEB method for detecting them. The WEB method consists of a three-step process; *their* words, *your* emotions, and *their* behavior.

Their **Words:** Their words can be an exaggerated positivity or extreme negative, derogatory words. There will be no middle ground.

Positive and Negative words: This consists of saying extreme negative things to people, or you, and exaggerated positivity to you or others. **Extremely positive** words include seductive tones or charming attitudes. Some examples of this are:

"You are amazing; I haven't met anyone like you."

"You are the best; I will make sure you get the best."

"Stay blessed because you deserve the world."

Notice how the positive words they are using are comparative. This positivity can turn **negative** quickly when you do something to upset them later on because they can quickly turn it around and use it to backtrack. Which then **can turn into** things like this:

"This person I know is really dumb, let me tell you why."

"I got rejected for my ideas at work; those people wouldn't know intelligence if it hit them in the face."

"I am going to come up with ways to get her fired; I can't wait to see the looks on people's faces when she does."

When they talk mean about people, or you, pay attention to the intent behind their words. Usually, they show signs of being thrilled about it.

Lack of empathy: As narcissists have lack of interest in sympathizing with people, they lack empathy. For example, if you explain something that really upset you, like a feeling for others, or getting rejected, they may dismiss your feelings about instantly. Instead, they will instantly reverse the conversation over to them, acting as if what you said has no effect on them, and your feelings are completely ignored.

Victimizing: Narcissists don't recognize when they have done something wrong or have emotion when they hurt you, as they take no responsibility for their words (and actions) because they feel superior. However, a narcissistic injury is when someone knocks their ego down a notch or two; when they don't feel so superior. Injuries can include being rejected, things not going as planned, or their way, and when you have dismissed them or ignored their wants or demands. This can lead them to become manipulative and strive to take power back. They become obsessed with destroying the person that hurt or "injured" them.

Your **Emotions:** Your emotions usually involve a vibe, or feeling you get when around this person. This is called your instinct and should always be listened to.

In the beginning, they may seem too great. One of the first signs is their actions and what they do. They can come off as charming, and make *you feel* on cloud nine, or extremely loved and may shower you with flattery and compliments. People who over-compliment you, or make you feel euphoric are usually never who they seem. Before getting involved with them, make sure their charm doesn't have a different intent. Did they pick you to be their victim? Or are they just naturally charming? Get to know them before diving in.

Do you sometimes (or all the time) feel less than, when next to them? It is automatic for a narcissist to build themselves up and brag. Often times, they don't realize the impact it is having on you, especially if they steal your light, or bring you down in the process of their own success. Eventually, with this constant treatment, you may be asking yourself questions like, "am I good enough?" "Will I ever be?" What do other people think of me?" These thoughts lead to negative feelings, which then lead to more problems such as depression or anxiety.

Are you drowning? Narcissists can take the air out of the room, and leave you trying to catch your breath (metaphorically). Because their attention is solely focused on themselves and what they are going to say next, they often take up the attention in the room. They need to be center stage. You also may feel like your suffocating because they have isolated you, and diminished all your needs, as they feel like they need to come first.

***Their* Behavior:** Narcissists often make a lot of people annoyed, frustrated, or left the conversation with some sort of negative feelings. When confronted with a narcissist, pay attention to their behavior, focusing on what they do, rather than the cover-up of words and phrases they say. When you take a glance into their lives, how many friends do they have? How many people do they associate with? How do they act for strangers? Most of all, how do they treat the people (and you) that they supposedly respect? When a narcissist is confronted with their actions or words, instead of taking responsibility and reflecting on the criticism, they defend it by saying things like, "How could you, after what I have done for you."

Test this theory by telling them one of your concerns, staying away from why they would - then your concern. Then create a solution of your own and see how they act. If they fulfill your request, it's a good sign, whereas if they ignore it, and continue to do what they please without hearing you out and dismissing your concerns - take action.

Whether there be conflict or not, a small problem or an imaginative one (one they created), narcissists are always looking to point blame. If they blame you for something they have done, or for their failures, it's called projection. For example, they may say, "I missed my phone call because you didn't remind me/ wake me up, and now it's your fault I miss out on this opportunity." So, just watch their behaviors and any red flags that come up, address them, and target your response.

Classic Narcissist

Also known as the *grandiose narcissist,* these are the people we think about when we hear the term narcissist. Everything we have learned thus far is what a classical narcissist is and what they look like. However, other narcissists share similarities but have distinct differences. A classic narcissist normally projects the blame to others while stealing the spotlight from you or someone else. They get bored rather quickly and are the biggest attention seekers among the rest. While all narcissists feel superior, the classical narcissist has the biggest ego.

It is important to note that just because you feel someone shares traits of a narcissist, doesn't mean they have the full-on disorder. According to the American Psychological Association, to be diagnosed as having a narcissistic personality disorder, you must develop instability in two out of the four psychological areas; cognitive - thoughts, effective - emotional, interpersonal - patterns of relating to others, and impulse control.

Malignant Narcissist

These types of narcissists are potentially the most damaging kind there is. Aside from having the classic traits of narcissism, they may be antisocial or inverted. They may develop a sadistic streak alongside the normal non-empathetic nature. Which means they thrive even more on torturing people and their victims. On the other hand, they also enjoy building you up to the highest point you can go, just so they can rip you down to the darkest place you imagined. Malignant narcissists are perhaps the most advanced in manipulation skills and find the experience empowering, as long as they get what they want no matter who they hurt in the process. If you are a victim or in the path of a malignant narcissist, you may feel a bunch of heartaches, emotional, and sometimes physical frustration, and mental exhaustion.

Aside from the obvious lack of empathy, a need for attention, sensitivity to criticism, charm, and egocentricity. Here are other traits a malignant narcissist develops that differs from the other types:

1. **Sadism** - A sadist is one who purposely performs pain, suffering, and humiliation onto others as a way to make themselves happy, or prideful. The distress they cause to you, makes them feel empowered and in control, which makes them gain self-esteem and happiness. They may act like this towards people and animals or watch victimizing videos and shows to get their fulfillment.

2. **Anticipatory Manipulation** - Malignant narcissists are so good at manipulation tactics, because they implement it, and practice it on a daily basis. Most manipulators will wait for an opportunity to arise, then strike with their manipulative methods. However, a malignant narcissist will not. They proactively manipulate every day, whenever they see fit to. This manipulation tactic is the most dangerous because, if you are the victim, at first you won't

realize you are being manipulated, and then eventually you will have been isolated, and torn down to a place where the perpetrator wants you to be. It happens so gradually, and by your own doing, that when you try to point the blame, the narcissist will then continue with this habit, and tell you that you are the one who made the decisions. This type of manipulation involves planning, calculating, and honing over years of practice to the narcissist.

3. **Anti-social** - Most narcissists are internally self-sabotagers, and so in this sense, it would make sense why they would develop some antisocial behaviors. They excel in lying, cheating, stealing, and have negative moods most of the time. They make for perfect con-artists, as they have a way with people from their charming attitude, and cool image.

4. **Paranoid** - Like someone who suffers from anxiety, a malignant narcissist feels like everyone is always out for their blood. Someone is always out to get them, and so they are suspicious and skeptical. With this trust boundary for others, they internally beat themselves up and show signs of confidence to gain a sense of power. They are never willing to get close enough to someone to have that someone peel back their layers, which helps them with their manipulation tactics and lack of empathy while doing it. Malignant narcissists often feel like they know what someone is doing or thinking, and so they create imaginary scenarios in their own minds, as a way to cause conflict with you. This, in turn, helps them seek control and make threats, so you don't do what their imaginary scenarios are, or so that maybe you do, and they can catch you. Meanwhile, you are doing nothing.

5. **Envy** - Malignant narcissists hate to see others succeed and have things that they don't, so they become envious. When they see others ahead of themselves, they will purposely try to sabotage it for their own selfish needs. So, if someone got a promotion they wanted, the malignant will then manipulate the boss, or the person into why themselves would be more fitting. They may even go as far as setting the person up, to make them look bad, and then be there for when the person fails, and the boss sees them as more fitting.

With their charming traits and their egotistic attitudes, alongside their manipulation tactics with the lack of responsibility natures, malignant narcissists are definitely ones to be the most concerned about. When they feel picked on, they take two steps ahead of you to return the favor or complete their goal. Which is usually to torment, cause stress, and leave you feeling unworthy.

Vulnerable Narcissist

Also known as the covert introvert narcissist. The biggest difference from this narcissist to the others is that they stray away from the spotlight and keep to themselves most of the time. Instead, they will attach themselves to another person (a host) and use them to their advantage to get what they need. They may show signs of excessive generosity to feel the attention and admiration back. However, if they do not get the attention they want and need, they may go to great lengths to suck it out of their host, or victim.

Aside from the other narcissistic traits, here is how to spot a covert narcissist:

1. **A cocky or dominant attitude** - A covert narcissist likes to observe their audience and behave through actions or body language. When they observe other's behavior, they silently judge and come up with ways of how and when they will strike or manipulate. When you talk, they listen but don't really pay attention, rather focus on their own thoughts. Their negative behavior comes from their body language showing signs like impolite yawns, low chuckles, eye-rolls, and obvious signs of boredom

2. **Passive Aggressive** - Most introverted narcissists will insult you, but make it sound like a compliment. They will also show signs that they are listening and respond with "whatever you would like me to do," then do the opposite, or ignore it altogether. When you address them, they may make excuses like they preferred their way or accuse you of coming up with a silly solution.

3. **They often feel victimized** - When you address a covert narcissist or give them your opinions on what you think would be best for them, they don't take it as advice; rather they feel victimized. They feel as though people are not giving them positive advice, but ideas to set themselves up for disaster. With this extremely highly sensitive attitude, they will dismiss you with their smug attitudes, and plot out ways to manipulate you to get what they want instead. Later, they will say their behavior is because of you as if you made them do what they did.

When you are dealing with, abused by, or facing one of these narcissists, you need to escape from their grasp. If it is a lover or someone you love, you may tell yourself that they can change, or that if you try this, or try that, things will get better. However, when you do this, you are actually setting yourself up for failure and enabling the abuse to continue. You must set healthy boundaries, and do not fall into their traps of when things are really good, and they make you feel euphoric because no matter what, they will bring you to a very unhealthy low. Look for support, reach out to therapists, and read self-help books, like this one, to know what you must do next. Continue reading for more information on how you can escape this unhealthy relationship and recover after you get away.

CHAPTER 2

The Surprising Impact Narcissistic Abuse Has on Your Brain and Reversing the Damage

Narcissistic abuse is one of the most damaging abuses out there because it affects you emotionally, and mentally. It can come in forms of physical, verbal, and mental abuse, so the quicker you catch the signs, and the faster you identify the narcissist, the better off you will be. Believe it or not, this kind of psychological abuse leads to the physical changing of the brain, according to recent studies. Because narcissists don't feel empathetic toward anyone's feelings, they don't see the consequences they cause or the damage they implement. It is proven that with long-term narcissistic abuse, part of your brain actually shrinks, and changes its shape. This leads to cognitive problems and mood disorders such as anxiety, depression, and even bipolar.

The two parts of the brain that change their form or shape with continuous narcissistic abuse, are the hippocampus, and the amygdala. The hippocampus is the region of the brain which focuses on memory and learning. The amygdala is the region of the brain that is responsible for forming and development of negative thoughts and emotions such as guilt, shame, fear, and envy. Over time, with constant abuse, comes the physical shrinking of the hippocampus, and swelling of the amygdala.

The Hippocampus

The hippocampus is part of the limbic system in the brain. The limbic system focuses mainly on processing and developing feelings and responding with actions or reactions. The limbic system also included the amygdala and the hypothalamus. The hypothalamus works together with the amygdala and creates the nervous system and the endocrine system. These systems regulate, balance, and control body functions. So, if the hippocampus is damaged, or the amygdala becomes disrupted, you may experience more suicidal thoughts, panic attacks, and flashbacks, or nightmares. This is out of your control when you have experienced such abuse for long periods of time. However, you can fix this by escaping your present nightmare and managing ways of dealing with stress and preventing yourself from enabling this type of relationship again.

Short-term memory is the first step to learning; without it, we wouldn't learn anything. The hippocampus stores these short-term memories, then later converts it into long-term memory or "permanent" memory. Stanford University and the University of New Orleans implemented a study, which found that there are strong links between high levels of cortisol (a stress hormone) and damaged or altered hippocampus. This means that the more damaged the hippocampus is (shrinking, swelling, etc.), the higher the possibility of high cortisol levels will surge through the nervous system. When we have high surges of cortisol pumping through us, we may feel things like dizziness, experience panic attacks, become moody, overthink, worry, fret, etc. Basically, the more stress you have, the smaller your hippocampus is, which is not a good thing.

Hippocampus is the core of our memories. We have two types of memories, which includes the declarative memories, and the spatial memories.

- **Declarative memories** relate to facts and events. An example would be learning the lines to a play, the lyrics to a song.

- **Spatial relationship memories** are more in-depth memories that involve pathways and routes. Some may say the spatial memory is our photographic memory. So, an example of this type would be that you memorized how to get from point A in a city you don't know to point B.

As talked about before, the hippocampus converts our short-term memories into long-term ones, then finds a different place in the brain for these long-term memories to be stored. What is interesting about the hippocampus, is that it is always generating new nerve cells, and continues to develop on a daily basis. So, it makes sense why long-term abuse would frustrate, or damage the development and shrink.

The shrinking of the hippocampus has been linked to long-term stress, or abuse, which then leads to trauma, which involves PTSD signs, and sometimes schizophrenia. Since evidence shows in recent studies that stress is one of the main causes for the shrinkage of the hippocampus, it makes sense why escaping narcissistic abuse is beneficial to start lowering stress and reversing the cortisol levels; you may experience when under this amount of pressure.

The Amygdala

The amygdala is mainly responsible for controlling our instinctual, core emotions, and functions. These include lust, fear, hate, love, along with heart rate, body temperature, breathing, and sugar levels, and blood pressures. When the amygdala is on high alert, it implements physical symptoms to the rest of the body, which is where the "fight or flight" response comes in. The fight or flight response is a response the body reacts to sending symptoms like trembling, sweating, feverish, dizziness, etc.

These symptoms can be alarming, but most of the time, they are "false alarms." Narcissists keep their victims on high amygdala alert, making it difficult for their victims to manage stress. So, when the hippocampus shrinks, it produces excess cortisol levels, and then the amygdala becomes triggered, it also sends out the same response that cortisol will apply. With this in mind, the hippocampus has now stored short-term memories into long-term memories, which are triggered by the abuse resulting in PTSD. When the amygdala is swollen as a result of the narcissistic abuse, anything can trigger this "fight or flight" response. So, you are stuck in a downward spiral of panic, and fear over the smallest things, which can be smells, sights, and even feelings. This is because what we see and experience, our brains are trying to relate to what has happened from before - pulling from our memories - and if those memories are traumatic, it triggers the amygdala to apply uncomfortable, disabling symptoms.

In short, the amygdala is the reason we are afraid of things or the reason we love things. It controls how we react or perceive the world around us. Based on our experiences through life, the amygdala is our control for how we respond to events that cause our emotions. If the amygdala is swollen, we will most likely react to everything - or small things - with fear and see them as a threat.

So, say you managed to escape the wrath of a narcissist. If you were in the relationship (parent, spouse, employer, etc....) for a long period of time, you would have developed PTSD, heightened fear, phobias, panic attacks, or depression. This is because the stress that the narcissist caused, caused your amygdala to swell, which then the amygdala has gotten used to living with heightened awareness, and seeing everything as threatening. While in the relationship, the victim (you, for example) will use coping mechanisms such as bending reality defense strategies. These are as follows:

- **Projection:** You may convince yourself that your abuser has goodness in them and that if you try harder, be better, or "bow" to them more, they will treat you better, but you are just struggling right now. With narcissists, this is rarely the case, and all you are doing is making excuses to stay in the relationship longer.

- **Compartmentalization:** You may only be focusing on the positive side of the relationship, completely ignoring the abuse and the negative, thus still defending your abuser. By doing this, you are telling yourself that this type of behavior is okay, thus training your brain that this way of heightened fear and the way you are living is normal. Hence the lasting effects of the narcissist.

- **Denial:** Because you feel it is easier to live with the abuse, rather than confront it, or escape from it, you may make excuses for yourself like, it's not as bad as it seems or as it feels.

The process where your brain has to create new neural pathways comes strictly from the hippocampus. Everything we do, learn, know, read, and understand is all the responsibilities that the hippocampus takes care of. With a shrunken hippocampus, it becomes harder to focus, takes longer to understand and learn, and we have to put more effort into doing things that were easy to us before. We may lose interest in things that we loved, partially because we don't have the drive, motivation, or energy to do it. This can all happen from narcissistic abuse.

The hippocampus shrinks due to the increased hormone surges of cortisol (the stress hormone response). The cortisol then stimulates the amygdala or triggers it, which is the cause for our thoughts to become fretful and anxious. So, it is essential to learn stress-reducing techniques to prevent this from spiraling - even if you aren't associated with a narcissist.

Reversing the Impact | Preventing the Spiral

As with most disorders, chemical imbalances, and therapeutic methods, there is usually a cure or a "way out." Of course, it takes drive and dedication, but when you want something bad enough, you will be able to get it. Techniques like Eye Movement Desensitization and Reprocessing therapy (EMDR) is good for learning how to cope or overcome PTSD or trauma symptoms. EMDR calms the amygdala, which allows room for your brain to react and respond to situations more rationally and logically.

Other methods include aromatherapy with essential oils, meditation and mindfulness, acts of altruism, and Emotional Freedom Technique (EFT). EMDR and EFT are explained in more detail in chapter six of this book. Before you can start practicing these techniques and coping methods, you first need to escape the narcissistic abuse.

Why You Feel You Can't Leave a Narcissist

Abuse is everywhere, and more often than not, implemented in most relationships. Sometimes we do it to our spouse, colleagues, friends, or children, and we may not even notice. Other times, we are the ones being abused. However, narcissistic abuse is the most damaging to our psychological state. Oftentimes, people have a hard time leaving an abusive relationship because leaving would be changing, and change is a scary thing for most people.

Here are the most common reasons people don't leave abusive relationships, narcissistic or not.

1. **Our society acts as if it is normal, so an abusive relationship is hard to understand or accept** - Since there are so many people going through abuse, our society, plus the media, creates abuse as something normal. As a relationship starts, it's normal to feel the euphoric highs, and the lows don't start until later on. But when the abuse starts to happen, we often don't realize until it's too late, and when we do notice, we fear the change of leaving and don't accept the situation we are in.

2. **Self-esteem becomes less than before, so starting fresh becomes even scarier than normal.** - Long-term emotional, and psychological abuse, like narcissistic abuse, changes our thinking patterns making it difficult to build self-confidence. Because you aren't physically abused, you may not feel as though the abuse you are going through is even as bad. However, mental abuse, in most cases, is actually worse than or equal to physical abuse. Once you have in your head that you are worthless, you may actually feel you deserve this life and find it easier to stick around rather than leave.

3. **Abusive cycles happen; after every abusive incident or fight, a make-up phase follows.** - After a real low, the abuser will then apologize, or do things to make up for their crappy behavior. This leads us to believe that there is hope and that your relationship can last. So, you tell yourself that because they are sorry, they don't deserve to be left behind. Then you come up with more excuses for them, which results in sticking it out longer. Then the abuse happens again, and so the real lows, are followed by the high highs again, repeating this process.

4. **Sometimes it is dangerous to leave, and the victim may be more afraid to leave than stay.** - Especially in physically abusive relationships, men or women are more likely to be killed after a break-up has happened, over the time of the relationship. A malignant narcissist has the same thought pattern as a killer, so the victim may be terrified to leave, so they stay for their safety.

5. **Society expects people to survive "no matter what" when in a relationship** - The pressure of having a "perfect" relationship means that we stay no matter what. We may feel judged or looked down upon if we leave our spouse. Loyalty is shown to be of the utmost importance with the "ride or die" attitudes in society.

6. **"Gaslit" behavior from our abuser keeps us in the relationship longer.** - Gaslighting means that the abuser will turn the blame or a situation around on you, and make you think something is your fault when it actually isn't. With, this being done constantly, the victim (you), may feel the need to stay as if their behavior is somehow your responsibility.

7. **"Things will change."** - How many times have you said this to yourself, or maybe your friends? We have this perceived notion that things were good once upon a time, and so with the right attitude, and both of you trying, things can get back to that. Maybe you think your partner is only acting like this because things are hard, or stressful, and with the right actions, and you taking on more responsibilities, things can go back to normal. The fact of the matter is, these are excuses, and we make excuses because we are scared to leave. An abuser's behavior won't change, because let's face it life is stressful, and there will always be problems. It is not up to you or anyone else to change your partner or change for your partner in hopes of things getting better.

8. **You share your lives together** - So, this is maybe the number one reason people stay. They feel familiar, and a sense of security with their spouse. Maybe they got married, had children, bought a house, shared expenses, and this is all they know. A life without this person by their side would look or potentially feel even more miserable than they already are, so they stay. The truth of this belief is that even though you share your life with this person, you don't have to finish your life with them. Abuse makes people codependent, and so the victim doesn't feel confident to leave and live a life of their own. In these cases, it is best to get a lawyer, or therapist's advice, to help you make the change.

When you are under the control of a narcissist, they are master manipulators. This means that they isolate you, make you feel weak and vulnerable, then convince you that they are all you need by building you up and setting others up to make you think twice about your friends. Then when you fight or have arguments, you can never win, and never escape because you are isolated, and they control you. Your mind no longer becomes as happy and fulfilled as it once was, your drive becomes unmotivated, and your life seems to fit only with their schedule.

To fight back, we often make five horrible mistakes.

- **Blaming yourself** - Because of the belief that we are to blame, (narcissists doing), we put the blame on ourselves which drives us to try harder, do more, and push ourselves past what we are capable of. However, the battle never seems to end, so we are abusing ourselves by enabling their behavior and letting it affect us. Meanwhile, they are sitting there laughing on the inside.

- **Making threats** - To gain some self-esteem or some sort of power back, we may look or search for their weaknesses and exploit them, causing us to have to make threats. However, threats only work if they are followed through, when you don't follow through, you lose your power. On the other hand, if you do follow through, you may feel even more lost than you did before for having to stoop that low, so you apologize, and the cycle starts again.

- **Trying to be understood** - Have you sat there trying to interpret messages, or body language, or words and sentences your spouse or narcissist has spun? You are making your best effort to relate to them, come up with solutions, and give them what they need, but want them to do the same. So, in your efforts of trying to understand them, you make the mistake of getting them to understand you. You may try repeating yourself, showing them what you mean, or even rephrasing what you are trying to say. However, they continue to return the attention back on themselves to make their own point. The true fact here is that they do understand you. They know what you mean, or what you are talking about. However, they only care that they are heard, they don't care about coming up with solutions for you, as there is no compromise with them. They simply just care about themselves.

- **Withdrawal** - After a long night, days, or maybe even weeks of fighting with them, you finally just give in. You become numb to feelings, and your own emotions and your energy has run out. So, you give up. While this helps with saving your energy and mental exhaustion, it does not get you out of the situation you are in.

- **Denial** - When we are confronted by our friends and people who love us about our relationship, we make excuses, or lie to hide the abuse. By doing this, you are only letting the narcissist win, because as long as you continue to make excuses for them, you show them that their abuse is secretive, which only gives them more power over you.

The truth is, is that you will never be able to deal with a narcissist. When you try something, they will always turn it around on you, When you give into them, they will somehow make you feel like your efforts are unnoticed, or that you are still at fault. Basically, no matter what you try to do, you will always be in the wrong in their eyes, and they never will be. The best method on dealing with a narcissist is to escape their wrath, and become independent, by learning personal growth strategies to get where you want and need to be. You must learn to live without them.

Hoovering

Here is a perfect example of what hoovering is: you and your ex have been over for a while. You haven't heard from them, and they haven't heard from you. You are finally getting on track to where you need to be; you may be going to school and making new friends. Maybe you are finally eating healthy and patched a broken friendship from before. Your life is finally heading in the direction you want. You will always remember the love and care for your ex, and you are finally moving on. All is right in the world. But then, out of the blue, you get a text or a call from your ex. It says, "I need you, I am in a dark place, and I just want to die. Please help me." Your heart speeds up, you swallow your throat, and butterflies flutter in your stomach. Against your better judgment, you answer with "what do you need?" Flashbacks of the abuse and your relationship come to your mind, along with all the good times that happened in your relationship.

This is hoovering. The minute you answer to them, you have fallen right back into their trap. Hoovering is a manipulative tactic that a narcissist will use to draw you back in. Think of hoovering as "sucking" you back in. Hoovering is done when some time has passed, and the narcissist will target their victim's weaknesses or vulnerabilities to get back what they had or want. When you give in to this manipulative tactic, they have won, and you fall back into the cycle you tried to escape from.

Narcissists hoover because they need to regain control. For whatever reason they have to draw you back in, most times, it's because you are an easy target. From being an easy target, they know they can get sex, validation, attention, affection, money, and even power. Perhaps the most defined reason they hoover is because they feel empty. Narcissists, as mentioned, need to feel wanted, or superior. When they aren't getting this attention, they hoover you, to get what they want as a way to fill that void inside them.

Narcissists are hungry for attention, to the point of it becoming their first and last thought of every day. When they don't get or have attention, and they can't seem to find it with anyone else, they will pick on their exes to have it back - meaning you become their victim again. They pick on their exes because they already know things about them, and most of the time, their exes are easy "prey." Because they know you; or, they think that they do, and they will exploit your weaknesses and have you coming to them. This continues, until they get bored of you, or find something better, then leave you, in which case you have fallen back into the abusive cycle again. The problem as to why you get hoovered is because you care too much, or have too much empathy for them, not realizing that they don't have or share the same feelings. They don't care, they just want what they want, and when they don't have it, they destroy to get it.

Types of Hoovering

There are many types of hoovering. However, some of these forms of hoovering may be done currently by the person you recently ended things with. One objective of hoovering is that is almost always done by a narcissist, with no other intent than to suck you back in, so that they can take advantage of you all over again. If an ex is doing this or has done these following hoovering techniques, it's best to ask yourself one thing. Is my ex a narcissist? If they were not, and things were just up and down, then your ex is not hoovering you, they are only trying to win you back after all this time. On the other hand, if your answer is yes, pay close attention to the following kinds of hoovering. When reading them, think of it like the way your ex is thinking, not yourself.

1. **Pretending or acting as if nothing happened.** - Narcissists will pretend as if everything is okay like nothing has happened, and that you are still in a relationship. They will ignore your requests to cut ties and may show up at your house, work, or even your family members house to reach you. They will send happy faces in a text and leave complimentary messages on your voicemail. This is one hoovering technique.

2. **Sending gifts** - Attempting to win you over again, they will go out of their way to send you things. This may include your favorite flowers, chocolates, gift cards, movie tickets, concert tickets, and even money.

3. **Apologizing** - They will apologize for everything they have done. They may even write a letter explaining in great detail about how "sorry" they are. As convincing as they are, there is only one thing you need to do. Think back to the beginning of your relationship - the honeymoon stage. If they are saying or doing the same things they did to win you over in the first place, it's fake.

4. **Indirect manipulation** - If you have managed to ignore all their attempts thus far, they may think outside the box and contact people you know, such as friends and family that are close to you. They will either tell your close relations lies so that the message will get back to you, so you feel the need to correct them, or talk to them, and at this very point you have been

hooked, and reeled in. Or, they will start to send really happy positive things to your family, in an attempt to show them they are trying, and have your family say that you should talk to them for closure reasons. Don't do this. The most effective, or manipulative message for if you have children with the narcissist, is that they will get your children to lure you back home.

5. **Declaring love** - Since love is such a strong emotion, they may send you love letters, write you poems, or explain in great detail all the good of what they remember what had happened. They will express their deepest feelings in the most romantic way. This is a powerful hoovering technique and should be ignored at all costs.

6. **Sending "out of the blue" messages** - You may see random texts saying things like,

   "Please wish *John* a happy birthday for me."

   "Are you going to that social event we talked about? It's tonight."

   "I am at the place we went to on our third date. I remember what you were wearing, and how romantic it was, do you?"

7. **Faking the need for help** - This is perhaps one of the nastiest tricks they can pull, and usually do it when they feel absolutely desperate. You may get a text or voicemail saying that they are going to kill themselves because they are at an all-time low. They may make up some fake illness like cancer, or heart issues so that you will come back to them out of feeling obligated or guilty. This technique preys on the natural instinct most people have for compassion.

Note that hoovering is a narcissists way to "suck" you back into the abusive relationship. They will do whatever it takes to remind you that what you had was good. Because most of us are empathetic and like to reason or try to our best efforts, they know this and prey on these instincts. Hoovering is lying techniques, manipulative methods, and disguises to get you to come back. With this in mind, you can ignore the behavior, and get a restraining or protection order of some sort so that you never have to deal with it again.

The Beginning of Recovery

Recovering from any type of abuse is hard, but escaping, and recovering from narcissistic abuse takes patience and dedication. You will have to continuously remind yourself of all the benefits, and the setbacks. Relapses will happen, and it may take a few tries to leave. once you have finally escaped their wrath, it is about commitment to yourself for a better life. I will explain briefly about the six stages for recovering from narcissistic abuse, which are as follows:

Stage One: Devastation

This stage is the first stage in moving on. You may feel emptiness, shock, depression, find it difficult to concentrate, or hold conversations, anger, and some bitterness. At first, you may feel number, and disappointed, maybe a little confused, and your mind will be flooded with the positive sides of your relationship. Memories of you laughing or going on dates may make you want to turn back, but it is crucial to understand that a narcissist will not change if they don't want to. It is also unfair to ask anyone to change themselves, and so this part of the process is needed.

If you detach yourself or withdraw from the world, this is okay. Give yourself time to release all this energy and feel the feelings that arise during this stage. It may feel like working becomes a hard task, eating becomes difficult, or binge eating becomes a habit. This happens because you will feel numb, lost, and like you have lost all control. The confusion comes from the loss of your relationship, wondering why it couldn't work, remembering the many things you did or didn't do. This is the first stage of moving on, while you experience signs of withdrawal, it's like a drug that you need to get away from. This step is normal, however, if it lost for a long period of time, seeking professional help may be in your best interest.

Sometimes, in this stage, you may be holding onto guilt or shame. This is because the narcissist still has a hold on you. They have manipulated your mind and twisted your words so many times, that even after they are gone, there is a part of you that believes you deserve this pain. Don't let their grasp keep you thinking you are nothing, worthless, or even crazy. You are not, and as long as you feel and think this way, they have won. The best revenge is showing them that you can survive without them.

Stage Two: Allowing yourself to grieve and be angry

So, after finding out that you are a victim of narcissistic abuse, you may feel that the relationship was one-sided and that you should not allow yourself to feel angry or grieve the relationship. This is false. Absolutely let yourself grieve. Let yourself be angry, and miss the relationship, just don't allow yourself to go back, or give into their hoover efforts. If you don't let yourself be angry and grieve, then you could actually be setting yourself up to fall into another abusive relationship down the road. Here are other things that could potentially happen if you don't allow yourself to be angry and grieve:

- Staying stuck in the devastation process longer than you should.

- Anger builds up. Temper problems.

- Trust issues.

- Unnecessary exhaustion, and depression, or stress for prolonged periods.

- Addiction.

- Avoidance patterns and habits.

- Chronic pain or illness.

- Obesity or eating disorders.

Once you have felt the anger, and carried the grief, allow yourself to move forward. Although, this may take some time, remember to continue to beat this one day at a time, Some days will feel harder than others, and other days will seem easy. The next step is to take care of yourself, no matter what.

Stage Three: Taking care of yourself

As we have learned, emotional, stress, or any type of stress can damage the brain. So, as you are grieving, and going through the waves of depressive states, to anger, bitterness, and finally acceptance, you need to make sure to take care of yourself. Read self-help books, and positive quotes every day to start feeling better and growing in your personal life. Surround yourself with positive and supportive people. When you are ready, get out and meet new people again. The emotions you feel is your mind and body's way of processing the stress and complexity of the situation. So, learning how to regulate your physical response to your emotional reactions is key to becoming healthy again. Some things you can do to take care of yourself are as follows:

- **Meditate and practice mindfulness whenever you can**. It is proven that when you meditate or become aware of the present moment, you can reverse the symptoms from the abuse you experienced. Go somewhere quiet, take in ten deep breaths (breathing with your stomach), and calming your mind by enforcing positive thoughts, and mantras.

- **Exercise every day.** This is crucial because when we exercise, like going for a run, take a nature walk, do some light yoga, etc. we don't focus on the breakup, anymore, but rather focus more on what we are doing. Exercise releases endorphins, which are feel-good hormones that our minds need to feel good about ourselves. The goal is to let go of the emotional energy by learning to love exercise and getting rid of the negative baggage in a healthy way.

- **Get enough sleep.** It's bad enough that the emotions that have you spiraling down are keeping you exhausted. Ensuring that you get enough rest is one of the fastest ways your body can recover from withdrawals and the emotional heartache you feel. If you cannot sleep, listen to guided meditation exercises, and let follow all the steps until you feel calm. Remember, there is always tomorrow that you can think of all the things your mind is telling you right now.

- **Eat healthy.** taking care of yourself means that you take care of your body as well. Nine times out of ten, the reason why people develop such mood disorders is because they don't eat right. Healing your gut heals your mind, which develops good chemicals, and helps balance your emotions.

Stage Four: Objective analysis phase

This phase happens when you have pushed past the devastation, felt the anger, and now all that seems like a distant friend or foe. This is where you need to be thankful for everything that has happened because it has shaped you into the strong person you now are. You can finally look back, without the attached feelings post-breakup. This is the stage where you are ready to get out of the slump you were in and help others who are suffering, or who have suffered the same as you. At this stage, you may find yourself having old feelings come slipping through the cracks. And this is normal, but the feelings won't seem so overwhelming or uncontrollable as you have tried hard to rebuild yourself so that the emotions don't have such a strong hold of you anymore. This will be a good feeling.

Stage Five: Acceptance and reintegration phase

Acceptance is about seeing things for the way they are instead of having a clouded vision or the "wool pulled over your eyes." The narcissist no longer has a hold on you, and you have accepted that what was can never be again. You understand your worth, and you know what to look for, and what not to fall into. At this point, you know all the signs, and realize that the grasp of the narcissist was unhealthy, and so if another unhealthy relationship starts to happen, you will be able to take action. Trust your instincts.

Stage Six: Ensure that you never become abused again

The last stage of your recovery is to make sure that you never have to go through something like that again. Oftentimes, people that have not healed fully from an abusive partner, or from the trauma, will accidentally or automatically fall right into another abusive situation. Researching and finding out the main areas or concepts of narcissism is not the answer to ensuring you don't fall into their trap again. The main reason for falling back into an unhealthy relationship is because we have not developed personal growth, or have fully healed from the last one, and so when our gut instincts scream at us "no," we ignore it, and just do it anyway because it's all we know.

Because all narcissists are not the same, the second narcissistic relationship you fall into will implement some other tricks, and without the previous wound is completely healed, you could fall into their trap again and result in having another terrible traumatic relationship .It's best to heal the wound completely so that this pattern doesn't continue.

So, do the inner work needed to heal your heart, educate your mind, and take good care of yourself through every step. Be cautious but not too cautious because you could miss out on great opportunities. Focus on getting rid of the garbage, and heal your mind, body, and spirit to release this negative energy and spot signs of narcissism early on. Continue reading for in-depth strategies on how to overcome and rid yourself of narcissistic abuse.

CHAPTER 3

Coping With Narcissistic Abuse

If you have ever been in a relationship with, or are experiencing narcissistic abuse, then you probably know how hard it is to leave. You know what you need to do, you think about the ways you can escape, and you gain the courage to do it, but then, you don't. You don't because something brings you back in. You sit there and think of all the good memories, then think about what would happen after you actually left, then you think about all the things that haven't happened yet, or maybe if you stayed things would get better due to whatever excuse you come up with. This is another form of fear. Your mind has you trapped as a result of the abuse to the point where, when you do decide to or try to leave, you feel a flood of panic. The fear is something many of us can't seem to overcome, so we stay in the relationship hoping that things will get better, or that things will be okay. But it never does, so you start from the beginning, getting ready to leave again. It's a vicious cycle that no one should have to go through. If you find yourself sitting there most of the time asking yourself, "should I stay, should I go," then you most likely already know the answer to this, and should go. Things don't get better; they only repeat themselves. The narcissist you are involved with will always make promises they can't keep, and they will always build you up for the main purpose of thrashing you down.

In the previous chapter, we talked about the stages one will go through once they finally leave for good. As much as the first stage is painful and hard, I hope you see why it's needed for the final stage to happen successfully. Devastation is difficult to manage, but with the right support, you will get through and finish all the stages, and be at a point where you view your ex as a person you knew but has no hold over you. I promise you that if you reclaim your power after getting through the dark side of your breakup, you will come to a realization that without sacrifices, you will stay stuck. No one likes to be stuck, and no one needs to feel the way you do right now. So, get up, release yourself, and become one with who you are by starting the first stage of the breakup.

Devastation

So, we have already talked about devastation, but did we talk about ways to get through it the easiest way possible? No. When we are devastated, we don't want to do anything, eat anything, speak to anyone, and we would rather drown our sorrows under cozy blankets, and cry into our pillows. The devastation comes in a few different stages and can come all at once, or one by one. First (or last) comes the shock that you are actually done, that your relationship is actually over. Memories will pool inside your mind and flush you back to what was. Next, you may feel numb, or cry (a lot), with the feeling of not caring about anything. Your eyes may hurt, you may not be able to sleep, which makes you unable to concentrate on anything, and you could withdraw from the rest of the world because you would rather do this alone then have anyone see you as pathetic as you feel. Next, anger will set in. You may become bitter to people around you and forget to take care of your needs like clean the house or get dressed. Anger will consume you if you let it, but this is part of the process of healing. To get past this feeling, you feel like a "rebound," will help you get out of this slump. So, you put on a fake smile, get dressed up, and go out on the town to get under someone else, so that you feel the affection you crave so much. This is called denial. You are in denial about your feelings. You think you are ready, but you are not. If you do this, you most likely end up with the same type of person you were just with, thus resulting in more damage to yourself later down the road.

As much as devastation hurts, and you may want to do everything to stop feeling that aching pain in your chest. Have the flashbacks go away every time you hear a song, turn the TV on, or go out; you can't. The best way to get through this stage is to learn techniques that will help you deal with these overwhelming emotions. It is important to remember that although this stage is needed for a successful final stage if you let yourself feel this way for too long, you will never recover. So, instead of remembering your lowest point, reminiscing about the good and bad memories, remembering all your fights, and all your efforts, or trying to come with answers to why you were so badly treated, stop. If you continue to do this, the pain only escalates and keeps you in the devastation stage longer than you need to be there.

Instead, try these tactics to help you speed up the process of devastation:

1. Closure

The stage of devastation may be so hard for some people that they often go back to their spouse in this stage. After all the crying, and the anger, maybe a couple of rebounds, and they decide to go back. This is not healthy, because next time you leave, you will have to start this process all over again, and I don't need to remind you what happens to our brains when we are under this type of stress. So, just end it. If you have made the decision to leave, then do that. Get your closure, write letters (send them or don't), say your goodbyes (physically or to yourself), and do whatever you need to gain some sort of closure. Then, don't go back.

2. Externalize

This stage is the mindful stage - in which we will talk more in detail about later. However, it revolves around knowing and understanding how you feel and being patient with these feelings. It's about accepting the hurt that you feel, but not clinging to it. Knowing that there will be better days, and right now, it is okay to let it all out.

3. Appropriate process

This is a necessary process to help you cope with the devastation because it allows you to make sure you are not obsessing over the breakup and your feelings. It comes in five steps:

a. Admit the pain, or anger

b. Vent, and let it out to the people who are most supportive - or write about it.

c. Determine your response to your emotions (are you going to sit here and feel sorry for yourself, or are you going to try to get up and take care of yourself today?)

d. Stick to your goals, and your plan to recovering and making it through this first stage of devastation

e. Forget it. Shift your thoughts to something else, something more positive. You can only learn to forget once the other steps are taken care of.

4. Distraction

Devastation will destroy your sense of accomplishment and hold you from doing things you used to enjoy. This stage in the process is to fight back - do the opposite of what you feel. So, if you feel like sitting in bed all day, get up and sit on the couch, or outside for the day. Distract your mind with telephone calls to loved ones, play crosswords, exercise, write, draw, etc. Do something creative, and don't allow yourself to sit with this pain.

5. Maintain your schedule

Whatever your routine was before, continue with it. If it is hard to fully maintain a routine right now, just do a couple a day, then gradually increase your strength to move on to the next thing you used to do. For example, if you used to wake up and go for a run, come home shower, get ready for work, go to work, come home and make dinner, then read a book. Start by just getting up and going for a light walk and having a brisk shower. Day by day, increase your routine to one more thing on that list.

6. Find a place that doesn't trigger you.

If your breakup consisted of them moving, and you are stuck with all the memories no matter where you look, consider moving or staying with a friend for a while. If you had to move, and it hurts to go out and see the places you guys walked or went on dates, avoid these places, and find somewhere new to go. Just don't avoid it forever.

7. Give in to the need for closeness - without sexual contact

The fastest way to get through this stage is physical closeness. So, if you have a child, cuddle them, if you have a best friend, ask for lots of hugs. When you need a shoulder to cry on, reach out to someone you trust. Along with this physical closeness, bonding with people you trust is a bonus in this recovery.

8. Avoid all things sexual

Although physical closeness is essential for recovering from a narcissist breakup, sexual entanglement with someone can make things worse. If you haven't completely moved, on you may feel shame, guilt, and even more anger. We want to avoid this as much as possible.

Devastation is the first stage of recovery, and it may also be the hardest. However, when you make it through this stage, you can move on to start taking better care of yourself, which will make you feel good. In short, you must let your feelings sink in, don't fight them, take care of your well-being, and stay off the internet or forums (at least for now). The last thing you want to do is overwhelm yourself with research that reminds you of your narcissistic relationship.

Allow Yourself to Grieve

Believe it or not, crying, and tears are beneficial to your recovery. Crying is scientifically proven to rid your body of stress. When you let your other emotions in, this also helps with the grieving process. However, if you hold your emotions in, you are making connections in your brain that suggests holding it in is a better solution and will actually cause more problems for you later. When people hold their tears, and anger in, they never learn to release or let go. Instead they teach themselves that it is okay to hold it in, which can result in an outburst later. Have you ever cried so hard, then after you get this foggy feeling, but it feels as though a weight has almost lifted? This is because you have relieved yourself of the tension or stress that you feel.

Tears are our body's way of releasing stress, fear, grief, anxiety, and frustration. Tears can come in many forms or feelings like tears of joy when a child is born, or tears of relief when something has ended for the better. For some people, they don't cry or release the tension in this way because they feel weak or pathetic when they do. Crying, and shedding a few tears is not by any means a sign of weakness, they are signs of strength and authenticity. Tears have more than one purpose other than just relieving stress. They contain antibodies that fight pathogenic microbes and remove irritants. There are three types of tears; reflex, emotional, and continuous.

- **Reflex;** These types of tears well up in our eyes to remove irritants like smoke, or exhaust fumes.

- **Continuous:** This tear contains a chemical called "lysozyme," and are there always to keep our eyes lubricated to avoid them drying out. Lysozyme protects our eyes form from getting infections.

- **Emotional:** Emotional tears are the ones we release for stress and anger, as already explained. They happen when we are sad, angry, stressed, or overwhelmed, etc.

Tears travel through the tear duct and into our noses to keep that section bacteria free. Ever noticed after crying, you may be able to breathe better, and your heart rate decreases? That's because of the emotional stress we released; we enter a calm or emotional state. It could also be because crying can be exhausting, but it does make you feel better. Dr. William Frey at the Ramsey Medical Center - an expert on tears - says that emotional tears have a buildup of stress hormones in them. So, when we cry, we release them, which, in an additional study, says that by releasing the stress through our tears, it gets replaced with an endorphin - the happy hormone.

Reclaiming Your Power after Narcissistic Abuse

Think back to what you went through, from the ages of 0-12. During this stage in our lives, we are constantly learning and growing into ourselves. To understand today, you need to first understand what happened in those years of childhood. For example, if you were abused, neglected, abandoned, lived in foster care, etc. through the learning stages of your life, you may feel like you need affection or become codependent now. Narcissists can pick this type of vulnerable person out of a crowd and give them what they need so that the narcissist benefits. So, it's time to ask yourself about you. What about you? Narcissists will make you feel as what you need, and what you want doesn't matter.

They set or hold high expectations of you, tell you to shut up, sit down, and just do your job which is to give in to their needs. They make you feel as what you say and do doesn't matter, which then causes or is the result of codependency. So, when someone tries to tell you what to do, or dismiss your thoughts and feelings, re-evaluate the situation and out loud or internally say, "what about me?"

This is why it is so important to figure out the "template" of what you have been brought up by. For example, if you have been ignored, or seen as invisible through the ages of 0-12, then you probably sought attention, and have been bred into letting go of your own needs for those around you. Which are what codependents do, they drop the needs of themselves to please and constantly put the needs of others in front of themselves for the hope that they will be seen for their efforts.

When you try to leave a narcissist, they may try throwing in your face "how could you," or "if you loved me you would do … or wouldn't do …" It is up to you to fight back with creating boundaries and looking out for number one - which is you. If your spouse or loved one doesn't see that you have needs as well, then they are either a narcissist or are not looking out for your best interests. You need to be able to confidently and assertively say "if you loved me, you wouldn't demand these things of me," or "you would instead ask how I felt, or if I can or even wanted to." By reclaiming power this way, you set boundaries, and are also teaching yourself that you are important too. Learning to respect ourselves by setting boundaries, and not giving into the narcissist's tricks gives us our power back. It also teaches the other person boundaries, and which you are putting your foot down about. In the future, when you sit down and ask yourself and your spouse, "what about me?" it will show you are also thinking of your own needs. If your relationship respects you, they will take a minute and understand that, or they won't. This doesn't necessarily mean that you don't have to do what was requested of you, but first, before making sacrifices, you must make sure that whomever you are associating with you thinks about your needs, wants, and feelings attached to the request as well.

Shifting Into Your True Powerful Self

The one thing most people don't realize is that everyone has lower self-esteem that whatever happens to us externally, triggers our internal defectiveness. What I mean by this, is that we all have that powerless self, we all have those thoughts that we may not be good enough. It's the narcissist's expertise to pick these powerless, and uncontrollable "flaws" about us and exploit them. They intentionally find our weaknesses, and blow them up, then convince us that they can help us and fix those qualities. For a while it works, then without them, you feel powerless again, and eventually, you feel powerless all the time because even with them, they make you feel as you couldn't make it without them. You are simply powerless.

To take back your power, you need to understand your true self. Your true self consists of feeling no pain, but rather, acceptance, joy, and wholeness. It is the non-judgmental part of you that exists without reaching out to other people to take our pain away. When we give the power to someone else to help us find and heal ourselves, we fall back into the same codependent trap, and never truly feel one with ourselves. The key to reclaiming your power is to overcome each stage of moving forward and dropping the person you were when you were with the narcissist. Let go of the victimized soul that you used to be, and strive for happiness, and confidence that you are stronger than this. If we can't do this, then we give into the powerlessness from what the abuser made us feel. Now to get through this, we need to figure out what is haunting us the most on the inside and tackle it. If we feel empty or abandoned, we look for ways to overcome these feelings in the most healthy and positive way we can. We never stop working on ourselves, and we never give the power to someone else to fix us and what is inside. Otherwise, the patterns that we implement throughout our lives will never change.

And this is the final step to reclaiming your power, is to be true to yourself and be honest with whom you are. Take control and tackle the "defective" qualities within.

Common Roadblocks you may face during the Recovery Process

Escaping narcissistic abuse is not easy; in fact, it may be one of the toughest things you can break free of. With their control, extremely impressive manipulative ways, and hoovering techniques, you may find yourself going back to them more than you want or staying in the relationship longer than you should. This chapter heading was designed so that you avoid making the common mistakes most make when trying to recover or move one. By following the next steps, you will stop wasting time, and be able to recover quicker.

1. **Believing that researching more about narcissists will make you better** - This belief stops you from moving forward because it triggers the abuse that you just went through, thus stopping your process from succeeding. This is because the rational and logical analyzing part of your brain has no direct access or contact with the emotional part of your brain - I like to call it the wise mind, vs. the emotional mind. For example, Say you got shot in the leg, then you research about guns, shooting, leg wounds, etc. Researching about it doesn't stop it from happening, and it doesn't take away the pain, or the damage already done. So, the more we focus on our trauma,

the more work we are going to have to take to get to the next step, which is healing from the trauma, rather than focusing on it.

2. **Assigning blame** - Blame is what you do when you feel someone is right, or when someone is wrong. The problem with blame is that we are blaming our narcissistic relationship for what they did to us. This childish notion stems back to when we were in our learning concepts of youth and giving the power to someone else to give us what we feel to be anger, sadness, joy, or other emotions. Instead, we shall not blame (even ourselves), but just accept that most of our actions were a cause from ourselves. We got into the relationship, and we stayed longer than we should have. We are in charge of our decisions, and whether or not we made the right or wrong choices, we learned from them. The main reason we blame others for providing or not providing for us what we need is because we haven't yet learned to provide it for ourselves, which gives us codependency and the habits of being with people that seek out our weaknesses for exploitation purposes.

3. **Staying busy to distract ourselves from the pain** - If we cannot heal ourselves and face the pain head on, and deal with it, then how can we expect anyone else to love us. Distracting ourselves away from the trauma the narcissist caused only implements more hurt down the road, and we never truly heal. It's like if we ignore our car breaking down, or a leak in our roof, and pretend it's not there. just to find out when we come back to it, the damage is still there. If we don't want to live with the pain or damage that the leak has caused, then we will fix it, or otherwise, confront the problem. This goes in the same way as us. If we are damaged and don't manage the feelings or cope with our trauma, when we sit alone by ourselves, the trauma, pain, and damage are still there, as we have not dealt with it yet, thus getting triggered again.

4. **Replacing the love of another with the love of someone else** - Most people would call this a "rebound," in which case it is. We want the love and attention of someone else, because we were so badly hurt by our narcissistic spouse or loved one. One of the problems that could happen with this type of behavior is that when you try to replace your narcissist partner, you may come up short, which then makes you crave the attention of the narcissist even more. Another problem is by doing this, you could actually damage your brain, or emotions even more, which could result in permanent self-esteem issues or at least more codependent tendencies. We cannot let someone else love us or give us affection if we don't put forth that example for ourselves. What is most attractive to a non-narcissistic person is a person who can care for themselves and provide their needs both physically and mentally.

5. **Keeping tabs on the narcissist** - One of the most destructive things we can do in our recovery is to figure out what the narcissist is up to. It only keeps their hold on you and makes you want them more. The trick is to completely let go of your life with them by providing no contact to get better and thrive on your own. Questions like "do they still love me, miss me, care for me, think about me," are pointless because instead of focusing on ourselves, we are putting the focus back onto them, and our trauma. One thing about narcissists is certain. They don't care, they never did, they used you for their own benefit, and they would do it again if they had the chance. If we don't feel like we are good enough to be loved, we will constantly seek validation and reassurance of our worth from another. We need to learn the worthiness of ourselves, by practicing self-healing before moving onto another person, and that is the key to reclaiming our power as well.

In short, the things we want to do, like check up on the narcissist, replace their love, assign blame, become distracted from the pain, and constantly researching about narcissists is contradicting to our healing process. As long as we don't do those things, and focus solely on love for ourselves, positivity in our minds, and taking care of ourselves, we can put the narcissistic abuse aside, and finally, grow into who we know we can be.

A few bonus roadblocks to your recovery process is as follows.

1. **Not admitting to yourself that the narcissist is dangerous to your emotional and physical well-being.** - This stems back to the "wise mind" vs.. "emotional mind." Our emotional mind is obsessed with coming up with excuses or reasons why it is impossible to leave. Why you should stay, and why it will work out if you did this, tried this, etc. We get trapped in the notion that the narcissist can change, or that they will want to. That maybe they aren't a narcissist, and the highs and lows you are going through are normal. However, if you feel like you constantly need to prove yourself to your partner, or if you tried harder, or whatever excuse you want to become real, then you are living with a narcissist. Healthy relationships don't ask you to prove your worth. Instead, they accept you for who you are and move in the same line, same path, and same expectations together. If you see yourself as a victim, you will always be one. On the other hand, if you see yourself as successful, you will be. It's called "Law of Attraction."

2. **Unrealistic expectations of the amount of time needed to recover** - Because of the feelings that we want to be loved, held, and noticed, we often try to rush the recovery and healing stages. Just when we start to feel better, we may think that it's all done, and then jump into something else faster than we should. When we expect the process to take a certain amount of time, we set

ourselves up for failure. However, when we just let things be, and continue to work on ourselves and let whatever happens come naturally, we forget about the expectations of how long, and eventually we are just "better."

3. **Avoiding the hard work to move forward** - the trick in moving on, is you have to be ready to. You have to *want* to. If you are not ready and don't want to, then you are forcing yourself into the recovery process without putting your full heart or effort into. Sometimes, people stay in the relationship because this is what they know. It feels good to get the sympathy and attention from others that they aren't getting from their loved one, and almost feel as though that would end too. But this is why it is important to give to yourself what you expect or want or are getting from others. Since moving on, and changing your life is so hard, you may become fearful of the whole process, and stay where things are easy. But look at it this way; are things actually easier if you stay? or could you put in as much effort as you are into this relationship as you could in yourself? In fact, being true to yourself, and letting yourself heal and go through the process of loving yourself takes a lot less stress than staying with a narcissistic partner. If you are not ready to walk away just yet, know that there will come a day where enough will be enough, and from there, you can finally face the future to move forward with no fear, because enough will be just that. Enough.

Throughout the recovery process, and with more information you are about to read, make sure to remind yourself that you deserve happiness. Remind yourself that you are the only one in control of where your life leads you. Be a good example for the people around you and be the positive self-caring image for yourself and what you need. If you are still unsure about what you should do next, the next chapter should answer all your questions about your relationship and yourself.

WAIT!!!

READ THIS BEFORE GOING ANY FURTHER!

How would you like to get your next eBook **FREE** <u>and</u> get new books for **FREE** too before they are publicly released?

Join our Self Empowerment Team today and receive your next (and future) books for **FREE**! Signing up is easy and completely free!!

Check out this page for more info!

www.SelfEmpowermentTeam.com/SignUp

Just a Friendly Reminder...

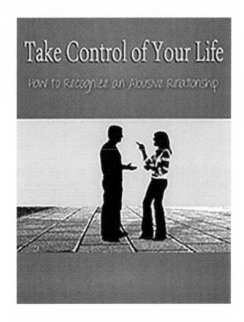

I'd like to offer you this amazing resource which my clients pay for. It is a report I written when I first began my journey.

Click on the picture above or navigate to the website below to join my exclusive email list. Upon joining, you will receive this incredible report on how to recognize an abusive relationship.

If you ask most people on the street what an abusive relationship is, chances are you'd get a description of physical abuse. And yes, that is most certainly an abusive relationship. However, abuse comes in many forms. The actual meaning of abuse is when someone exerts control over another person.

Find out more about recognizing an abusive relationship and learn how to take control over your life by clicking on the book above or by going to this link:

http://tinyurl.com/RecognizeAbusiveRelationship

CHAPTER 4

Common Questions Asked by People Recovering from Narcissistic Abuse

When we dive into something new, we are often fearful of the changes that lie ahead. Our emotional mind attacks us with questions and can often keep us awake at night pondering about all the things our future holds. We may fight with ourselves about whether or not to go back, tell ourselves lies or beliefs that things could be different, and even defend our betrayal against others. The truth is, is that we cannot get along with everyone, and so when we get involved with someone, and fall for them, it is natural to have arguments, disagreements, and lows. Every relationship goes through these things, whether you are intertwined with a narcissist or not. However, the dangerous signs of a relationship are when our arguments become ultimatums, our disagreements become fearful fights, and the lows outweigh the highs. Relationships are difficult as it is, and normally when you care about someone and love someone, it is natural to want to keep your relationship together and fight for everything so that the years are not lost. But, like the last chapter says, "what about me?" If your relationship feels one-sided, and with all your efforts, the other person has to **want** to change and **want** to walk the same path by your side as well. Narcissists don't think about your feelings, and they don't **want to**. That is the key factor when addressing your thoughts and asking yourself questions that you need to be aware of.

No matter which type of narcissistic relationship you have experienced, or may be currently in right now, you are most likely questioning the same things most in your position are. The common questions every narcissism victim has asked themselves are as follows:

1. **How do I get the narcissist to change?** - The thing about change is that when we try to change someone else, we are actually "accidentally" trying to control them. The truth here is that you can **never** change someone. You can only change your own actions and responses to their

behavior. The thing that most people forget to do over time with their spouse, friend, coworker, etc. is that they forget to accept the person for who they are. If you cannot accept them for who they are, then you may want to try techniques to change them. Nonetheless, this is the wrong approach. If you can't accept how they are now, then you need to ask yourself if you can deal with this person how they are now without anything changing for a lifetime. If your answer happens to be no, then you are the only one in control of your next action to this response.

2. **How can I keep my children from being abused or hurt by a narcissist?** - Have you ever heard of *"monkey see monkey do?"* Children spend most of their time learning how to act, what to say, or who to be from their influences. If your co-parent's actions and behavior revolve around narcissistic ways - manipulation, lying, lack of empathy, neglect, etc. then you may be dealing with alienation syndrome. Most narcissistic parents will use their narcissistic ways to influence children to reject the other parent. Most of these strategies that the narcissist will use are brainwashing techniques, which can do serious damage to your parent-child relationship.

So, if you are the parent on the other end of the narcissist, and it is impossible to limit the other parent's influence on your child, then follow these next suggestions;

- Teach your child critical thinking knowledge

- Role model a positive and safe environment for your child - avoiding becoming controlling, neglectful, and fearful experiences.

- Spend quality time with your children to get to know them on a deeper level. Build and grow your bond.

- Relax. Enjoy your life with your kids, without living in fear of what the narcissistic parent is doing behind your back.

- Be an adult. Meaning, do not put yourself in the same position as your children or give power to your co-parent.

- Seek support from a professional, like a therapist, or counselor. Go through family therapy to figure the best option for what you can do in your situation.

3. **How do I respond to a text message or a call from the narcissist?** - As hard as this answer may be for some of you to accept, the best approach is to cut off all contact. This may make you scared or fearful of what they will do if you ignore them. It may make you in your head about

what game they want to play next, or how they are going to plot against you. However, by responding to them, you are giving them what they want - attention. It is best to block them from everything, text, calls, social media, etc. If you bump into them in public, avoid contact with them as well.

If they are a co-parent, family member, boss, or someone of the sort where you have to keep in contact, keep the conversation on point. Keep it short, and sweet, simple and straightforward. The goal here is to not let the narcissist hoover you back to them or manipulate you more. If you are new to this process, ask a third party to help you with the messages, as they won't be involved, and will be able to tell the difference between manipulation and straight forward talks.

4. **How do I manage "silent treatment?"** - The silent treatment is another way of a narcissist to hoover you or manipulate you. If you understand this and recognize the signs or the intent behind the silent treatment of your abuser, then you **must** avoid this behavior. Do not respond or associate contact with them. The silent treatment is a hurtful control tactic from the narcissist to get under your skin. When you ignore it and don't let it bother you, you are gaining some of your control back. Which will show them that this will not be tolerated. If you cannot get away from this person, distract yourself with something else. It is important to note not to take things personally and remember that the silent treatment is just another form of abuse. It is not about something you did or didn't do, and it's not something you deserve or earned.

5. **How do I co-parent with a narcissist?** - It can be extremely difficult to co-parent with a narcissist or someone who has traits of the sort. The best approach to answer this question is to set up some sort of legal documents on the time that is spent, and how parenting will work. That way, when it comes down to it, you won't have to contact this person as much, and it will be legalized so there are fewer fights about it. Another route is to set up family counselors or attend parenting classes together.

6. **How do I break free from a narcissist relationship?** - The reason it may feel impossible to get away from the narcissist is not only to do with love, but you have developed a "trauma bond." As "Good Therapy" explains, and I quote[1] *"The "addiction" to the person with narcissism is really an addiction to the brain chemistry attached to the anticipation and traumatic bonding within the relationship."* What this means is that narcissists are addictive because of the constant up-down cycle they put you through. When we are abused, or brought down very low by our

---

[1] https://www.goodtherapy.org/blog/common-questions-asked-by-people-healing-from-narcissistic-abuse-0507184

abuser, the only way to get through the low, is when our abuser brings us up again. This creates the "trauma bond," which becomes addictive, and can be a difficult process to escape from due to some withdrawal effects.

To work through this, you must follow the stages and take care of yourself. It will be hard at first, and it always gets hard before it gets easier. This is where friends, family, therapists, and other supports can be a real benefit to you. You may feel like you want to withdraw from the world, or only talk to the narcissist themselves, however, fighting these feelings is the only way to break free.

7. **How do I heal from growing up with a narcissist?** - This takes time and practice, and it basically stems down to getting to know yourself internally. Children that are raised by narcissistic parents have learned to use their parent as a guide of how to act, speak, and behave. Look inside yourself for the answers, A few steps to try are these:

   a. Find your voice.

   b. Learn if you have dissociated or developed other "serves" to manage and cope with your childhood

   c. Be kind to yourself. Be inspirational and positive for yourself.

   d. Create positive affirmations to tell yourself every day - "I am enough," "I am not responsible for anyone else's feelings."

   e. Surround yourself with positive and 'safe' people.

   f. Talk to a counselor, or psychologist.

   g. Join support groups.

8. **How do I recover from estrangement with my child?** - Perhaps the most painful thing that can happen to a parent is estrangement from their children. Your emotional mind is going to want to kick in and explain to your child the truth, in hopes that they would turn to you again. However, by doing this, you are stopping to the narcissist level to get your child to turn on them, which will only make your child confused, and matters worse. So, you may be stuck with grief, sadness, despair, and hopelessness. Seek guidance from a counselor in which they can help you with the following:

   a. Reminding you that it's not your fault.

b. Live life to the fullest of your ability.

c. Keep communication lines open.

d. Learning assertiveness and boundaries.

e. Not allowing yourself to be abused by your children.

f. Listen to your child non-judgmentally, even if their truth isn't the truth. Listen with kindness and empathy while not tolerating disrespect.

g. Practice self-care and self-kindness.

h. Offer your help or love to others or paying it forward.

i. Do not give up hope. Tomorrow is always a new day, and it's best to live each moment with an open and ready heart.

As hard as narcissistic personalities may be to handle or manage, you need to be stronger than the abuse they make you feel. You can only do that by learning and growing for yourself every day. Every day is a new opportunity to do something new, face your fears, and challenge yourself to grow.

Why is it Difficult to admit that I have suffered from Narcissistic Abuse?

Denial is the first part to any breakup. It's also the main reason why it can seem so difficult to admit to the narcissistic abuse you just went through. Regardless of if you are still in a relationship with them or not, the attachment is still there, and the games that they play are still taking control of you. If you have caught yourself thinking 'they will come back,' or 'one day they will wake up and realize what they did was wrong.' You are in the denial stage. Even though you have foregone the abuse, it's like without them, you are still holding onto the idea of you being together again. As long as you hold onto this thought, they still gain and have power over you. Denial minimizes the truth of what is right now. Meaning, what is happening right now is that you and your spouse have now become ex's, or the relationship is over and has been for a while. You just haven't come to the realization of accepting this yet, because anything past this point is scary and new.

How Long Does it Take to Heal from Narcissistic Abuse?

How long it takes is not the question, but what do I need to do to heal? - is a better one. Pain is the barrier which causes *how long* the healing will take. So, when you focus on healing the pain, is when you can start understanding how long it will take to heal from the abuse. If we sit there and pretend that the pain does not exist, or we distract ourselves from the pain by being with someone else, or diving into work, the healing process will take forever - literally. It can feel like you are taking two steps forward, and then three steps back, to be put in the exact place you were trying to avoid in the first place. This happens when you don't deal with the emotional pain that the narcissist has caused.

Anxiety, depression, and other mood disorders like PTSD all stem from trauma and pain that we haven't dealt with. It's our body's way of telling us that the pain is not going anywhere and give us the opportunity to take the trauma and turn it into lessons that we can grow from. The process in dealing with our pain and trauma or abuse is to feel it, hold it, and then release it in healthy ways by taking care of ourselves. Eventually, we will learn that through these dark times in our lives, and how we manage to get through them is who we truly are on the inside. Our experiences shape us to who we are going to become, and everything that has happened to us up to this point shaped us to who we are today.

Talking and venting about our pain to other people is not going to fix the pain or heal our problems; it will give us a short release, and a quick endorphin rush. However, you may find that when you are alone, the pain just gets worse, and this is because we aren't dealing with it ourselves. We lie to ourselves and convince our souls that we are fine, that it's just a little problem, and that we don't need to put the work in to get where we need to be because we aren't actually that bad. This is not the case, and it's a lie we tell ourselves to avoid the pain and hard work that we need to put in.

There are three things you can do to deal with your pain:

- Going towards the pain and feelings associated with the pain

- Completely feeling the pain, and the emotions

- Opening our heart with love and non-judgment to it

The pain does not go away if we distract ourselves or tell ourselves that we are okay. The truth is we need to accept that we are not okay, we need to understand that we are upset, and we need to be patient with ourselves for the time it takes to tackle each emotion that comes forth. When we have thoughts of diminishing ourselves, bullying or beating ourselves up for what could have been done, or what should have done, we are only making the pain worse, and the healing process will take longer than it needs to. In short, treat yourself for how you would treat someone you loved unconditionally who would be going through this, like your children. What would you say to your best friend if they told themselves what you were to yourself? As though this may not feel like it would work for you, write two letters. One letter from yourself, to yourself, then the response as if you were righting back to a friend. Everything you say in the response letter you need to actually implement through the process of dealing with your pain.

Why Can't I Stop Thinking About the Narcissist?

So, we have researched, read about, talked to, and tried our best to get over or through our narcissistic abuse or trauma. We have finally reached inner peace, and may even start to feel a bit better, however, the answer to this question - why can I not stop thinking about my abuser? Is this; you are addicted to love. You are addicted to how you felt when you were with the narcissist. The way a narcissist "loves" us, is them finding out our weaknesses, exploiting them, and giving us validation in a way that we never experienced before. We get this behavior confused with 'love' because it's a good and addictive feeling. But one thing is for certain. Narcissists don't feel love. They may think about or implement love in other ways, but mostly they just 'love' you because they are getting what they want from you by manipulating you into believing you are getting what you want.

And, we are attracted to or pulled in by the narcissist so easily because what we experienced love was as children, or in our early development years, is all we know, and all we know what to look for. If our childhoods were traumatic, and we failed to get the attention we needed, then we crave it all the time. When the narcissist gets a grasp of us, they feed into our desires and show us a different way or world about what love is. And this could be different for everyone.

When we are children, we model after our parents, and so if they treat each other wrong, or judgmentally, then we will observe with judgment and treat people wrong as well. If our parents are too lenient on us, then we learn to use people or whine to get our way, and never grow up past this point. Then we will go through life behaving as if we are superior; this is how a narcissist is born. Also, if our parents are too strict, then we may feel as though we aren't good enough, and everything we do becomes dismissed, which then we want to continuously please people. We look for love in others that our parents could not give to us because we have not been taught how to love and take care of ourselves; this is how a codependent is born.

So, the reason for why you can't stop thinking about the narcissist is because they either gave you the love you never had, or the attention you crave, or the feeling you missed with anyone else. Or, you are stuck wanting to please people and be respectful, or good, or enough for someone and the narcissist made you feel as though you weren't good enough. They were an example of what you had lived within your early development years, which would make sense for why you question yourself now. This is because you haven't learned how to properly take care of yourself and love yourself unconditionally for who you are today.

How Do I Overcome Loneliness After Narcissistic Abuse?

As most things do, loneliness also stems from childhood, early development years. As children loneliness can stem from neglect, or abandonment from our parents, or caretakers. Then unconsciously, unaware when we become adults, we fall into abusive relationships because they cover up the 'wound' that we have buried inside us - loneliness. Then we are afraid to leave, for the feeling that with almost every abusive relationship we have been in, they have isolated us, and took us away from our friends and family, in which case they become all we have. So, when they are gone, we are back to feeling lonely again, which may be a feeling we feel impossible to overcome.

When we are left to be alone, with maybe one or two people by our side, this often does not become enough. So, we will actively look for companionship, or someone to be around so that we can escape this loneliness. This cycle is essential for our growth to be able to break it. The answer to the question is to embrace the loneliness and to let it in. Just like pain. We need to learn how to deal with the discomfort of loneliness. You can be alone without feeling lonely, or you can be around a bunch of people and feel like the loneliest one there. You have to be willing to be alone so that you don't fall into the cycle of getting into abusive relationships in the future. Because, when you are alone, you get to be with yourself, and get to understand yourself on a deeper level, which is when you can do the most healing.

However, being alone is not the same thing as being lonely. Being alone is when you are not with other people, you are not surrounded by anyone else. Being lonely is an emotional state. So, you can also be alone without feeling lonely, and this is the goal we need to achieve. It is also best to stop complaining that you are always alone. Do not seek attention on social media, or vent to people all the time about how you are so lonely. The last thing you would want is to have a narcissist nearby, and then target you, which then you fall into another abusive relationship time and time again.

There are two cures to loneliness:

- **Presence:** Meaning to be completely here with the here and now. Being completely mindful of what you are doing right down to the literal sense. What are your toes doing? what color is the room you're in? If you are eating, what does it taste like? Be completely in the present moment. It's not overthinking, worrying, or obsessing over things you cannot control, but being completely one with this moment right now. When you find yourself distracted or focusing on something else, bring yourself back by asking, "where am I?"

- **Authenticity:** Meaning being 100% you and who you are. Standing up for what you believe in, and just being completely authentic to who you are, and escalating the vibe externally. It does not please others, becoming the person that someone else expects you to be, doing what others want you to do, holding inside what you want to say, etc. You need to feel completely free and comfortable to be who you are. The question to bring yourself to being authentic is "who am I?" Think of three adjectives that describe you for your ideal self.

The last little bit that you can do to break through the feelings of loneliness is to take time for yourself. This is truly beneficial when you put time aside to look after you. It is not selfish, but, instead, it is responsibly selfish to understand your importance and needs. You need to look out for yourself, otherwise, how can you focus on work, college, relationships, parenting, etc. If you are looking for others to take care of you. At the end of the day, you should be the only one that is there for you. When everyone else leaves, and things don't go as planned. It is only when you take care of yourself that you find true internal happiness.

If this hasn't helped so far, the next best thing is to find companionship in an animal. A dog or a pet can be beneficial for many reasons and will never betray you. Animals are great healing mechanisms you can enjoy. I suggest a dog, because you can train them, bond with them, go for walks with them, talk to them, and they will only show you loyalty and respect back.

How Do I Get Back into a Healthy Relationship After a Narcissistic Abusive Relationship?

The answer to this question is dynamic, because when you are in a relationship with a narcissist, they attack your confidence, your power, self-esteem, and isolate you to feel worthless. If you haven't done the work to fix what the narcissist broke, then you won't have a healthy relationship, because you will be looking for in your next partner what they took from you, which can result in getting involved with another narcissist or abusive partner.

To get involved with another relationship that is healthy, you first must address the CPTSD - Complex Post Traumatic Stress Disorder. CPTSD happens when you repeat the process of an abusive relationship, such as being with a narcissist which can make you think or have triggered emotional flashbacks. CPTSD can be stemmed from childhood trauma when you are emotionally neglected, (or any other form of abuse), and if you haven't been in a childhood traumatic situation, the narcissist can make you suffer from this as well. It is a type of disorder that is an ongoing trauma that implements intrusive, unpleasant, and repetitive memories that fire off like alarms. In short, your brain literally screams at you to "look at this," "think about this," "then this happened," "you need to think about it first." CPTSD also implements overwhelming, and unwanted emotions that seem to come out of the blue, because your brain has made connections subconsciously to the triggers that you may be facing from the past trauma you experienced.

Another thing that can happen from being in a narcissistic relationship is that your 'super-ego' gets hijacked. In short, your super-ego controls your ego. So, it tells your ego how to act, what is right, what is wrong, and so forth. If you have been the victim of emotional trauma or abuse, your super-ego will become inflamed and damaged, which then your rights become wrongs and vice versa. It will send you negative messages about who you are, and also send you emotional flashbacks that you can no longer control. Which results in CPTSD.

So, the question here is, what do we do if we want to get into a loving relationship that is healthy for us? We have to reduce the emotional flashbacks, and if we don't do this, then we will constantly be triggered by our past, in which we will put the blame onto our new partner, which will cloud our vision of who they truly are. Also, when you are vulnerable or stay in this CPTSD state, the more likely you will fall into another narcissistic relationship again. Because what they will do is spot these weaknesses, and put you where they want you to be, to stay stuck in this mind state. The next thing you must focus on is healing your super-ego. If we haven't healed the inner critic part of us, then you will also likely fall back into a similar relationship. This is because your intrusive thoughts will tell you that you deserve this, and when you believe that you actually deserve the abuse, you are settling for less than what you can have - a healthy, loving partnership. If you don't work on the superego part of your brain, then your perception of love will always feel as though belittling, gaslighting, not being good enough, trying unnaturally hard, is love. It is not.

You basically want to get to a state where you can easily process, feel, and own your own emotions, so learn about emotional intelligence as quickly as possible. When you learn emotional intelligence, you will easily be able to pick out an abuser aside from a lover, as you will know and pick up on the cues and be more in tune with your own personal instincts.

Three things you must do, and when you search for support through therapy, you can achieve these goals for gaining a healthy relationship. Heal the inner critic - super-ego, take care of your CPTSD, and finally learn emotional intelligence.

Should I Forgive the Narcissist?

Most of us say to ourselves, or others that we want to forgive our abuser, but somehow, we just can't. The answer to if you ever will honestly doesn't matter. Whether you do, or you don't, it's entirely up to you and makes no difference if you did or not. The reasons why forgiveness is not always the answer are as follows.

1. **You need to move on.** - Just like the hoovering techniques, a narcissist will use, focusing on whether or not you should forgive is actually one of them. The reason for this is, once you forgive them, you are more likely to go back to them, as they will convince you that if you can forgive them, things will change, and it's needed for the relationship to grow. However, narcissists have a disorder. Disorders do not just 'change.' It takes realization, and then a few stages to go through before accepting that the disorder is here, which takes years of work. If you follow them through these years of personal growth, you will only be hoovered back in to get abused more until that happens IF that happens.

2. **It's time to focus on you** - When you ponder the thought about forgiveness or not, you are avoiding, or procrastinating self-care. Self-care is one of the most beneficial and quickest healing processes you can do to move on. When we learn how to love ourselves, it becomes quite difficult for a narcissist to break through. This is because narcissists have no love for themselves, and do not understand someone having the power that they need or crave for themselves. So, they would rather pick on a different victim.

3. **Forgive yourself instead** - The main forgiveness you need to focus on is forgiving yourself. Forgive yourself for putting yourself through the abuse for longer than you should have. Forgive yourself for not being able to take care of who you are. Forgive yourself for being a lesser version of yourself. Finally, forgive yourself for the lack of effort you gave yourself for growing and being 'powerful' again. Use this opportunity to make up for the things you forgive yourself for.

4. **You need to heal** - Everything that has been said prior to this chapter is everything that you need to do for yourself to heal. Feel every emotion that comes with devastation, feel, and grow with your alter egos, or super-ego. Tackle the CPTSD trauma you implemented. Take care of yourself and fight back on those negative self-images. The faster you heal, the better off you will be. Sitting there focusing on forgiving your abuser, may or may not make you feel better, but you have far more things to work on than forgiving someone else. It is time to put yourself first.

In short, the forgiveness of the narcissist is entirely up to you. If it makes you feel better, go for it, if it doesn't serve you, then don't. However, in order for success, and the answer to most of your questions come from within. When you ask questions about the relationship or trauma, or abuse, or the future, or people you care about, whatever it may be. Know that you have the answers already, and just need to look inside yourself to find them.

CHAPTER 5

Getting Back on Track with Trust

Living with a narcissist or implementing a real relationship with a darker personality disorder person can leave you second guessing everything. This is because you no longer trust yourself or others around you and is why it is so crucial to heal through personal growth, to get past this. The biggest reasons why trust seems so difficult after a narcissistic relationship is because you are fearful that it will happen again, being alone has now become very new, and new things can be scary, and the narcissist has damaged your perception of life, and so you see everyone as a narcissist. If trust already doesn't come easy to you, then learning to trust again, may be even more difficult.

Depression, anxiety, and CPTSD are common side effects when you go through narcissistic or emotional abuse. Some tactics of an abuser include negative criticism, control, verbal threats or punishment, belittling, gaslighting, mind games, lack of trust or loyalty, isolation, and ignoring. The consequences for staying in these types of relationships can put an emotional strain on the body and the mind where the victim is left to believe they are unable to be on their own or 'survive' without their narcissistic spouse.

Luckily there are things we can do to get better, gain our trust back, let go of fear, and accept change. The following are just a few suggestions to get started.

1. **Take your time** - Time is power, and power is what a narcissist will try to take from you. It is completely normal to feel even more threatened or afraid once you leave the relationship. This is because during your relationship, your abusive partner 'allowed' you to go when they told you, you may have constantly been questioned or controlled, what you believed in wasn't good enough, and they became unsupportive of your beliefs. Now that you have escaped the relationship, you may constantly be looking over your shoulder, or checking your phone, in case they are in the dark depths of every corner of your life like they used to be.

The truth about taking your time is that the abuser may have made you feel lost, confused, alone, and questioning what you should do and where you should go. You may be used to being told what to do, so you search for the acceptance of others before you do something. Your life is yours to live, not theirs, and regardless if you are in a relationship or not, it's only your choice on what you do, how you do it, who you spend your time one, and where your path is leading you. These are all things the narcissist makes you question about, and if you have stayed longer than you should when it's over, you may be untrustworthy of the what, where, who, when, and how. Self-care and healing take time after a relationship like that, and you need to take your time with it. Don't question the process, or how long it will take until you trust again, just start healing, and trust will come naturally to you as gradually as it is going to take. Accepting this is your first step.

2. **Create boundaries or revisit them** - Boundaries teach yourself and others how to respect you. Through boundaries, you can start healthy relationships, promote confidence, and become accountable, or hold others accountable for actions. The thing you need to understand is that your needs matter and the only person who is going to make your needs happen is yourself. Again, it is your life, and only your choice who you want in it, and how you want to spend your life with those people in it.

3. **Be knowledgeable** - It is not the best solution to start researching and learning all you can about abuse and narcissism right away after your breakup. However, when you are ready (when you start to feel better), start learning about what you went through, not as a way for revenge or selfish purposes, but as a guide in what to look out for. When you do research, focus not so much on the abuse, but more on how to love and take care of yourself, look for how to guides on how to be better and live better by avoiding such relationships. You can reach out to counselors, life coaches, workshops, classes, and support groups.

4. **Take back your story** - In an emotionally abusive relationship, the abuser will force false narratives onto the victim to justify their behavior. Which makes the abuser right, and the victim in a place where they feel they have no say about anything that happens through the relationship. The narcissist will often gaslight you in a way that alters your perception or reality about how you view the world and see yourself. This can cause long-lasting damaging effects on your mind, and on loving yourself because you have been told something false by someone you love.

Taking back your story is about undoing the abuser's lies and manipulations by being truthful with yourself. What you believe is the only thing that matters, or that should matter. As though this process can be difficult, it is possible and can be done only when you have successfully completed the stages of healing after the relationship is over.

How to Trust Others and Yourself Again

If you are in the process of leaving the narcissist, then you may be feeling pretty numb with devastation right about now. Life might seem so dark right now that you really don't know where to start picking up the pieces. The thing to try to remember in this state is where were you mentally before your encounter with the narcissist? You were probably confident, or more confident than you are now, believed in the good of others, You may have even been a little assertive with your own boundaries. You put these in place so that you wouldn't fall into an abusive relationship. Now that the relationship is over, part of what you feel may be just the fact that you can never trust someone else again due to the betrayal and hurt you went through. If you let yourself stay in this dark place, without opening your mind to the possibility that not all people are like that, then you will stay unpleasant and become bitter.

The new question is, how do you learn to trust again? Here are the steps.

1. Forgiveness

Through the abuse and trauma you may feel terribly stupid and beat yourself up a lot about how you could let yourself go through it all, You may be very negative one your self-image for not acknowledging the signs or staying longer. However, this can hurt your ego, and superego even more than what the narcissist put you through. The first step is to completely feel and take in every emotion you are going to undergo. Then be patient with yourself, time heals most wounds, but forgiveness is the strongest antidote. Instead of being your own worst nightmare, become your best friend, and really get to know yourself by forgiving yourself for the torture you suffered from. Take care of yourself through forgiveness and self-love, is one of the best ways you can get past such a difficult time.

When those negative thoughts of self-loathe pop into your mind, learn to acknowledge them, let them happen, and non-judgmentally watch them pass on. When they don't seem to go away, replace them with positive affirmations and mantras like "I got this." Also, the abuse was never your fault. The reason the abuse happened was that the narcissist is so insecure in his own skin that they attacked your weaknesses to make themselves feel powerful. There is nothing wrong with you, so forgive yourself for feeling this way too. Use this break-up as an opportunity to listen to your intuition more and grow more into who you are supposed to be, and who you want to be.

2. Listen to your gut (intuitive instincts)

Intuition is when your body gives you warning signs when something is wrong, or when you should be cautious before proceeding. Intuition can come in forms of racing thoughts right before you are about to do something, a feeling that you should run or freeze, or a vibe like chills or hairs standing up on your neck. Maybe a chill rush down your spine. Have you ever done something dangerous, or been in the line-up to a rollercoaster ride? That feeling you get as you step closer to the ride; your body and mind may be screaming at you not to go through with this. Or maybe your first kiss or date with someone you just met, that feeling you get right before your lips meet, or the feeling you have when you're sitting across a table from them on your date. This is your intuition. Sometimes your instincts scream at you to continue going, and other times, it tells you no. Learning to listen to it takes practice and life experience as you go through the roles of the ups and downs. Can you remember what you felt the minute you met your last girlfriend or boyfriend? The first impression is a judgment we make, usually right after our intuition speaks to us.

Has there been a time where you knew exactly what your insides were telling you, but you went against them anyways? Then what you feared would happen did? This is another form of intuition. So, when you think back to all the times you ignored your gut feeling about something, or someone, learn to listen to it next time.

3. Building new confidence

If you had confidence before your relationship, then it is likely that the narcissist has taken that away from you. The most daunting task in your recovery process is to build a new sense of confidence, different than you had before. This can only come as you build your self-esteem and your perception of who you are and who you want to be. So, maybe you didn't have a bunch of confidence back then either, which is why it is crucial to start building it now so that you can feel what you do deserve - worthy and appreciated from yourself. The good news is that by following the last two suggestion, forgiving yourself, and learning to listen to your intuition, you will be also building self- awareness, which promotes confidence. Your goals through these three steps bring your awareness levels to a place where you can look at how the narcissist hurt you, and which areas you need to work on the most. Which will tell you your strengths and weaknesses, and in the process of working through your weaknesses, with every one you overcome, your confidence level will go up as well.

This last stage in the process of building confidence cannot be completely done right unless you really look into the traumatic experiences you endured even before the narcissistic relationship. It could stem from childhood, and learn to break down, and walk through these barriers will help you see just how strong you really are, which will build a new level of confidence. Reaching out to support systems and teams like groups, classes, therapies, family, and friends, you will learn how to develop self-reflection. Self-reflection is crucial in learning more about yourself, and how you can see all the beautiful qualities the narcissist made you blind to. Take the pain that you feel, and use it to learn more about yourself, and you may just find out new things you never have seen about yourself before. By lighting up this whole new perception of yourself, you will find success and inner peace, which often leads to happiness.

Learning how to trust again is no easy task, but with patience and self-kindness, and the help of others, it is possible. By following the given steps, you will find that in time, you will develop authentic self-trust. When you have successfully learned how to reach inside yourself and trust who matters, then you can start putting your trust in new people who come into your life. This is because with the trust you feel inside yourself, you can trust that you know best when you are going to put your faith in someone else. This happens when you are perfectly in tune with your intuition. When you are in tune with your intuition, you will only follow your own gut instinct if you have the confidence to believe that you are right. And with forgiveness of your mistakes, you make along the way and patience to overcome whatever problems lie ahead for you, you will finally learn the true meaning of trust in yourself and in others.

CHAPTER 6

Ultimate Strategies to Overcome Narcissistic Abuse

You have made it this far, and may be wondering, so how exactly do I get past this devastation stage? How do I feel better? What are the exact things to do to get to a state where I have completely grown? There may be so many questions running through your head at this point. One of the first steps you can take is to cut off all ties, use the no contact rule - no matter what. Then it's all about self-care, and making a routine for yourself, like exercise which will greatly help you with the pain and stress you are feeling. Acts of kindness go hand in hand with self-awareness methods like how to be in the now with being mindful. Being mindful of your thoughts, feelings, and behavior can really help you to understand the behavior and feelings of others and has many more benefits. Then, there is EFT, Emotional Freedom Technique, which teaches us grounding methods, breathing techniques, mantra repeating, and other beneficial things you can do to make yourself feel better on those really tough days.

As briefly discussed in the previous chapters, EMDR Therapy is great for helping out with overcoming and pushing past feelings resulting from narcissistic abuse. And, while all of those are mainly to help your mental state, it is also good to work on your physical state with what you feed yourself, and what you can smell, opening up all your five senses. A diet plan, along with aromatherapy, can really speed the process when combined with the other mental methods.

No Contact

Perhaps, the first and most important thing to do when getting through a narcissist break up is to cut off ties completely. This means absolutely no contact - no matter what. Look at it as a no-contact order, except you are giving yourself this. Having no contact may hurt at first, but if you keep with it, it can really teach you things like self-respect, self-discipline, and will give you the much-needed space and time to do you for a while. As you got through the waves on devastation, some days may be harder, so it may be best to come up with a safety phrase when you are having trouble fighting the urge to reach out. Phrases like "he will just continue to hurt me if I reach out" or "What's the benefits of talking to them? It will do me no good, and I will be back where I started." You are so fragile at this point in time, so having no contact will give you both time to accept that it's really over, so you both can move on.

No contact may seem really difficult, or almost impossible, simply because they are all you know, you have lived your life with them whether they were a spouse, parent, or friend, and now it feels strange to live without them. You may be half in and half out about doing what you need to do to get better because you still have beliefs things could work. The mantra you need to repeat to yourself is, "narcissists won't change, because they can't unless they are willing to accept they are a narcissist." Which they won't because they don't see that there even is a problem. However, if no contact is not an option, there are other things you can do to avoid them. If you are co-parenting with them, then safety precautions need to be taken, and if they are a family member where you will see them at family events, you need to set serious boundaries.

What Exactly is No Contact?

There are some definite guidelines on the no contact thing and must be followed at all costs. When they contact you, for their hoovering methods, you need to really use skills you learn to ignore them at all costs. When you have urges to contact them, be mindful of them, and distract yourself by calling someone else or doing something else, and if those methods don't work, do an excellent workout to get you out of your head. Here are the guidelines:

- Block their number and all social media communication.

- Do not respond to any messages or emails that you receive.

- Not reading or responding to letters or cards. Fight the urge.

- Do not answer your door when they come over unexpectedly.

- Let your boss know that you are not available if they call you at work or show up at your work.

- Do not engage in external resources, like if they reach out to other people, you care about to get a rise out of you.

- Avoiding people who do not support your decisions and respect your boundaries about not talking about the narcissist.

How No Contact Supports and Promotes your Recovery

Healing is essential, and by following the no contact rule, you can finally gain a sense of peace (in time), with massive benefits to your mental health. Here is how;

1. Acceptance

Relationships can really shape your life regardless of if they are healthy or not. Every person in your life becomes a part of your experiences that you go through. Our experiences shape who we were, who we are today, and who is going to be or want to be. Every negative thing that you go through is an opportunity to implement positivity and engagement in self-growth. In healthy relationships, you are respected and honored without judgment.

When you get involved with a narcissist, quite the opposite happens. They make you become dependent on them, and take your strength from you, so that you feel trapped, or that you have to rely on you. This is their intention. Once this has taken place, and they have isolated you, and gotten you to a place of pure codependency, you feel as though you need them in your life. You feel as though even the abuse is hard, one day they will change if this, or if that. They won't then you are stuck in a vicious cycle living a nightmare. Acceptance is about accepting that the relationship is over, and you can gain this opportunity through no contact to do right for yourself.

a. **Letting all hope go** - The pattern that gets stuck on repeat from the narcissist is idolize, devalue, then discard. Without feeling any sense of empathy for you or your self-worth, the narcissist will cycle through this pattern indefinitely, leaving you feeling worthless. They put you on a pedestal and make you feel absolutely wonderful, then instantly drag you down, and discard your feelings by implementing blame. There is never a real conversation in between the arguments, and there are never real reasons they can give you to justify their behavior. This is never your fault. As long as you still hold what they need, or possess traits they can exploit, they will always hoover you or come back to poison you more.

The process of letting go of hope for them is that you can recognize this pattern, and reality should set in. If this sounds all too familiar, then all hope is lost for change, or "working things out." By holding onto this sense of hope, you are procrastinating your recovery, and sadly, it is false hope.

2. Addiction –

With acceptance, you must understand that you are not "in love," or "holding on" for a reason. You are simply addicted to the emotions that the narcissist makes you feel. How much time do you spend a day thinking about the narcissist? How do you feel when they punish you for it? Think about the silent treatments, for example. Do you feel pain when you think about how they treat you as opposed to how you treat them? Do you feel insane? or even physically ill?

These feelings you feel have now caused you to feel addicted to them. It's called trauma bonding in which they implement to keep you around. To keep you thinking about them. In the idolizing phase, they keep you 'high' on the highs of the relationship through their actions, once they know everything is okay, and you are hooked all over again, they shift into the devaluation phase. Which is the mental abuse stage where they tell you everything that's wrong with you and can even set you up to do what they want you to do, so that when you do it, they can devalue you even more. Then, to keep you from running away, they implement little doses of love through the torture. Which sets you up to stay addicted. To recover, **no contact at all** is best.

    a. **Behavioral conditioning** - You crave the narc's attention and validation, and despite the abuse, you continue to chase the next high they give to you because it feels as though it outweighs all the bad. The narc then gives you your "hit," by hoovering you or baiting you back in through the first stage of idolization once again. This is done to you deliberately so that when they call, you are programmed to respond. If you don't respond, you feel as though you are in danger, or something seriously wrong could happen. This is how they form your actions to behave, think, and feel the way they want you to. It's also called a brainwashing technique.

    By breaking this cycle through no contact, you can reprogram your own mind, and take control and power back from your abuser.

3. Heart, mind, and soul aid –

Behaviors are driven by what you think, and how you feel or manage your emotions. Narcissistic abuse represents cognitive dissonance and denial. Cognitive dissonance means that you have conflicting beliefs to what you originally believed. Which results in confusion, distress, and to get out of it, you are driven to fix the contradiction you feel. So, this is why trust is necessary so that you don't question your beliefs, and you are confident that they cannot be countered by a narcissist. From the confusion of everything you once believed to now being everything you are unsure of if you should believe causes you to live in survival mode. In which you may feel depressed, anxious, panic, restless, lack of trust, paranoia, fear, social isolations, obsessive or intrusive thoughts, anger, night terrors, or nightmares, and numbness.

Whatever you feel, you cannot start your healing process until you work through the pain and every emotion that comes with the pain. This cannot happen until there are no more ties between you and the narcissist. From the moment you implement no contact with your narcissist, you can start to embrace the positive healing measure that you must take to become healthy again. Just remember, when you grieve and become devastated, you have started healing. It may not feel like it, but it's better this way.

How Exercise can help you Heal from Narcissistic Abuse

Exercise can help with many disorders such as depression, anxiety, and mood disorders because the endorphins that rush through your body helps heal your body, mind, and soul. Exercise can also work to heal from abuse as well. Chronic abuse or narcissistic abuse shrinks the prefrontal cortex (front part of the brain) and medial temporal cortex (deep, center part of the brain). Anxiety results from long term stress, which includes problems with planning, decision-making, and socializing. When we undergo narcissistic abuse or bullying for a long period of time, our brain changes, which is not your fault or your control. The brain does this, to set up natural, and instinctive defense mechanisms against the abuse. When we exercise, it increases the thickness of our brain, which is essential for healing it.

However, every exercise has its own effect on the brain, and you must understand which exercises you do for proper brain structure and healing. It has to be a certain exercise designed, especially for healing the brain. Follow the next steps to start healing your brain with these specific exercises.

Step One - Choose an exercise from the list

- Brisk walking, jogging, or running

- Stepping stairs, or marching

- Bike riding

- Elliptical training.

The reasons these exercises are implemented strictly for brain development is because they are simple and repetitive. They all use patterns, which in order for your brain to grow, and heal, it is essential to have predictable measures be taken. This is because, with the emotional abuse that has happened, your life has been sporadic and unpredictable. Using high-stress exercises (anything that puts stress on your body), actually produces the cortisol chemicals to release, and can cause more anxiety at this very vulnerable state.

Step Two - Get started

Basically, you have to get the will or overpower the urge to sit around, and just start doing the exercise that you picked. If you feel uncomfortable and want to stop, fight that urge too. Exercise may be uncomfortable because, in the first two minutes of the exercise, your body is getting used to it, which means you might experience your heart rate increase, and your breath to quicken. This is a good sign because it means your brain is getting used to the idea of the pattern and predictable exercise.

Vow to yourself, you will do this every day for half an hour or more. After ten minutes into your workout, the 'feel good' chemicals will kick in, and your exercise will become easier. After ten minutes, with the endorphin surge, the prefrontal cortex (responsible for stress management) relaxes, which creates a controlled environment that your brain has been craving. Then you need to stay in this 'zone' for twenty minutes or more to get the best results. When you practice these exercises every day, you create a routine, which is also essential for brain healing from the abuse you implemented.

If you cannot go for twenty minutes at first, don't sit down, or relax, slow down, or just take a stepping break (where you step in one place), while focusing on your breathing. Go at your own pace, but keep it steady, and make challenges along the way. The goal of the exercise is to feel a sense of euphoria afterward because your brain is getting more oxygen and blood flow. This is a short-term effect that you can feel right away.

However, a long-term healing exercise for greater effects, and better releases of endorphins, you will need to practice this thirty-minute exercise for three to four weeks, about five times a week. The brain requires constant engagement and will not heal as you need it to after abuse has taken place if you don't commit to this.

Acts of Kindness

Acts of kindness mean that you do things for other people, for no reason, and having no expectation of getting it in return. Kindness is contagious in the very aspect that people who witnessed the act of kindness become inspired or motivated to want to do the same thing. This will make the chances of 'paying it forward' increase at a higher level. Then when you do something kind for someone else, you will also feel good, as it causes a feel-good emotion to stem right in the base of your brain. When you do kind things for other people in front of a group of people, you have just caused a domino effect, because they will feel inspired to do the same thing.

Here is a list of the massive benefits that acts of kindness associated with:

- **Increases the 'love' hormone** - Witnessing acts of kindness produces the oxytocin hormone (which is what you feel after or during a sexual act) This hormone lowers blood pressure and improves heart health. Oxytocin increases our self-esteem and confidence levels, as well.

- **Increases energy** - At the *"Greater Good Science Center,"* they did a study where they observed participants who helped others or acted generously to others. The participants reported feeling stronger, calmer, and less depressed. This also increases feelings of self-worth.

- **Increase in lifespan** - Volunteer work as a result of helping people for free tends to lower aches and pains. After sifting out contributing factors to health like exercise, gender, habits, marital status, etc. people 55 years of age and older who volunteered had a 44% increase in living longer. Which is stronger than the effect of exercising daily and eating healthy your whole life.

- **Increases Pleasure** - Recent research implemented from *'Emory University,'* that when you help someone, your brain's reward centers light up, leaving you with what's called a 'helper's high.'

- **Increase in serotonin levels** - Serotonin is a chemical in your brain needed to promote feelings of balanced happiness. Low levels of serotonin are one of the reasons why people suffer from anxiety and depression. Kindness stimulates or activates this chemical and calms you down, heals you, and makes you happy.

- **Decrease in pain** - Endorphins are the brain's natural painkiller. When you help others, or 'pay it forward,' you produce more endorphins and get endorphin rushes. Also, endorphin rushes come from exercise as well.

- **Stress Decrease** -   It is known that acts of kindness or generous people have 23% less cortisol running through their body. Cortisol is a stress hormone, and so when it is not being produced enough, you are a happier person.

- **A decrease in feelings of anxiety** - Anxiety sufferers accomplished helping others for six days a week. After one month, their moods increased, there was an increase in relationship satisfaction and a decrease in social isolation.

- **A decrease in blood pressure** - According to Dr. David R Hamilton, acts of kindness create emotional warmth, which releases the hormone oxytocin. Oxytocin released the chemical called nitric oxide, which dilates the blood vessels. The dilation of blood vessels reduces blood pressure, which makes sense that we can now look at oxytocin as a "cardioprotective" hormone.

What is EFT?

EFT stands for Emotional Freedom Techniques. EFT is used to help heal and recover from narcissistic abuse. This technique does not need to be guided by a professional therapist and can be done all on your own, wherever, and whenever you need.

EFT was founded by Gary Craig who was a Stanford trained engineer which he studied multiple acupressure techniques used for healing. The problem was that acupressure from what therapists used were complicated combinations of acupuncture points. So, Craig developed an easy formula called "tapping" on main acupressure/puncture points while concentrating on a problem. Using the system Craig found, happens to be considered effective for issues like anxiety, depression, abuse, phobias, and even PTSD or physical illnesses.

Five Ways EFT for Narcissistic Abuse Recovery Helps

1. **EFT helps reduce stress, depression, and anxiety** - In Traditional Chinese Medicine (TCM) negative feelings and emotions such as depression and anxiety are a result of blocked energy called "meridian" channels. The tapping in EFT forms and regulates new energy (chi) and removes emotional blockages.

2. **EFT helps lower cortisol levels (a stress hormone)** - After you get chi flowing from Craig's tapping technique, the newfound energy can reduce cortisol. Since cortisol put weight on the belly, and in the gut, it can also help you lose weight if you aren't developing so much.

3. **EFT helps decrease PTSD symptoms** - Panic attacks nightmares and phobias are very responsive to EFT treatment. However, do not rely solely on EFT for reducing these

symptoms, as it takes therapy and exposure therapy methods to help cope with it. In severe cases with PTSD, consider seeing an EFT practitioner.

4. **EFT helps physical pain associated from narcissistic abuse** - Studies have proven to show that EFT helps extraordinarily with physical pain.

5. **EFT helps in healing childhood wounds or trauma.** - Narcissists look for people who have childhood wounds and trauma, so that they can exploit these symptoms and make matters worse. They do this because people that have childhood trauma are easy victims to get them to do whatever they want. EFT can build self-esteem, and by building your self-esteem, your old wounds will gradually recover and worked on.

Tips on Using EFT to Heal

You will need numerous sessions of EFT to heal from narcissistic abuse. There are layers to EFT, which is called "aspects." EFT can heal some problems, as shown above, instantly, for in-depth or deeper issues. You will need to undergo the "aspects" of EFT to fully or almost fully heal from narcissistic abuse. After tapping on one aspect, or layer using EFT, if you don't find it helpful, try a different layer or aspect until you find the right fit. For example, if you tapped on fear due to a car accident, and it only helped slightly, you would then focus on tapping on something more specific like feeling trapped. This way, you have hit a breakthrough into your true healing when implementing EFT.

What are Grounding Techniques?

Grounding techniques are a form of mindfulness to bring you back to the present moment. It is practiced for the purpose of training your brain to focus on what is here, and now instead of focusing and worrying about the past or future. In your case. Worrying about the past trauma, or the future about what the narcissist is going to do, now that it is over. Grounding is usually taught to you by a therapist and can be used to cope with and manage anxiety, depression, panic attacks, PTSD or C-PTSD, among other disorders.

Anxiety sufferers, or people who suffer from mood disorders, or abuse, and trauma, usually find themselves lying awake at night due to excessive, and uncontrolled thoughts. These thoughts worry about everything you could have or should have done in the past. Also, worrying about what is going to happen in the future. This is where grounding techniques come in. To bring you back to the present. Most grounding techniques focus on all five of your senses, touch, smell, sound, sight, and taste. However, there are no right or wrong methods to use when using grounding strategies. The following grounding techniques are the most beneficial for anxiety and trauma from recovering from narcissistic abuse.

1. **Concentrate on your breath** - You are intentionally, and without changing your breath, focusing solely on your breath. When you feel anxious or overwhelmed, your breath may be short and shallow, causing you to hyperventilate. You may not even notice it, and so when you intentionally bring your attention to your breath, focus on the rhythm of it. If it is short and shallow, gradually bring it back to normal. Like mindfulness breathing, the goal of grounding yourself when you are in a frenzied state, you take in a breath, count to ten, hold it for a couple of seconds, then release. At first, it may make you dizzy, but just make it a point to focus on your breath and breathing patterns. It will center you and bring you back to this present moment.

2. **Physically hold something.** - Grab something such as a stuffed animal, a cup, a rock, or anything that you can see, feel, and use your senses with. Look at this item as if you were seeing it for the first time. For example, imagine you are caveman holding an eraser for the first time ever. What does it smell like, feel like, taste like, does it make a sound? What does it do? What color is it? What does it look like? Think about this item, where did it come from? How was it made? Being completely in this moment with the eraser, focus solely on the object you are holding.

3. **Repeat a mantra** - Think of a calm word, or phrase, and repeat this in your head until you feel calmer. It could be as simple as "toasty," or "warm." It could be as intricate as "I am okay, this is a false alarm," when having a panic attack. Or it could be as uplifting as "I got this, I am strong." Whatever mantra you choose, make sure it is either uplifting, simple, or makes you feel good.

4. **The 5,4,3,2,1 exercise** - This exercise brings you to the present moment by helping you focus on your surroundings. It gets you out of your head and back to what is happening now and around you. The great thing about this exercise is that you can do it anywhere at any time, and write it down, or just do it. The exercise includes:

   a. **Five** things you can see

   b. **Four** things you can feel

   c. **Three** things you can hear

d. **Two** things you can smell

e. **One** good thing about yourself

5. **Get up and do something physical** - So, imagine you are in a bubble about an arms width all around you. Whatever is upsetting you outside this bubble, may make you want to change scenery. When you feel flustered or upset, changing your surroundings may be the best until you feel better. You could go to the bathroom and run water on your hands. While focusing on the texture, or the way it feels on your skin. You could rub lotion on your hands, continuing to rub it in until there is no more, counting how long it takes to disappear. Make a cup of tea, and focus on the warmth of the mug, the color of your mug and the taste of your tea. You could literally do anything and focus on absolutely everything you are doing.

The more grounding techniques you do, the easier it will be to continue to stay in the moment while you are doing things. If you practice this all the time, it will come to you as second nature, and you may even notice that you are completely present in everything you do. The grounding methods are strictly for those days where you are having a difficult time with flashbacks, or obsessive thoughts about your ex, or what could happen. When the what, the why and the how gets the best of you, think about a grounding technique and practice it.

What is EMDR Therapy?

EMDR (Eye Movement Desensitization and Reprocessing Therapy) is a type of therapy used in PTSD and C-PTSD recovery. It reduces the physiological distress accompanied by traumatic memories or flashbacks. This is when participants intentionally focus on their memories, while at the same time concentrating their attention outside themselves. It is a way to control your memories instead of them controlling you. For example, say you abused as a child, your therapist would ask you to close your eyes, go into a room in your mind, and play the memory. While asking you to take a deep breath, without you saying anything, they would guide you on how you control the memory. Some instructions they would say are pausing the memory, rewind the memory, change the color of the memory, fast forward. Then repeat.

If done successfully, you teach your brain that you are no longer back there, and you are an adult now looking at your memories in a third person type of view. They ask you how you feel about the memory, and then ask you how you feel now. Then gradually get you to feel different about your memory and perceive it differently so you can get relief from the power or control it has over you now.

Another example of this would be to have your eyes open but focus on your therapist's hand tapping, while also remembering what happened to you before. EMDR has been thoroughly studied[2] and has proven to be very effective for coping with or managing a series of traumatic events. It works well because the rapid eye movement allows neural networks in the brain to open up, allowing access to memories. These memories can be re-thought about and reprocessed about how we see these memories while being in a safe environment, as opposed to where the traumatic event took place. Then the memories become replaced by how you feel about it. Instead of being terrified, or panicky about it, you would then associate the memory with uplifting, powerful, and empowering thoughts and feelings, because you gain control back. When this happens successfully, the nightmares and anxiety attacks associated with the memories are then reversed, or not present.

How EMDR Can Help Someone Who Has Experienced Abuse

Someone who has experienced physical, emotional, mental, verbal, or sexual abuse may have many negative memories attached to their experiences. During an EMDR session, the person is asked to focus on the details of their trauma and abuse while also watching the therapist make some form of movement for several seconds or minutes. While this is happening, the therapist may generate or ask you to focus on positive affirmations or thoughts about how the memory or trauma feels.

The goal for the session is that the details of the memories fade, the experience may feel less traumatizing, and the emotional impact may decrease. For example, the abused may now see the abuser as someone who is ridiculous brought on by humor or pity, in which the memories suddenly don't feel as much of a big deal to think about or to get upset about anymore.

This happens because the brain is open to the experience and becomes unblocked in which the participant now thinks differently about their past experience. This teaches us control.

Can EMDR be helpful for Narcissistic Abuse?

Narcissists implement all types of abuse to get what they want, as discussed. It's basically the means of what most people think about when they hear the word abuse. However, narcissistic abuse is dangerous, and the recovery may not be healed in a few short sessions of EMDR because the damage that is done is worse than the damage that stems from normal abuse. Narcissists will add a layer of abuse on top of the "normal" abuse because they intentionally deceive you, brainwash you, repeat

---

[2] https://www.ncbi.nlm.nih.gov/pmc/articles/PMC3951033/

certain behaviors to trap you, and so forth. They mess with someone's core identity and make them believe something other than what they are supposed to or brought up believing.

You can never tell what a narcissist's true intentions are, whether they are telling the truth or not, who they really are, what their pasts were like, what they think about, basically everything you will question yourself about when it comes right down to who they are. When you ask questions, they may seem irritated, or allow you to know the minimum details. They lie not just to others and you, but mainly to themselves. The same methods or tactics used in cults, a narcissist will use to brainwash their partners or victims.

Most of it happens without actually causing "memories" to happen. And so, when the abuser tries to explain the wrong or think about the wrong that has happened, they can't. Mainly because the narcissist takes advantage of the cognitive dissonances that develop in you, and they do this by using intermittent reinforcement. It's the little things that they do over time that build up and build up into what feels traumatic, but when you think of something or try to think of one thing, it seems petty, or very minor. This is how they betray, and trick and trap your mind into staying because they haven't actually done anything wrong - in their opinion.

EMDR helps by focusing instead on the memories, but the feelings attached to the narcissist, and the therapist guides you through the many minor events that have happened. Then teaches you how to control or perceive the events, or feelings differently. You can diminish their devaluation through EMDR, which results in having more confidence and a stronger sense of self-esteem.

What are Positive Affirmations?

Positive affirmations are phrases or statements that challenge negative or unhelpful thoughts. Basically, you come up with something motivating, inspiring, or something that builds your self-esteem and you repeat it. Kind of like a mantra. These affirmations can be encouraging, motivational, or anything positive that boosts your confidence and promotes a positive change in your life. If you want to make a long-term change about the way you feel and think, positive affirmations are what you need to practice daily. Here are some of the main benefits of positive self-talk:

- Self-affirmations have been proven to decrease stress.

- Self-affirmations have been used in interventions which lead to physical behavior.

- They can make us dismiss, or become noticeable to harmful health messages, and responding with positive change rather than staying in the negative surroundings.

- Affirmations have been linked to academic achievement implemented by the students that feel "left out."

Positive Affirmations for Victims of Narcissistic Abuse

One sure fire way to recover from the mental and emotional abuse that the narcissist has distilled into you is positive self-affirmation. When you talk nicely and be kind to yourself every day, you will start to love yourself for who you are, which creates a reversal effect of what the narcissist has made you believe. This creates a strong mental state in which you become more resilient to hurt, blame, and harmful inflictions inflicted on you from this point forward. Tell yourself the following affirmations daily, and you will regain a sense of empowerment, and speed up your recovery process.

1. **I am healing gradually. One day at a time. One step at a time.** - Reminding yourself that you are healing not only decreases the pain but reminds yourself that you are stronger than you think and will heal one day at a time. It gives you something to look forward to, so that one day you won't have to say this but can replace it with something else more positive.

2. **I am focusing on my future while leaving the past behind** - Almost always, you will think about the past events from what the narcissist made you think and believe. You may catch yourself thinking about your relationship with them, the good and the bad. By saying this to yourself, when you catch yourself in that moment, you may find that it will help you to stay on track and focus on what is to come.

3. **I am loved and will be loved. I deserve love, care, affection, and respect** - When you catch yourself belittling your own self, or questioning yourself worth, repeating this affirmation to yourself should bring you back to what you do deserve. When you practice on how to trust and let go of the fear of something bad happening, this affirmation will do wonders for you and your recovery.

4. **I am making myself a priority through self-care** - So, most victims of narcissistic abuse put their own needs aside for the goodness, or to help their relationship. Not realizing that the narcissist has tricked you, or trapped you into these patterns, sometimes you may catch yourself putting your thoughts, and beliefs aside for someone else even now. Practicing this affirmation will remind you that you are important, and you deserve to come first.

5. **I know and trust myself** - Gaslighting, a certain technique an abuser will have you go through can make you become untrustworthy of yourself, and the good in others. This is so that you become dependent on them and stay under their control. By telling yourself that you trust yourself, you can move forward, believing that you do trust and know yourself well enough to follow your instincts and live an abuse-free life.

6. **I have created strict boundaries that I am going to stick to** - When you separate from a narcissist, they will inevitably try to hoover you back in. This is why it is crucial to keep the no contact and set boundaries. By setting boundaries, and sticking to them, you can block out their attempts at "winning" you back. Most of the time, the reason why a narcissist will come back into your life is because your boundaries are not strong enough to push them out. This affirmation will remind you that you have set these boundaries, making it easier to ignore their hoovering techniques.

7. **I have the support of the most important people in my life** - A lot of people have a hard time asking for help, but when you say this to yourself, it will be a positive reminder that when you need it, your support system will be there. Take a look at everyone you know and contact the closest bonds you have. Then, ask them for the much-needed support to help you get through this difficult devastation time.

What is Aromatherapy?

Aromatherapy is a healing treatment that comes in the form of oil, called "essential oils." The oils are extracted from plants to promote health and well-being. It has gained more recognition for the science of medicine and healing. Aromatherapy has been used for healing purposes for thousands of years, stemming back to ancient cultures in China, India, and Egypt, among many other places. The natural plant extract can calm in balms, resins, and oils, and are known to have positive physical and psychological benefits.

The following list is a list of products in which the aromatherapy works through your sense of smell or rubbing the oils into your skin.

- Diffusers

- Aromatic spritzers

- Inhalers

- Bathing Salts

- Body oils, creams, lotions, or topical applications.

- Facial steamers

- Hot and cold compresses

- Clay masks

There are over one hundred different types of oils, and each has specific benefits for specific problems. For example, when you are sick, you would diffuse eucalyptus oil, or when you are anxious, you will rub or infuse bergamot into your pores.

The benefits of aromatherapy are as follows:

- Pain management

- Increase in sleep, and the quality of sleep

- Stress reduction, irritation, and anxiety

- Joint pain

- Reduction in headaches and migraines

- Helps manage the pain from birth labor

- Fight illnesses and speeds recovery

- Helps with digestion

- Boosts immunity

Aromatherapy can help with narcissistic abuse recovery because some oils make you feel calmer, and more at ease with the complications in life. It helps by managing or helping you cope with your emotions.

The Most Popular Essential Oils for Healing

As mentioned earlier, narcissistic abuse can take massive negative effects on the brain. So, to release emotional trauma from the baggage of your previous relationship, you must stimulate the amygdala for proper healing. Our sense of smell is the only five senses that we have that are directly linked to our frontal lobe area in our brain. The frontal lobe controls our emotions, which greatly affects the limbic system. The limbic system, as mentioned, is responsible for controlling your emotions such as fear, anger, depression, and anxiety.

The following list provides you with information about the most important essential oils for healing your brain when you have undergone such a traumatic and abusive narcissistic relationship.

1. Basi

This essential oil is helpful for coping with feelings of anxiety, panic, and uneasiness. It promotes calmness, provides strength and peace in mind, and body. It may be helpful when it comes to addictions as well. Which is essential for helping you overcome the self-sabotaging thoughts or behaviors that were implemented from your narcissistic relationship.

2. Cedarwood

When you go through change or a sudden crisis, this oil is for those times when you become overwhelmed, or fearful of the sudden adjustments in your life. The events of change can leave you feeling trapped or isolated. Cedarwood implements the effect of leaving you to feel grounded and stable. Cedarwood may leave you feeling focused, happy, and hopeful.

3. Lavender

Lavender oil is very beneficial in helping you manage a number of emotions. It is proven to help with anxiety, depression, irritability, panic attacks, and stress reduction. Lavender enhances the beta waves inside the brain, which helps to calm your mind and make you feel more relaxed.

4. Inner Child

These oil releases stress from our mental, emotional, and physical bodies. This oil helps with PTSD, managing feelings of abandonment, rejection, and neglect. An inner child brings you peace, feelings of "in love," and acceptance to yourself, as well as feelings of shock, and grief.

5. Bergamot

Bergamot is a natural antidepressant. When we feel like we are unlovable, or when something is extremely wrong with us, bergamot is our friend when we cannot get out of our heads. It is the oil that helps us realize things about ourselves. We may feel self-love, self-acceptance while getting rid of self-judgment, and self-loathing. Bergamot releases feelings of fear, blame, the craving for approval, shame, and emotional pain.

6. Frankincense

This oil implement feelings of truth. It invites the individual to let go of negative energy or vibes and cleanses the spirit and soul. It promotes feelings of peace and enlightenment.

7. Hyssop

Hyssop enables clarity and helps you connect to yourself, encouraging well-being. Hyssop rids your body of the stressful, emotional uncleanliness, removing feelings of guilt, and fear.

8. Melissa - Lemon Balm

Lemon balm is an immune boosting essential oil used for emotional turmoil and combats stress and feelings of being overwhelmed. This is helpful for people who isolate themselves and shut down or withdraw from the world.

Through recovery from essential oils, no contact, EFT, EMDR, positive affirmations, exercise and grounding techniques which you will learn through being mindful, your process of healing will take less time than if you weren't to practice these strategies. Narcissists poison your mind, they make you believe different from your own beliefs, and they never feel as though they do anything wrong. They hurt you through gaslighting and become your worst nightmare even after your relationship ends because of the effect they have on your mind. The strategies in this chapter are sure to bring you back on track and help you go into the direction you need to go. It will help you to identify future narcissists and set you up for a healthier and positive relationship in your future.

CHAPTER 7

Indications that you are Recovering from Narcissistic Trauma and Abuse

With everything that we have learned so far, whether or not you have started your recovery from the abuse, you may be wondering if you have even taken steps forward. Sometimes, it can feel as though you have taken steps forward, but many steps back. With this frame of mind, you may feel motivated to strive for success, and less inspired if you don't feel any different than when you started. The truth is, with every step forward, practicing the many techniques and strategies in this book, you will be on the right path, even when it doesn't feel like it. You may question whether or not you have made any progress because you still may be thinking or wondering about your abuser. You may miss the moments you shared due to the cognitive dissonances the narcissist has implemented. This will cloud your vision and taking any more steps forward may feel like an impossible task.

So, the question is, how do you know where you are in the progress of your recovery? Pay attention to the following signs, as these signs are clear indications that you are recovering.

1. **You realize and understand that self-care is an everyday priority** - This first sign is that you have finally come to the acceptance that when you put yourself first, you are making steps forward. Self-care is perhaps the utmost importance in recovering from your past trauma and abuse. Self-care may include things like saying no more often, taking a nap when you feel overwhelmed or tired, eating healthier, exercising daily, creating boundaries, and making wiser decisions. You are done making excuses as to why you can't, or reasons why you should be back together. Instead, you are so focused on putting yourself first, that you don't feel like you have time for anyone else's "drama."

2. **You do everything you have to, to protect your physical and mental well-being** - You notice the identity of a narcissist, and you realize that their feelings were never real. You understand the pain you went through, or are going through currently, and have vowed to not let it happen again. You do not allow yourself to respond to their hoovering techniques and understand that if you continue down this path, things will get better. You have come to terms with the fact that you will no longer tolerate or accept being around negative influences and going back into a narcissistic relationship. You have a new sense of peace and have set up boundaries to continue feeling happier than you were.

3. **You don't care about what your ex thinks.** - Remember the time where you were sitting there, after your separation, and you wondered if they were thinking about you, what they were doing, and how they were living their lives without you. Maybe you missed them and wondered if they missed you too. You are now in a place where you don't think about or wonder those things because you are fulfilling your own dreams, desires, ambitions, etc. You no longer spend time thinking about their hold over you, or what they think, because you don't have the time or patience to.

4. **You are more focused on your own life than what your ex is doing with theirs.** - Because you know that if you go back to your ex, you will only be living with the repeated abuse that you experienced before, you no longer care to be engaged with them. You are at a state where you have worked really hard to get where you are now and realize that the most important thing is to take care of yourself.

5. **You come up with solutions, rather than focus on your problems.** - You have come to a realization that you have the power, and strength to change your circumstances. You have accepted that control, and power is in your hands, and not theirs. For every action, there is a reaction, and it's your choice how you decide to respond. If you get an email from your abuser, instead of having the urge to read it, you just delete it. When you get a text, you find it easy to ignore it. When you see them or run into them, there are no longer the "in love" feelings you once had.

6. **You see the past abuse as an opportunity, rather than a punishment like you once had.** - Regardless if your low self-esteem or unconfident behaviors were stemmed from your childhood, or not, you now realize that going through the relationship of a narcissist was an opportunity to overcome these weaknesses. You no longer look at your ex, or anyone else for approval, or appreciation. You have come to a state of mind where you are strong enough to

walk away from anyone who makes you believe against your beliefs and devalue who you are. You have officially become your own best friend, instead of your worst enemy, and you are now clear about why you experienced the abuse and forgive yourself because where you are now is where you need to be.

WAIT!!!

READ THIS BEFORE GOING ANY FURTHER!

How would you like to get your next eBook **FREE** <u>and</u> get new books for **FREE** too before they are publicly released?

Join our Self Empowerment Team today and receive your next (and future) books for **FREE**! Signing up is easy and completely free!!

Check out this page for more info!

www.SelfEmpowermentTeam.com/SignUp

Thank you for reading my book...

Don't forget to leave an honest review...

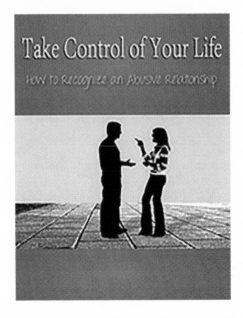

I'd like to offer you this amazing resource which my clients pay for. It is a report I written when I first began my journey.

Click on the picture above or navigate to the website below to join my exclusive email list. Upon joining, you will receive this incredible report on how to recognize an abusive relationship.

If you ask most people on the street what an abusive relationship is, chances are you'd get a description of physical abuse. And yes, that is most certainly an abusive relationship. However, abuse comes in many forms. The actual meaning of abuse is when someone exerts control over another person.

Find out more about recognizing an abusive relationship and learn how to take control over your life by clicking on the book above or by going to this link:

http://tinyurl.com/RecognizeAbusiveRelationship

CONCLUSION

Narcissistic abuse is perhaps one of the most extreme and damaging relationships you could ever experience due to the power they hold over you, and then the work you need to do to get better afterward. The main reason why people stay in narcissistic relationships is that they do not want to do the work to heal themselves. But, what they don't realize is that by staying in the relationship longer than they should, they will never have the opportunity to become a stronger, more peaceful self. The main reason you were a victim, is because you are self-conscious, and have questioned many things about yourself. It is so important to work on yourself now, during an abusive relationship, and years to come. Never stop working on yourself, to become the individual you were meant to be.

This book is the ultimate guide to help you get to where you have always been. So, take your trauma, and look at it as an opportunity to do something better for yourself. Be that strong, confident person you have always wanted to be. Do the work it takes to get the fulfillment you need. Fight the fear of change and ask yourself the important questions that will move you forward. Do I want to live in a bad relationship forever? What is the main benefit to me by allowing this behavior to happen? Who do I want to be? Everything you possibly imagined that you could have wanted is why you are in a narcissistic relationship. It is why you grabbed this book and read it to the end. Where you are in your life right now is exactly where you are supposed to be. The next step is what you choose. What kind of change will you make for yourself right now? What decisions will you make to make your future brighter?

The next steps may seem hard, but the decision is the easiest decision you will make. It should be simple. You want to make a difference in your life. You want to set a good example for your kids. You want to be the best version of yourself that you can be. You have a mountain to climb, but when you reach the top, it will have been the most worth fight you have ever done before.

So, what are you waiting for, make the next thing you do a step to a better future?

Cheers.

References

A Conscious Rethink – 12 Signs You're Dealing With a Malignant Narcissist (2018, June 07) Retrieved from https://www.aconsciousrethink.com/7145/malignant-narcissist/

A Conscious Rethink – 7 Healing Affirmations For Victims of Narcissistic Abuse (2019, February 26) Retrieved from https://www.aconsciousrethink.com/3949/7-healing-affirmations-victims-narcissistic-abuse/

Amygdala – The Brain Made Simple (2019, May 25) Retrieved from http://brainmadesimple.com/amygdala.html

Caroline Strawson – The Top Three Mistakes That Stop People From Healing From A Narcissistic Relationship (2018, June 10). Retrieved from https://www.carolinestrawson.com/the-top-three-mistakes-that-stop-people-healing-from-a-narcissistic-relationship/

Everyday Feminism – 5 ways to Rebuild and Love Yourself After An Emotionally Abusive Relationship (2018, July 27) Retrieved from https://everydayfeminism.com/2018/09/love-yourself-emotionally-abusive-relationship/

Fairy Tale Shadows – How EMDR Therapy Can Help with Narcissistic Abuse (2019, May 10) Retrieved from https://fairytaleshadows.com/how-emdr-therapy-help-with-narcissistic-abuse/

Good Therapy.org Therapy Blog – Common Questions Asked by People Healing from Narcissistic Abuse (2018, December 03) Retrieved from https://www.goodtherapy.org/blog/common-questions-asked-by-people-healing-from-narcissistic-abuse-0507184

Hack Spirit – Neuroscience reveals the shocking impact narcissistic abuse has on the brain (2019, May 19) Retrieved from https://hackspirit.com/3859-2/

Health Direct – Causes of Narcissistic Personality Disorder (NPD) (2019, May 23) Retrieved from https://www.healthdirect.gov.au/causes-of-npd

References

Healthline – What is Aromatherapy and How does It Help Me (n.d.) Retrieved from
https://www.healthline.com/health/what-is-aromatherapy#side-effects

HelpGuide.org – Narcissistic Personality Disorder (201, March 21) Retrieved from
https://www.helpguide.org/articles/mental-disorders/narcissistic-personality-disorder.htm/

Kim Saeed: Narcissistic Abuse Recovery Program – 6 Steps to Emotional Healing after
Narcissistic Abuse (2018, January 05) Retrieved from https://kimsaeed.com/2014/08/27/6-
steps-to-emotional-healing-after-narcissistic-abuse-1-is-most-important/

Kim Saeed: Narcissistic Abuse Recovery Program – The Top 8 Essential Oils for Emotional
Healing (2018, January 03) Retrieved from https://kimsaeed.com/2016/03/21/the-top-8-
essential-oils-for-emotional-healing/

Loner Wolf – 8 Signs You're the Victim of an Abusive Hoovering Narcissist (2019, April 29)
Retrieved from https://lonerwolf.com/hoovering/

Mayo Clinic – Narcissistic personality disorder (2017, November 18) Retrieved from
https://www.mayoclinic.org/diseases-conditions/narcissistic-personality-disorder/symptoms-
causes/syc-20366662

Medical News Today – Hippocampus: Function, size, and problems (2017, December 07)
Retrieved from https://www.medicalnewstoday.com/articles/313295.php

Mindbodygreen – When Forgiveness Isn't a Good Idea: A psychologist explains. (2018, March
12) Retrieved from https://www.mindbodygreen.com/articles/why-you-shouldnt-forgive-a-
narcissist

Mindcology – 8 Types of Narcissists – Including One to Stay Away From at all Costs (2018,
October 24) Retrieved from https://mindcology.com/narcissist/8-types-narcissists-including-
one-stay-away-costs/

Narc Wise – Grounding Techniques for Panic attacks when Recovering from Narcissistic Abuse
(2019, April 08) Retrieved from https://narcwise.com/2019/04/08/grounding-techniques-panic-
attacks-narcissistic-abuse/

Narc Wise – How No Contact Supports Narcissistic Abuse Recovery (2019, January 27) Retrieved
from https://narcwise.com/2018/04/02/no-contact-recovery-narcissistic-abuse/

Narcissism Recovery and Relationship Blog – 4 Key Stages of Healing After Narcissistic Abuse
(2018, December 01) Retrieved from https://blog.melanietoniaevans.com/4-key-stages-of-
healing-after-narcissistic-abuse/

Narcissism Recovery and Relationship Blog – Claiming Your Authentic Power After Narcissistic Abuse (2016, September 19) Retrieved from https://blog.melanietoniaevans.com/claiming-your-authentic-power-after-narcissistic-abuse/

One Love Foundation – 11 Reasons Why People in Abusive Relationships Can't Just Leave (2019, May 25) Retrieved from https://www.joinonelove.org/learn/why_leaving_abuse_is_hard/

Positive Psychology Program – Positive Daily Affirmations: Is There Science Behind It? (2019, March 05) Retrieved from https://positivepsychologyprogram.com/daily-affirmations/#science

Psych Central – 5 Emotional Freedom Technique Benefits in Narcissistic Abuse Recovery (2017, December 01) Retrieved from https://blogs.psychcentral.com/liberation/2017/12/5-emotional-freedom-technique-benefits-in-narcissistic-abuse-recovery/

Psychology Today – 3 Steps to Identifying a Narcissist (2019, May 23) Retrieved from https://www.psychologytoday.com/us/blog/5-types-people-who-can-ruin-your-life/201808/3-steps-identifying-narcissist

Psychology Today – 7 signs of a Covert Introvert Narcissist (2019, May 24) Retrieved from https://www.psychologytoday.com/us/blog/communication-success/201601/7-signs-covert-introvert-narcissist

Psychology Today – The Health Benefits of Tears (n.d.) Retrieved from https://www.psychologytoday.com/us/blog/emotional-freedom/201007/the-health-benefits-tears

Psychopath Free – Trust After Emotional Abuse (n.d.) Retrieved from https://www.psychopathfree.com/articles/trust-after-emotional-abuse.284/

Random Acts of Kindness – Make Kindness the Norm (n.d.) Retrieved from https://www.randomactsofkindness.org/the-science-of-kindness

Ravishly – 4 Stages Of Recovery From Narcissistic Abuse (2019, May 25) Retrieved from https://ravishly.com/4-stages-recovery-narcissistic-abuse

The Compatibility Code – The Compatibility Code (n.d.) Retrieved from https://www.compatibilitycode.com/book-resources/devastation/

The Minds Journal – 7 Signs You've Arrived as a Survivor of Narcissistic Abuse (2018, September 07) Retrieved from https://themindsjournal.com/7-signs-youve-arrived-as-a-survivor-of-narcissistic-abuse/

Verywell Mind – Are You Dealing With a Malignant Narcissist? (2018, November 08) Retrieved from https://www.verywellmind.com/how-to-recognize-a-narcissist-4164528

References

Wikipedia – Narcissistic Abuse (2019, May 13) Retrieved from
https://en.wikipedia.org/wiki/Narcissistic_abuse

World of Psychology – How to Use Exercise to Overcome Abuse and Bullying and Heal you
Brain (2018, July 08) Retrieved from https://psychcentral.com/blog/how-to-use-exercise-to-
overcome-abuse-and-bullying-and-heal-your-brain/

YouTube – Getting Back in a Healthy Relationship After Narcissistic Abuse Pointer. (2018,
August 18) Retrieved from: https://www.youtube.com/watch?v=kKxujjGMmm0

YouTube – Narcissist, Abuse Recovery: How Long Will It Take? (2017, March 30) retrieved from
https://www.youtube.com/watch?v=mMxMsk-U1to

YouTube – Overcoming Loneliness After Narcissistic Abuse (2017, April 14) Retrieved from
https://www.youtube.com/watch?v=jiDNJeUHG9c

YouTube - Reclaim Your Personal Power After Narcissistic Abuse – Codependents and Empaths.
(2015, September 08) Retrieved from https://www.youtube.com/watch?v=bqmydqU-lqY

YouTube – The 5 Most Common Narcissistic Abuse Recovery Mistakes (2018, July 11).
Retrieved from https://www.youtube.com/watch?v=cAOIdOKcFy8

YouTube – Why Can't I Stop Thinking About the Narcissist? (2017, September 13) Retrieved
from https://www.youtube.com/watch?v=zxIzdXJ-eWg

PART III

GASLIGHTING

*How to Classify, Counter, and
Conquer the Covert Control of Others*

PRISCILLA POSEY

INTRODUCTION

*"Remember, a fact is a fact, no matter how hard the liars
amongst you might try hushing it up." - Billy Childish*

The first thing to know about gaslighting is that you, as a victim, feel stifled and used. It is a powerfully dangerous form of emotional abuse where you are made to feel worthless and believe that the world is likely to be a better place without you. As a victim, you think that you are a useless person in any kind of relationship. Unfortunately, these imagined feelings are a result of someone else who has such immeasurable control over your life that you don't even realize it.

You are so blind to the manipulation that is happening in your life that you don't believe, not even for a second, that you are a victim. You are so caught up in pleasing and keeping the 'manipulator' happy that you forget that your life is not yours anymore. And yet, there is a deep sense of yearning to be free. Here are some classic signs of being under the control of a manipulator in your life:

- You feel that you are giving your best, and yet, you are not happy at all.

- You are confused about the relationship in question. For example, you think you have a good husband, and yet you cannot find happiness in the marriage.

- You feel you cannot work any better than this, and still, you don't stop trying to do better.

- You have problems making decisions, even the simplest ones, and are continually second-guessing yourself.

- You have absolutely no time and energy to invest in yourself.

- You don't care how you look, talk, or behave with other people except when the manipulator comments on these aspects of your personality.

- You don't care what others are saying about you. You only worry about what the manipulator is thinking of you and your behavior.

- You keep making excuses for the other person's mistakes.

- You start talking with the concerned individual, but end up feeling like you wished you hadn't started the conversation at all.

- You are obsessively worried about one or two flaws in your personality and character so much so that you begin to believe that they will become your nemesis.

- You yearn to break free but cannot find the courage and strength to do so.

And how do I know all this? Because I lived like this for many, many years before enlightenment struck me and I found the power to break free from such a pitiable existence to live my life fully and meaningfully. Here is my story.

My first encounter with a narcissist started when I was 19 years old, and lasted a seemingly interminable decade. In the days of my youth, thanks to the raging hormones and his stylish charm and wit, I fell hook, line, and sinker for this absolutely handsome man who went on to become my husband even as he worked extremely hard to make my life one living hell.

And mind you, for a very long time, I did not even realize that something was wrong with my charmer of a husband. I kept telling myself that something was wrong with me, and he was right in expecting the impossible from me. I'm sorry I've gone ahead in time. Allow me to complete my story from the very beginning.

I met him at a college party, and his electrifying smile was enough to light up the entire room. When I first looked into his captivating eyes, there seemed to be an instant connection between us. Despite being a crowded party scene, the two of us spent the entire night by ourselves and away from all the other people.

We talked the whole night and exchanged a lot of personal information. I told him why I joined a college far away from my home. It was to put as much distance as I could between me and my overbearing parents. As we spoke, we found many common likes and dislikes like, for example, we both realized that we loved the tacos sold from an almost neglected stand just off of the college campus. Very few students found the time to walk that distance for a taco!

We also spoke at length about my dreams and desires, and it looked like we had set off a lifelong friendship. He also spoke about his life until then, and his dreams and desires. The attraction between us was so strong that within two weeks of our first meeting, we were dating exclusively, and within just four months, he proposed marriage, which I accepted delightedly thinking that an idyllic life was all set for me with this wonderful man in my life. We got married very soon, and within a couple of months, I was pregnant too.

Things took a nasty turn after our marriage. My newly-acquired husband didn't need to put on any pretense of niceties (though I understood this much later in life). He started finding fault with everything I did or wanted to do.

If I didn't score 100%, he told me I was worthless and that there was no need to waste tuition money for college. Unilaterally, he pulled me out of college telling me that I should be a stay-at-home parent for the family. At that time, it made sense to me, and I thought his expectations were reasonable.

However, things got slowly but steadily out of hand. If he didn't like the dinner I prepared, he would empty his plate into the garbage and order pizza for himself. On the other hand, even if, on rare occasions, he cooked and burned the dish, I was not allowed to eat the burned food without complaining. He would become uncontrollably livid if I made any attempt to point out his mistakes.

If his clothes were not ironed well enough to meet his stringent expectations, he would not hesitate to command me to wake up in the morning to correct these 'mistakes.' This unpleasant attitude was displayed even at the cost of waking up our baby daughter at an unearthly hour.

All my protests were drowned in the unilateral argument that it was my job to look after him and do everything in my power to meet his needs and requirements. I was expected to be perfect in everything I did; care for him and our daughter and get perfect scores. That he didn't have to do these things was an accepted law between us, which I also took with little or no protest of any kind.

It was amazing how he was able to make it look like everything was happening naturally and correctly.

I truly believed that I was not worthy of going to college, and my only job was to take care of his needs, and to do that perfectly. I convinced myself that, after all, he was going to work to provide for us, and it was my duty to take care of our home, our daughter, and my husband's needs to perfection.

At that point in time, it made sense to me that this was his way of displaying his love for me. He wanted me to be a cut above the rest and achieve higher standards than the average.

Over time, things got worse. His criticisms were direct and hurtful. For example, he would call me fat if I ate something against his wishes. He would command me to change my dress if he believed that it had a low-cut neck more than necessary. He would tell me to adjust or even remove my makeup if he thought it was excessive! If I protested or fought against these mean attitudes, he would accuse me of cheating on him.

And eventually, my life reached such abysmal limits that I could do nothing without getting my husband's (thankfully, ex now) approval or consent. Suddenly one day, I woke up to the realization that I couldn't do this anymore, and once this idea hit me, I felt a sense of liberation, and consequently, I found the courage to open up about my feelings and life experiences to my friends.

After listening to my anecdotes and experiences, one friend told me to read up and learn about narcissism. I was amazed at the number of attitudinal references to the narcissism that I could easily identify in my husband's behavior. The deeper I delved into the subject of narcissistic personality disorder, the greater was my realization of my husband's personality problems, and the more I realized how I had been living the life of a completely ignorant fool blaming myself for all the problems of my life. I was completely under the control of a manipulative and controlling person without realizing that he had a personality disorder, and I was at the receiving end of it.

And with this realization came the power to slowly but steadily disentangle myself from the claws of my husband until he became my ex and I was completely free of his influence over my life. The only way out for me was to get out of the highly toxic relationship.

However, for some of you, this 'finality' need not be the case. Fortunately, some of you could be in a place from which you could salvage and repair things and set right all concerned stakeholders, including the person with the manipulative personality disorder.

This book is written with the intention of passing on my learning and the little wisdom I gained through my experiences and consultations with experts in the field to people in need of this kind of advice. This book is my comprehensive guide to what narcissistic minds are, how to best engage a narcissist, how to interact with others in regard to supporting you in your journey, and some bonus chapters that I found might provide some useful content. Hopefully, you will find this book useful as you begin your journey to understanding the narcissistic mind, and you will find valuable insight into why narcissists do what they do. Read on, and I sincerely hope this book will help you break your leash and find freedom and happiness, slowly but surely.

WAIT!!!

READ THIS BEFORE GOING ANY FURTHER!

How would you like to get your next eBook **FREE** <u>and</u> get new books for **FREE** too before they are publicly released?

Join our Self Empowerment Team today and receive your next (and future) books for **FREE**! Signing up is easy and completely free!!

Check out this page for more info!

www.SelfEmpowermentTeam.com/SignUp

As A Token
of My Gratitude...

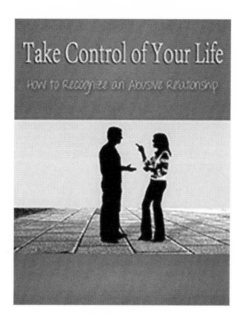

I'd like to offer you this amazing resource which my clients pay for. It is a report I written when I first began my journey.

Click on the picture above or navigate to the website below to join my exclusive email list. Upon joining, you will receive this incredible report on how to recognize an abusive relationship.

If you ask most people on the street what an abusive relationship is, chances are you'd get a description of physical abuse. And yes, that is most certainly an abusive relationship. However, abuse comes in many forms. The actual meaning of abuse is when someone exerts control over another person.

Find out more about recognizing an abusive relationship and learn how to take control over your life by clicking on the book above or by going to this link:

https://tinyurl.com/RecognizeAbusiveRelationship

CHAPTER 1

Understanding the Ins and Outs
of Gaslighting

In 1944, a movie called *Gaslight* was released that changed the way people thought about manipulation and its immense power. This movie shows the story of a husband character that manipulates his wife and her life to such an extent that she begins to believe that she has become insane.

In this movie too, just like in my life, the wife, Paula, gets completely caught up with the charms of Gregory, the man who woos and wins her. After a whirlwind romance, they get married, and then the tragedy begins. Gregory begins to show his true personality so subtly that Paula begins to think that everything is alright with her husband and that she is going crazy.

The husband in the film dimmed the gas lights in the house and insisted that the wife imagined that the light was dim. His insistence and manipulation were so powerful that the poor, hapless woman begins to think that she is going crazy. And so, the name gaslighting came to be used for such devious and evil manipulative tactics to deliberately steer people away from their real lives and life experiences.

The movie itself is based on a 1938 play of the same name. The ultimate aim of the villainous husband was, of course, to drive his wife to insanity so that he could put her away in a mental institution and claim her inheritance.

Gaslighting is the name used by psychologists to refer to the tactics used by people with a personality disorder to control and manipulate the lives of other people, either individuals or a group of people. These tactics are so strong and go so deep that the manipulated people tend to doubt and question everything in their own lives; their reality, perceptions, feelings, experiences, and interpretations of these experiences. If someone can have this kind of maniacal control over your life, then there is little doubt that your life and sanity are in danger.

At this juncture, it is important to differentiate gaslighting from those tactics that many people use to annoy and irritate the people around them. Gaslighting tactics have a dark quality that annoying but innocuous behavior of certain people doesn't have. It is imperative that you clearly differentiate between the two so that you don't end up judging everyone you come across wrongly.

But you must know for certain that gaslighting is a very serious problem, and you must learn to discern such behavior and stay as far away from such people as possible. After all, having your reality taken from you can be quite dangerous, and if not managed sensibly can prove disastrous for you and your loved ones.

The difficult thing about understanding gaslighting is that the behavioral signs might start out as something very small and insignificant. For example, the manipulator could correct a small detail in a story or life experience you are narrating. Of course, then his or her correction makes sense, and you accept it wholeheartedly. Slowly, that 'past victory' becomes the focal point and keeps rearing its ugly head in all your interactions with the concerned individual, and before you know it, you become his or her slave completely losing touch with your reality and life.

Deliberately, you will be pushed to such an extent that taking simple daily decisions might become difficult for you. Driven by the seeds of self-doubt sowed by the gaslighter, you could find yourself second-guessing every decision you make. Like I already told you in the introduction chapter, even the clothes I wore became my husband's decision. At some point, the victim is likely to feel that he or she cannot take any decision whatsoever and depends on every little thing on the manipulator.

Furthermore, the aggressor will slowly convince you that his or her behavior is also your fault. The more you apologize for your behavior, the greedier the aggressor's ego becomes, and the person demands an increasing level of apology and supplicating behavior from you.

The aggressor gets so deep into his or her gaslighting attitude that you will find it exceedingly difficult to reach out and seek help from other people in the fear that they will go against your aggressor. When you are completely and irrevocably under the aggressor's control, then the person dumps you and seeks new 'conquests.'

History of Gaslighting

While the term 'gaslighting' was introduced during the early 1940s, the concept of manipulative behavior for controlling people and altering people's imagined realties has been part of human history for a long time. The victims were simply 'diagnosed' with this condition. They simply withered away in a lunatic asylum or some other institution, alone, depressed, and completely neglected.

Can you recall the story of 'The Emperor Clothes?' What happened there? Did the smart salesman drive every observer on the street to believe that the emperor was clothed in the finest of garments when, in reality, he was stark naked? A little, guileless child saved the day for the rest of the people who believed that if they couldn't see the clothes on their emperor, then it was their fault.

In 1981, psychologist Edward Weinshel wrote an article entitled "Some Clinical Consequences of Introjection: Gaslighting," in which he explained the concept in the following way. The manipulator 'externalizes and projects' the image or thought, and the victim 'internalizes and assimilates' the information into his or her psyche unquestioningly. The 'victim' takes in all the faults, mistakes, and irrationality in such relationships.

Why Does Gaslighting Happen?

Simply put, gaslighting is all about having control. This need for control or domination could stem from personality disorders like narcissism, antisocial issues, unresolved childhood trauma, or any other reason.

Gaslighting behavior is usually seen between people involved in power dynamics where one person invariably wields more power than the other person or people in the relationship equation. The victim of gaslighting tactics is typically on a lower rung than the manipulator and is also terrified of losing something in the relationship. The target of the manipulative relationship is likely to be a codependent partner in the relationship.

For example, in a romantic relationship, the wife might feel the compulsion to put up with manipulative behavior because she WANTS to be in the relationship and/or desires the other things that it brings. Such people are ready to change their perceptions to align with those of the manipulative partner so as to avoid conflicts and to allow things to happen smoothly.

On the other hand, the manipulator continues to be one because he or she is scared of being seen as something less important or significant than desired. Another critical perspective of the gaslighter is that the person may not realize that he or she is behaving in ways that could harm or hurt the 'target.' They could be indulging in gaslighting tactics simply because they were reared like that.

For example, if a person was brought up by parents who believe in the concept of absolute certainty, then this person may not know that other perspectives can exist and that they can be right. Such people could be primed to think that anyone who has a different approach or perspective is wrong. Further, they could believe that people with these 'wrong' notions should be corrected, and thus resort to gaslighting tactics; an approach found commonly in a family and among loved ones.

And then, there are the ones who employ gaslighting to show off their dominance and power with little or no care toward the pain and agony inflicted on the target. Sometimes, the 'dominance and power' could also be a facade for the manipulator's insecurities and fears. Whatever it is, gaslighting is employed to dominate unfairly over other people.

Where Does Gaslighting Happen?

Gaslighting can happen and be experienced by anyone and everyone. For example, you could be a victim of such tactics from your spouse, partner, colleague, or sometimes, even a parent. In fact, gaslighting tactics are not restricted to the personal or professional realm.

Gaslighting strategies are used even in public life, affecting an entire group of people. There are multiple instances in which you can clearly see gaslighting techniques by President Donald Trump and his administration. Most experts agree that politics is a field where spreading lies is taken and accepted to be a stereotypical attitude. However, President Trump seems to have taken it a bit too far.

In the initial days of his office, President Trump - along with his administration staff - are believed to have lied so blatantly that there was a shade of arrogance and utter contempt for the intelligence of the American people. It was like the concerned officials were baiting the common people, telling them to rise up and revolt against the nastiness if you can; this was a clear sign of narcissistic personality disorder.

For instance, the administration lied about the crowd size at the Presidential swearing-in. It was clear that photos from President Obama's swearing-in were manipulated to look like the current one. It was so easy to detect this lie that for some people, it was like a war cry to the media, which was most likely to be discredited by Americans for putting such lies on their websites and publications.

At a personal level, gaslighting tactics are used by manipulative people who want to control the lives of their family members. Think of a physically and emotionally abusive spouse wreaking havoc on his or her partner or the children in the family, and you can easily discern gaslighting behavior.

Where is Gaslighting Typically Seen?

Geographically speaking, gaslighting behavior is not exclusive to any part of the world. Wherever power dynamics are in play and where the need and desire for control over people and resources exist, gaslighting behavior can be witnessed. Multiple studies reveal that this kind of unpleasant and dangerous behavior is prevalent not only in personal relationships but also at the workplace, and even in public life as in the way some politicians and their coterie interact with the common man on the street.

MHR, an HR services provider, conducted a survey in the UK which revealed some shocking numbers. Over 3000 people undertook the survey, and 58% of this group claimed that they had experienced what they believed was gas-lighting behavior at their workplace. About 30% said they did not experience such behavior while 12% said that they didn't know! The disturbing results of this survey poll reveal how widespread gaslighting is in the UK. Some examples of gaslighting behaviors at the workplace include:

- Taking credit for your work

- Mocking you, your behavior or dress style in front of other colleagues

- Setting unreasonable and unrealistic deadlines

- Deliberately withholding information that is crucial for the success of a project you are working on

Most of the elements mentioned above are seemingly insignificant but add up to a lot in retrospect. And moreover, unlike bullying, which is easily discernible, gaslighting behaviors are subtle and are meant to slowly but surely put doubt on your capabilities and value to the organization. Such attitudes cannot be caught until after the damage is done to the target's psyche.

Another US-based report says that 3 out of 4 people in the country are not aware of the term, and this state of ignorance is despite the widespread prevalence of gaslighting behavior in the entertainment and media industries where power-play dynamics are perhaps the strongest.

Nearly 75% of the surveyed people said that they had heard of the term but did not know its meaning. The study revealed that about a third of the female population had termed their romantic partners as 'crazy' or 'insane' in a very serious way. About 25% of the male population had also used these two words to describe their partners.

Therefore, gaslighting behavior is not restricted to any particular geography or industry, and can be witnessed in different countries, cultures, and industries.

Common Gaslighting Situations

Here are some common examples of gaslighting scenarios that could help you understand if and when you are being gaslighted by various perpetrators.

In a home environment - Alice's father, Andrew, is a bitter and angry man who is carrying a lot of negativity right from his childhood. His power play is most evident with Alice, thanks to her dependence on him for a lot of things. Alice's mother is the breadwinner in the family and is away most of the time at work.

Alice spent a lot more time with her father than her mother and had unwittingly built herself into a codependency situation with Andrew. She was highly sensitive to his mood swings and was always worried that some action or behavior of hers would bring on a dark mood in her father.

Whenever her father was in a dark mood, he would lash out at Alice by saying that 'You're worthless,' 'I wonder why you were born,' and quite frequently using foul language too. If Alice tried to argue back with him, he would laugh it off and say, 'Why are you so unnecessarily sensitive?'

Alice had become so accustomed to this situation at home that she did not even think it important enough to speak to her mother about it that was too busy with her work to find time for her daughter. Alice was completely under her father's control and even accepted it as natural. She believed that her father was only helping her toward self-improvement and that there was nothing wrong with him.

Another common situation is when adult children manipulate their old parents. Here is a sample case that you are likely to find in many homes. This topic is discussed in detail in the subsequent chapter.

In a romantic relationship - In the eyes of most people, Julie's life could be seen as being as ideal. Married for over five years to her first love who is now an adoring husband, financially secure (her husband, John, is an investment banker who rakes in the moolah), and with two beautiful children, Julie might look like there is no dearth of happiness in her life. And yet, she knows what she is going through. Before her marriage, Julie was an artist with some great skills.

After she got married, John did his best to prevent his wife from trying to advance her skills and make a name for herself in the art world. He always found fault with her work and made her feel worthless. Every time she tried to paint something, he would say, 'A lousy artist like you is not going to make it in the art world which is filled with brilliant artists. Your work will never match up to theirs. Don't waste time and money on this. Instead, just focus on looking after the family.'

Also, he would always bring up a bad experience that she had had during her early artist days. She had created a painting and wanted feedback from a famous artist who was a good friend of her husband's. The man had said that her skills were way below even an average artist and that she should not even try moving forward. Julie's husband never failed to bring up that comment and used it to make her believe that she was fit for nothing more than taking care of the family.

Julie's husband used that one bad experience and feedback to remind her of her worthlessness continually, and repeated practice and such habitual behavior enslaved her to her husband completely. Now, although she lives comfortably, she realizes that her life is actually empty. She wants to break free from her husband's manipulative ways, but he uses their children to strengthen his power over her.

In a workplace scenario - Jolly was a salesgirl in a large cosmetic showroom. After working for five years, she was given a promotion to work in another section, which not only gave her a higher salary but also opened up career growth prospects. Jolly was very happy with the promotion and started working with her new boss, Penny.

Initially, Jolly found Penny helpful and sweet. Slowly, Penny started passing on insignificant tasks to Jolly, who did them uncomplainingly. However, this did not stop at all and, in fact, increased so much that she had no time and energy to learn anything new at the job. She was just about able to finish all the work assigned by her boss, who kept her at arm's length and discouraged interactions of all kinds except with giving out tasks.

A department meeting was called one day, and Jolly was part of it. Penny addressed the other people and said, 'Meet Jolly, who has been with us for nearly three months now, and she has yet to learn the ropes of the new department. I hope she catches up soon or else we might have to send her back after demoting her.' Jolly turned red with embarrassment and shame at this open and unexpected insult from her boss. And she realized that she had unwittingly become a victim of gaslighting tactics!

Emotional Hot Spots that are targeted

Nearly anyone can be a target to gaslighting tactics considering the subtlety involved in the process. Very few people can really discern the difference between gaslighting and simple annoying behavior. Most often, people will tend to categorize gaslighting behaviors as a mere annoyance and tend to ignore it. Yet, there are certain types of people who become easy targets for gaslighting. Some of them are:

Empaths - Empaths are people who are extremely sensitive to everything that is happening around them. They can quickly, and most often, unwittingly absorb both positive and negative energies from their environment. Such people can be easy targets for gaslighters because it is quite easy to influence them. Just sending negative vibes to empaths can enhance their sensitivity to a gaslighter's needs.

Insecure people - Gaslighters typically target people with significant inferiority complexes. Men and women who feel insecure about themselves are easy targets considering that they are already in a vulnerable condition.

Moreover, insecure people are continuously looking for positive affirmation from others, which is exactly what gaslighters want in the initial stages of any new relationship. Gaslighting tactics start with heaping praise, often when it is not necessary and praises on the victims initially, and once they are trapped, the true color of gaslighters come to the fore.

And yet, it is time to reiterate that some gaslighters are so good at what they do that even the sanest and most sensible people can become their targets. Therefore, it makes sense to be aware of the concept of gaslighting tactics and their multiple negative effects and to be wary of such people.

CHAPTER 2

Illusion vs. Reality

So, now that you know the definition, history, and other basic aspects of gaslighting, we can go on to red flags that should help you understand whether you are a victim of gaslighting tactics. In addition to being aware of red flags, you must be able to identify different kinds of techniques used in gas-lighting tactics. This kind of knowledge will build your self-awareness and also guide you on how to handle such elements before they get out of hand.

It is imperative that you recognize the signs of gaslighting tactics as quickly as you can. Such situations if left unresolved can result in anxiety and depression, which, in turn, can lead to irrevocable, sometimes even fatal, outcomes. Victims are frequently known to have nervous breakdowns.

So, read on and be on your guard to ensure you lead a life free from being unduly victimized simply due to your naiveté. Build your mental and emotional strength with the power of knowledge.

Red Flags or Telltale Signs of Gaslighting

You 'feel' or 'sense that something is 'off' - It could be anyone; your partner, spouse, parent, sibling, friend, boss, or anybody else. You cannot place your finger on the core issue. But, you 'sense' that something is wrong about this person. If you keep thinking like this about a person, then it is definitely a tell-tale sign. Sometimes, it might be someone else you trust who can feel this way about the person you are getting eerily close to.

Here is an example to illustrate this. I had already told you that I met my ex-husband when I was just 19, and I was floored by his personality and behavior. I raved about him to my best friend, Betty, who, by the way, did not attend the party when I met him for the first time.

I was insistent that he meet my best friend as soon as possible. In fact, I had told him that I would bring her to meet him at our next date. He said okay then. But, he canceled our next date giving some weird excuse. Even though I felt uneasy, I left it like that.

When we were fixing up our date again, the first question was about Betty. He wanted to know if she would come. Coincidentally, she was busy and could not have come to meet him. He readily agreed to come for the next date. We met, and again, I came away completely swept off my feet. Now I look back, and I realize that he worked very hard to make sure that he did not meet Betty for nearly three months. Betty found his behavior strange and kept warning me about him saying that something was definitely off. I brushed it off, saying she was reading too much into a trivial thing.

Then, one fine day, Betty just turned up at one of our dates giving some feeble excuse that she was in the area, and wanted to drop in and say hello to my boyfriend. Incidentally, even I was unaware of her sudden appearance. But, my partner was livid and made it seem that I had deliberately set a trap for him to meet Betty. He didn't speak to me for nearly a week blaming me for the incident. I had to literally beg him to forgive me for doing something he did not like. You see, I had almost become the slave of his charm and good looks by then.

I have to give it to Betty for being honest with me and telling me to my face that she picked up negative vibes from my boyfriend and warned me about him. It was my error of judgment (I thought she was just jealous) that prevented me from heeding her warning.

Now when I look back, I realize that if a simple routine event of meeting my best friend could trigger an unreasonable reaction from my husband, shouldn't I have accepted that something was really 'off?'

You feel threatened by the concerned person, but you don't know why - Tom is your father, and you want to do things that make him happy. But, you also feel a deep sense of threat in his presence. He is smiling at you, and yet, you feel fearful. You don't know why. This seemingly inexplicable feeling is rooted in your instincts. However, you are not ready to heed your gut feelings because you are scared of losing the one man who seems to love you.

Here is another example of this kind of threatening to feel you could have experienced. Your husband appears to care for and love you. You can see him walking toward you with an affectionate smile on his face. But you flinch instinctively because you 'sense' he is going to hurt you. But you don't have any obvious or tangible reason to 'feel' like this.

You are frequently second-guessing your memory - One of the first things that gaslighting tactics target is your memory. Manipulators invariably start by doubting what you are saying. Look at the following conversation:

Victim - I must tell you about how I won an award for acting in my freshman year. I played the role of Lady Macbeth, and everyone raved about my acting skills. It's a memory I cherish, you know.

Manipulator - Really? I thought you told me you had stage fright and didn't particularly care for performing on stage? Remember that time in your school days that you told me about when you were so scared that you couldn't say a word and had to walk off the stage when the audience began to boo? You told me how embarrassed you felt about the entire incident.

Manipulator (continues, even as the victim is trying to recall this incident) - Are you sure you won the award because you were good or because there was no one else vying for the prize?

The victim feels flummoxed and tries to recall every minute detail of that event which is likely to make her or him unsure of what actually happened. Such manipulative and doubt-creating experiences are repeated frequently by the manipulator, and very soon, the victim begins to second-guess every memory from past life.

You feel disoriented and confused - You remember keeping the car keys in the bowl near the door when you returned from work yesterday. Now, you can't find them there, and your husband looks for them and finds the keys in the freezer! He tells you that this is not the first time you have put the keys there.

You are asking yourself if you really put the keys in the freezer. You can't believe you could do such a thing. Yet, the keys were there in the freezer. A few minutes ago you could vividly recall the scene where you remember dropping the keys in the designated bowl. But, now with the keys in the freezer, you cannot recall that memory anymore. You are confused and disoriented about your life.

You are always focusing on your character flaws - The primary purpose of a gaslighter is to make you feel less worthy of yourself, which is achieved by relentlessly focusing and reminding you of your faults. Continuous interactions with such people are likely to have made you focus excessively on your flaws rather than your strengths. Your self-esteem is likely to be at abysmally low levels.

So, if you find yourself always looking for your faults in any given situation, then it could be an important gaslighting tell-tale sign. For example, if you have had a fight with your partner and if you look back at the scene with the intention of how you could have done something differently to prevent the fight without thinking of your partner's mistakes, then it's time to wake up to reality. Again, retrospective thought in this way occasionally is fine. But, if you are doing at every instance, then it could be a cause for concern.

You always feel you should apologize - You are a good worker in the office, and your earlier bosses had always praised you for your dedication and hard work. However, with your new boss, Ben, you feel inadequate about your capabilities. He keeps finding fault with your work, and most often, you feel he is right. You feel compelled to keep apologizing to Ben for your mistakes.

You have completed a complex and multilayered report by Sunday evening working extremely hard right through the weekend. You send the report late Sunday night by mail to Ben. He responds almost immediately with a spelling error you made on the body of the email. You spelled report 'reprot.' Ben did not even open the attached report. Instead, he chose to find one little fault that hardly mattered.

Ordinarily, people would have lashed out at Ben for this email and would have reminded him that they had been working the entire weekend and he has the nerve to come back with a small spelling error! However, you feel the need to say sorry in such a situation! This is a sure sign of being a victim of gaslighting tactics.

Furthermore, when you apologized for the error, Ben's reply was to tell you not to overreact. He only pointed out an obvious mistake, he said. You again feel the need to apologize for overreacting. These conflicting emotions drive you nuts, and you don't know what to do.

You always feel you are not 'good enough' - Gaslighting victims are not restricted by gender. Both men and women can be caught in the web of deceit and lies. For example, I knew of a lady who was not just beautiful but also very talented. She could paint, draw, sing, and dance. She was the breadwinner in the family while her husband looked after the home.

In this kind of power dynamic, the lady friend, Brenda, used gaslighting tactics to control her husband. She kept reminding him of his 'average' money-earning capabilities. She never failed to tell him that if it was not for her ability to rake in the moolah, the family would have reeled in poverty.

The poor man was continually made to feel that he was not good enough for his wife. He always felt disappointed in himself and his capabilities. Consequently, he felt compelled to accept the humiliation and insult that Brenda wrought on him uncomplainingly. He felt that this was his way of contributing to the relationship.

If he had only stopped to think, he would have realized that she needed him more than he needed her. He was a qualified accountant and could have easily made a reasonably good amount of money for his family's sustenance. However, Brenda needed her husband to 'add' to her capabilities. Thanks to her seemingly happy family, the world thought that she was not only beautiful and talented but also ran a wonderful home!

You think you are going crazy - This feeling is not a simple 'going mad on a hectic day' kind of experience. When you are a victim of gaslighting tactics, you feel neurotic and begin to believe that something is wrong with your head and that you need help. Sometimes, this neurotic feeling is so deeply ensconced in your mind that you may think that nothing can help you anymore, and the only way out is 'going out,' which leads to suicidal tendencies.

'Feeling neurotic' is as close to the final target that the gaslighter wants you to reach. He or she is working slowly but surely towards making you feel that you cannot live without them. You find yourself unable to understand what is happening around you and that you need the gaslighter to interpret and spoon-feed you. You think you will die if he or she is not around you at all times.

You feel alone and hopeless - This is usually the final act of submission. You feel so alone and hopeless that your life seems empty. You begin to live like an automaton and don't find the power to connect with anyone, even those who truly care for and love you.

In fact, you feel so alone and hopeless that you believe that you are not worthy of love. So, if someone approaches you affectionately or even in a friendly manner, you either withdraw completely or lash out at them because these reactions become your surviving techniques. You choose to blank out all forms of emotion, hoping you feel less pain than before.

For example, as a wife, you could be the victim of gas-lighting tactics and be under the control of your manipulative husband. However, your parents and siblings truly care for you, and they realize that something is wrong in your life and want to help you. But, your sense of loneliness is so deep that you keep them out of your life and counter their moves to get close to you. Irrationally, you continue to hang on to your manipulative husband, thinking he is the only one who can remove the feeling of loneliness and hopelessness in your life.

Other tell-tale signs that should alert you to impending dangers of being a gaslighting victim are:

- You feel scared all the time and don't trust yourself to take the correct decision.

- You are scared of something but cannot pinpoint the cause of your fear.

- You tense up physically and mentally whenever the gaslighter is close by.

- You recall happy moments in your past life with sadness.

- You think you are not the same person you were in the past.

- You think your life has changed drastically. But, you are uncertain of what exactly has changed.

- Interestingly, you are also addicted to the grandiose attitude of your manipulator so much so that you need those brief moments of love and affection (even if it is fake) from him or her to be happy.

- You remember yourself to have been a bubbly, happy person who never thought twice about expressing opinions. However, nowadays, you feel scared of saying what you want to say and choose to remain silent most of the time.

Therefore, if you are experiencing any of the feelings mentioned above, don't believe you are going crazy. You could be the victim of gaslighting tactics. Think as objectively as you can and examine your life and your surroundings.

Manipulation Techniques Used by Gaslighters

So, how do manipulators manage to control people? Are there specific techniques they use? Yes, these techniques can be labeled and are easily discernible. Manipulators learn by experience and know which technique is the optimal choice in any given situation. Here are some of the techniques that manipulators employ for gaslighting:

Withholding - Gaslighters use the 'withholding' technique to hold back certain elements, including critical information in the relationship. Here are some examples:

- A husband refusing to acknowledge or pretending not to see the pain that his wife is going through is withholding an element that is essential to keep the relationship healthy.

- A mother who refuses to share her emotions with her teenage daughter is also holding back something that could help the latter cope with the struggles of adolescence.

- A boss pretending not to understand what his subordinate is telling him is a withholding tactic.

- A boss holding back important data that prevents the victim from achieving optimal results

- A partner who refuses to accept that he can help around the house is also employing withholding tactics.

One of the most significant consequences of the withholding tactic is to prevent people from getting a chance of a fair solution to problems and issues.

Blocking/Diverting - The abuser controls any given situation through the use of blocking or diverting. For example, an abusive parent could say things like, 'I'm not having this conversation tonight. We've spent a lot of time and energy on it already.' The parent closes the discussion by saying there's nothing more to discuss.

Trivializing - Also referred to as minimizing, this technique is used by gaslighters to trivialize your feelings and thoughts. For example, if you went to your boss and said, "I was hurt by your words," then a manipulator's typical reply would be, 'Why are you making such a big fuss about it?' Or 'Why are you so sensitive over something so trivial?' or 'I was only kidding. Why are you taking it so seriously?'

Not only do such replies enhance your feelings of hurt, but they could also make you feel quite stupid, increasing your sense of self-doubt. When the abuser repeatedly trivializes your feelings and thoughts, you begin to feel that you are overreacting, and soon, cease to talk about your feelings or opinions openly.

Forgetting or Being in Denial - Manipulators use the denial tactic by refusing to acknowledge your thoughts and feelings. They avoid your side of the story altogether either by conveniently forgetting or simply denying things that you might have spoken about earlier. In fact, denial tactics are used particularly in those instances in which the victim wants closure. Look at the following conversation between a husband and wife where the husband is the abuser.

Husband - What rubbish! You never said that you have a party to attend this weekend. You must have dreamed the conversation you had with me.

Wife - But, I did. I told you about it when we were having dinner on Wednesday.

Husband - Now, I've proof that you are dreaming up or lying about the conversation. I was traveling on Wednesday and did not return until midnight. How could we have had dinner that day?

Now, the wife is confused. Did she or did she not tell her husband about the party? When did she have dinner with him? Was it not Thursday? The seeds of self-doubt have been planted in her mind by her manipulative husband using the denial tactic.

Changing the subject - Another gaslighting technique commonly used by manipulators is to change the subject if you raise a subject they don't want to discuss. For example, if you were to ask him about a promise that he made to take you shopping today, he would turn around and ask you a completely different question like, 'Did you talk to your mother about babysitting our child while we attend the office party tonight?'

This sudden change of subject is likely to take your thoughts away from what you were asking him. And what's more, you could have genuinely forgotten to ask your mother. Now, the scene is set for him to attack you for your forgetfulness and reiterate his point that something is happening to you. Your self-doubt could take a big leap forward.

Twisting and reframing - Experienced manipulators are great at using this technique. They are skilled at taking a statement you made during an earlier conversation and twisting and reframing it to suit their needs and to their advantage. Abusers efficiently pick out sentences and place them out of context resulting in multiple consequences, including:

- You begin to second-guess yourself more often than before

- Your words would be twisted in such a way that you could be made out to be a villain, or worse still, crazy

For example, if you accused your abusive partner of hitting your son and confronted him, he could come up with something like this, 'I didn't hit your son. I only smacked him lightly at the back of his head. And anyway, it's good that someone was responsible enough to correct his behavior.'

Also, abusers use this technique to discredit you among your friends and loved ones as well.

Blame-shifting - Gaslighters use the blame-shifting technique regularly in their interactions with victims. All conversations and events are twisted in such a way that invariably, the blame for all the wrong consequences fall on you. Even when they have to explain their incorrigible behavior, they will say it happened because of something you did or said. Slowly but surely, gaslighters will make their targets believe that they are responsible and accountable for all the wrong things happening in their lives.

Isolating the victim - The gaslighter likes to corner his or her victim in such a way that there are no exits left. Moreover, if the victim has people who offer love and support during difficult times, then it becomes difficult for the abuser to control his or her life. The gaslighter works hard to make sure that he or she is the only reference point for the victim, and all other perspectives are closed.

One of the most effective ways this situation is achieved is through the isolation of the victim. Manipulators lie about your friends and family to turn you against them. Conveniently, only the manipulators will know about secrets about the people that they want you to hate. Repeated feeding of misinformation will lead you to a point where you will trust only the manipulator. When this condition is reached, you are in total surrender mode.

Using a mask of assertiveness or fake compassion - This masked behavior of abusers makes you believe that you have got it all wrong. They will say that they did not mean anything close to what you have interpreted from the interaction. You begin to believe them so much so that you doubt your own thinking process and accept their version as the true one and yours as the imagined one because you think you are going crazy. Here are illustrative statements commonly used by gaslighters:

- You know how much I love you and will never do anything to cause you any pain.

- You recall the time I stayed up with you the entire night when you were not well? Doesn't that mean anything? Doesn't that make you realize how much I love and care for you? (It would have been one instance when such a thing happened!)

- You are the most important person in my life, and I cannot live without you.

While these words seem loving and affectionate, the trick lies in the follow-up action. Ask yourself if the person's actions and behaviors are aligned with the true meaning of these words. Or are they simply hollow and fake words?

Manipulative Techniques Resembling Attention-Seeking Behaviors

Some manipulators are so smart that they end up using attention-seeking behaviors and attitudes to manipulate and control others. You would think that the manipulator was only throwing a tantrum and give in to his or her rantings. If you are not careful about repeatedly falling for this gimmick, you are likely to fall into the trap of manipulation very soon. Beware of the following attention-seeking behaviors that are actually disguised manipulative techniques.

Hysterical behavior - If an individual is reacting hysterically and creating histrionic outbursts to anything and everything around him or her, then you could be facing the threat of manipulation from this person. Typically, such outbursts are highly melodramatic and exaggerated. These kinds of attention-seeking outbursts are commonly used by manipulators to get what they want from you because you are caught in a highly embarrassing situation where everyone around is looking at you as if you are obliged to solve the manipulator's problem.

Playing the victim - Manipulators use the status of being a victim to appear above others. They may never have had a big problem in life. But their ability to convert the smallest issues into something big and describe how victimized they felt gets them a lot of attention. Through this habit of attention-seeking, these manipulators are skilled at viewing everything happening to them in a negative light, empowering them to get into the role of a victim all the time. Most people, especially gentle-hearted people who are easy manipulation targets, fall for these gimmicks, and actually, end up being the victim.

Playing the role of an indispensable friend - Manipulators have this amazing talent of playing the role of an indispensable friend and squeezing their way into the lives of vulnerable and weak people. The role of an indispensable friend is highly suited for manipulators as it gives them a status higher than others in the victim's life.

However, with time and concerted effort from the manipulator's side, these poor victims become so dependent on the manipulators that they end up getting exploited to the hilt. If a sensible person manages to see through such gimmicks and gets out of the clutches of such 'indispensable friends,' then these manipulators get nasty and disrespectful.

Pretending to be sick - Sickness is one of the most effective attention-seeking methods used by manipulators. As it is natural for people to feel sorry for sick people, most manipulators who use this technique quickly achieve their ends.

Manipulators tend to use either imaginary health problems or an existing issue (which is more likely to cause little or no harm) to garner attention for themselves in order to control people in their lives. In fact, some manipulators can go to the extent of harming themselves to seek attention and sympathy.

This attention-seeking method is usually adopted by introverted manipulators who are not skilled at other forms of manipulation. Such people resort to subtler means of gaining attention than those who use hysterics and drama. It is still as dangerous as any other form of manipulation.

Pretending to be busy all the time - There are people who pretend to be continuously busy and keep telling you that they wish they had an easy life like yours. This kind of manipulation tactic not only gets the attention but also puts down the victim who ends up feeling guilty for having an 'easy' life. Sooner rather than later, this manipulator has the victim dancing to his or her tunes.

Munchausen Syndrome by Proxy (MSBP) - This form of manipulation tactic is highly dangerous because it is triggered by a mental illness where the manipulator will actually cause harm to the victim (many times, serious harm), and then step in at the last minute as a savior to the victim. The ultimate purpose of this method is for the manipulator to get the glory and success that comes after the 'rescue.' Of course, the victim feels obliged to his or her rescuer and ends up in complete control of the manipulator.

It is important to note that this kind of gaslighting technique can actually be very dangerous as the intention to cause harm in the first place could go awry and end in fatality too. Imagine a manipulator using the tactic to trip a victim down a long flight of stairs thinking that he or she will quickly take the victim to the hospital, which would be seen as a rescue. It is highly possible that the victim could bang his or her head on the way down, and get irreparably injured or fatally wounded, right? The manipulators are really not in control of their actions in such cases.

The Key Elements of Gaslighting Success

Yes, the stealth and the subtlety of gaslighting tactics make it very difficult to identify and recognize this kind of dangerously manipulative behavior. Here are some key elements to help you break down your understanding of how gaslighters achieve success in their evil plans:

They undermine their victims stealthily and subtly - Stealth and subtlety are the foundation of gaslighting behavior. Gaslighters are such great liars that they can mess with the minds of their victims in such confounding and confusing ways that the hapless target cannot really detect that he or she is being manipulated. They use fake compassion and camouflaged affection, which tend to make the victims believe that they are being cared for and not manipulated in any way.

They are excellent deflectors of arguments and objections - Gaslighters are skilled at deflecting arguments and objections that victims raise. They brush aside victims' arguments lightheartedly and casually. They will say things like, 'What rubbish! Have you had problems sleeping recently? Have you taken your medication?' These statements are more likely to get the victim looking at their own mistakes rather than thinking they are being manipulated, right?

Manipulators make the victims question everything they believed was true - The ultimate goal of gaslighters is to get the victims to question their own reality. Gaslighters achieve this final purpose in stages. They start small and slowly and steadily reach a stage where their victims doubt every aspect of their lives and experiences.

- Phase 1 - Helena's boyfriend, Ben, began by telling her, 'You're not tired. You have had a good amount of sleep.' It is harmless enough to agree with Ben, right?

- Phase 2 - Ben says, 'Come, come, Helena. Now, you are trying to escape from your responsibility. How can you say you are tired after sleeping for more than 10 hours last night?' Now, the guilt in Helena's mind takes shape.

- Phase 3 - Ben says, 'You said the same thing last week too, and yet, you were able to sit and watch a movie without sleeping. If you could watch the movie, you could not have been tired. Are you trying to keep something from me?' Helena immediately jumps up and does what Ben wants her to do feeling totally guilty for having watched a movie instead of doing what her boyfriend told her to.

- Phase 4 - Ben's words have become sharper and stronger than before, and his demands from Helena are becoming increasingly difficult. But, Helena believes that he has her best interests at heart and does not think that Ben could be manipulating her in any way.

The above phases might happen over a few months, or sometimes, even over an entire year. There could have been a few occasions when Ben allowed Helena to have the benefit of the doubt. However, he made sure that such occasions were completely leveraged to his advantage in making sure Helena was under his total control!

Differences between Manipulation and Bad Behavior

Many times, especially for people who have already undergone the trauma of being gaslighting victims, it can get very difficult to discern between manipulative narcissism and simply bad behavior that is not only harmless but also can be cured easily. It is important to know the difference so that you don't lose out on a potentially good relationship and also to ensure that innocent people are not mistaken for being gaslighters merely due to their inability to behave nicely.

People who behave badly don't do it repeatedly, and there is hardly ever a discernible pattern that can be clearly seen. Lying occasionally because of embarrassment or guilt or genuine and occasional disagreements or even a perspective that is completely different from yours, cannot be categorized as manipulative behavior. Keep a lookout for a pattern that adds up to something dangerous or sinister, and if you come across such people, then you need to have your antennae up and alert. The others need not worry you excessively.

Keep a lookout for all the tell-tale and warning signs mentioned in this chapter so that you can quickly and effectively identify gaslighters who are trying to control you and your life. Yes, some may seem like a harmless annoyance. Yet, continue to watch and observe any suspicious activity and seek help or run when you realize that you are in any kind of a relationship with a manipulator. Learn to discern between illusion and reality and don't allow a manipulator to take this power away from you.

CHAPTER 3

Manipulation Where it is Least Expected

One of the biggest misunderstandings about gaslighting is it is a manipulative strategy that exists only between romantically involved partners. Well, I hope by the time you read this chapter, you will have accepted that this is not the case, and know that gaslighting is not restricted to any one kind of relationship. It can be seen everywhere and anywhere.

Gaslighting in Families

The scary thing about gaslighting occurring in parent-child relationships is that it is treated as normal behavior, and mostly accepted as being okay by society. It is believed that parents will never want anything but the best for their children, and therefore, any kind of behavior is allowed. To be brutally honest, this thought process is archaic and unscientific and has no logical foundation.

First, not all parents have the intention of the ultimate good for their kids. It would be naive to think that there are no parents who have abused and misused the power of parenthood, causing emotional, mental, and physical harm to their own kids. Moreover, even if the parents did have their kids' best interests at heart, gaslighting techniques would hardly be used to prove parental love.

Additionally, gaslighting in parenthood, regardless of true intent, can cause far more harm and good. The harmful effects can easily spill into the child's adult life. Such children tend to grow up with trust issues. They get very low self-confidence levels considering they have never been allowed to think, talk, and make decisions for themselves. Such kids invariably don't allow themselves the freedom to be independent because they doubt their capabilities.

Having said all that, it is equally important to remember that just strictness and discipline cannot be misinterpreted as gaslighting techniques. Like the suggestion made in the previous chapter, look out for abnormal patterns in behavior and then decide whether it is gaslighting that is happening or simple love, affection, and disciplinary behavior being displayed, perhaps, a bit overwhelmingly. Here are some lookout signs you can use:

Gaslighting parents tell you what to like and dislike - Here are some examples:

- What do you mean you don't like steak? Our whole family loves steak. There is not a single member who doesn't love his or her steak. Now, come on, shut up with your complaining and eat it up. And didn't you eat steak and enjoy it last Monday?

- Don't you like the beach? Now, what kind of dislike is that? Everyone in our family loves the beach. C'mon, get ready for the beach holiday this summer. It is going to be as much fun as the one that happened last summer.

Do you see the pattern? Such parents refuse to accept that their child could be different from them and others in the family. Tastes and preferences are natural and cannot be enforced. However, parents of this kind use such tactics to keep control over their children.

If your parents never allow you to like or dislike things that are not aligned with their choices, then it might be important for you to point out this discrepancy and see how the discussion goes.

Gaslighting parents don't really care for the happiness of their children - Parents using gaslighting techniques rarely try to solve the problems of their children. Not only this, they simply don't accept that the child has a problem at all in the first place. Parents use this excuse not to help their kids find happiness. Telling their children that crying is not for boys (yes, especially boys) is a way of dismissing the issues the child is facing.

Instructing children to 'hide' their feelings because showing emotions is not a civilized thing to do is a common way of brushing kids' problems under the carpet. If you see such an unrelenting behavioral pattern, then you could be dealing with a gaslighting parent.

They treat all your ideas as 'silly' - Parents commonly use this tactic to cover up their own ignorance. Power dynamics invariably play a big parent in a parent-child relationship, and accepting ignorance does not come easily to some parents. The child's ideas (particularly the ones that the parents cannot understand) are dismissed as silly and childish.

Imagine this situation. A much-loved dog in the family has just died, and the child is distraught shedding copious tears. His sadness is deep. In such a situation, if the father were to say, 'I don't know why you are making such a silly issue of it. Anyway, you did not like the dog very much.

Don't simply shed crocodile tears to impress people. I was the one who loved the dog more than you and looked after him. You should be ashamed that you are doing so little to help me.'

In one sweep, the child's feelings have been completely invalidated, and that poor kid will think that his tears are getting in the way of his father's happiness and feel guilty about his feelings. Also, the father has made it very clear that he, as a parent, is the more important member of the relationship.

Sometimes, parents use the term 'wild imagination' to dismiss the ideas and thoughts of their kids. Children brought up on a staple of such behavior find it exceedingly difficult to try out their ideas and, with time, even lose the ability to think on their own for fear of ridicule.

Gaslighting parents are always right, and the kids are always wrong - Parents employing gaslighting techniques never accept that they can be wrong. They insist that the kids are wrong and they themselves are always right. And the only 'evidence' to them being right is that they are older and wiser than the children. Of course, you have to be careful of name-calling because in some cases they could really be right. To reiterate an earlier point, remember to look for a pattern of negative and manipulative behavior.

A supportive parent is one who works hard to keep their children happy and healthy regardless of power dynamics and ego issues. It is extremely unfortunate that children are particularly vulnerable to gaslighting, considering that they look up to their parents for their opinions and perspectives. Manipulative parents commonly punish their children for real and imagined mistakes, and the poor child grows up believing that he or she is incapable of being right.

Here is a simple example that can be the initial stages of manipulative parent strategy. The mother yells at Sam in the morning, 'See, you are going to be late for school again. If you simply did what you were being told to you instead of mucking around, you are going to have this problem every day.' Sam is going to believe this statement whether he is in the wrong or not, and in the future, his perceptions and beliefs are going to be warped and totally messed up. He is going to be under the control of his mother all through his life.

Gaslighting by Adult Children

Even though this can be categorized under 'gaslighting in families,' it makes sense to give it a separate heading considering how common this problem is around the world. Adult children can be master manipulators taking advantage of their desperate parents who always try hard to keep their children happy. Adult children are masters at using guilt to manipulate their older parents. Here are a couple of examples:

- Oh! So, you won't help me? Then, I am going to land on the street and get killed by someone.

- You keep telling me to work hard and get a job. Stop pressuring me. I cannot do this, and if you don't back off, I might just kill myself.

The frustrated parent(s) feels so guilty that he or she gives in to all the unreasonable demands of the adult child. Here are some ways that adult children hold their parents to ransom to get what they want:

Adult children use emotional blackmail - The child will threaten to kill himself or herself if parents don't give in. While genuine problematic cases where the person is not in the right frame of mind and can cause self-harm should be taken seriously, repeated pressure tactics of self-harm require to be handled firmly. As a responsible parent, you must put your foot down when you know that these tactics are ways to run away from accountability.

Your child is lying using selective memory - You clearly remember having an important conversation about something with your child. You also remember the promise that he or she made to you. But, suddenly, your child recalls that conversation in an entirely new light. He or she is twisting it to make it appear the exact opposite of what happened. Your child is extremely good with selective memory techniques and conveniently forgets certain vital elements that could alter the meaning and outcome of the conversation drastically. If you see this repeatedly, then you know you are being manipulated by your adult child.

You are dealing with all the problems of your adult child - Thanks to your adult child's inertia and complete lack of responsibility, in your old age, you are taking on a second job so you can feed an extra mouth, you are bearing your child's debts, etc. Your child's responsibilities have become yours while he or she continues to behave irresponsibly without a care in the world. If this is the case in your life, then you know you are being taken for a sucker by your adult child.

Your adult child is continually borrowing money from you - You are helping your child financially month in and month out. He or she might call it 'borrowing,' but, you haven't got a penny back from your child. All this is because your adult child is so lazy that he or she cannot work hard and keep a consistent job, and needs a new job every few months. While helping your child with money occasionally is fine, exploiting you is not! It is nothing short of manipulative behavior.

You do not expect respect any more - This situation is when you have almost reached the ultimate purpose of your manipulative adult child. After repeated attempts at trying to get your child to change, you have finally given up so much that you don't even expect respect from him or her anymore. Remember to get out of the rut before you reach this stage of no-return.

Gaslighting in Relationships

There is little doubt that gaslighting is highly prevalent in romantic relationships of all kinds, including married, unmarried, live-in, same-sex, and more. Here are a few illustrations to help you understand how manipulative controls work in any relationship.

Example 1 - Your partner may have promised you that he will get something done for you on Saturday. When you try to remind him via text message or phone call, the manipulative person is likely to say, 'No silly, I said Sunday, not Saturday. I'm busy the whole of Saturday.'

By itself, this statement is quite harmless and cannot really be called gaslighting. In fact, it is likely you misheard or misinterpreted the meaning. However, the same thing is repeated for an unreasonable number of times, and then you need to start questioning your status in the relationship.

Example 2 - You had chosen a Thai restaurant for your anniversary dinner because you heard your girlfriend say she loves Thai. But, a manipulative person would like to respond in the following way, 'I don't particularly like Thai cuisine. But, I know of one great Mexican restaurant that we must try.'

You begin to doubt what you had heard earlier. Did she say she liked or disliked Thai food? Manipulative people use this technique of saying one thing and then backtracking to shame you or make you feel guilty of not paying attention in conversations.

Example 3 - Look at the following conversation where the gaslighting technique has reached deep levels, and your manipulative partner is actually making you believe that you are backtracking on an already agreed condition.

- You: I am so excited about us going to meet my partners for the Easter weekend. They are dying to see you.

- Your partner: Didn't we agree that we will wait for a little while longer before we meet your people?

- You: We spoke last week, and you said you are perfectly ready to meet with them.

- Your partner: We did speak, and I said I'd be happy to meet them. But I also said, let's do it after a month. But, now that you have already told them, I can't do anything but come. I don't want to disappoint your family.

You see the way the episode is panning out? It now seems that your partner is accommodating your mistake, which automatically puts you on the defensive. Such people will keep this instance in mind and will use to control an important decision in the future.

Gaslighting at the Workplace

Gaslighting at the workplace is all about keeping and holding power. Here are a couple of illustrations to help you understand gaslighting tactics commonly employed at the workplace.

Example 1 - Suppose you go to your boss to report that you have completed a given task, a manipulative person is likely to respond like this, 'Why did you waste your time doing that thing when I told him specifically to do this task?'

Now, any average person is going to get agitated with this comment, and you will respond in a fumbling, or perhaps, angry tone. Your manipulative boss is going to say, 'Aren't you overreacting to this just a wee bit more than necessary? Now, go and work on that other task.'

Example 2 - You are sure to connect with classic workplace gaslighting tactic. Suppose your boss promised you a raise the coming May. You approach him or her promptly and remind him just before the pay rises are to be decided. Your boss says this, 'I didn't promise you a raise. I only said that you could get a raise if your performance gets better. Sadly to say, there are many elements still lacking in that aspect.' You know you have been taken for a ride.

Example 3 - A colleague of yours is trying hard to get one-up on you. She makes you jittery with statements like, 'I heard that the boss is not very happy with your report. I am sure you are in trouble.' The colleague walks away knowing full well that she has sown the seeds of self-doubt in your mind.

If you fought back a bit, this person would respond with, 'I only wanted to warn you so that you can be prepared. God! Someone is really feeling very sensitive today.'

Example 4 - Another colleague-triggered gaslighting statement could go something like this, 'Weren't you marked on that mail? Well, maybe the boss doesn't yet trust you with such important things, I suppose.'

Gaslighting tactics at the workplace can also happen through actions and are not restricted to verbal abuse. Your colleague could come and shut down your computer simply without reason. It is quite likely that you forgot to save your work at that time. Imagine the pain and agony.

Alternately, he or she could move an important file from the place you normally keep it to another place, and it takes a bit of time for you to find it. This loss of time might happen exactly when your boss is demanding that file right now. Your boss is not likely to take your 'tardiness' lightly. Although you don't have proof, deep down, you feel that something is not right.

And yet, all these instances add up and create weakness, fear, and self-doubt in your mind. You believe you are not worthy of your job, and sooner rather than later, you could simply call it quits. Beware of such situations!

Gaslighting in Public Life and Politics

Politicians all over the world are known to use gaslighting tactics to control how they are viewed by the public. For example, in a speech on July 2018, Trump lashed out at his imagined opponents for 'distorting, doctoring, and fudging' his tape using advanced technology to make him look bad in the public eye. He refused to back down on these allegations even when journalists published the entire transcript and the untampered full video.

What was Trump doing? He was making the public question their own experiences so that they felt confused and confounded and didn't know what to believe. He was making the public doubt their memories, realities, and perception by sowing the seeds of confusion. If this is not gaslighting, then what else can it be called?

Moreover, this is not the first time Trump is believed to have been using gaslighting tactics to confound the American public. The use of Russian intelligence and intervention to affect voting patterns in the 2016 presidential election was also dismissed as 'fake.' Trump knows that for an uninformed public, it just comes down to his word against the word of ordinary journalists who are out to 'defame and demean' him in the public eye.

Therefore, gaslighting is not restricted to being between two people. One person with the backing of political and financial strength can gaslight an entire nation.

WAIT!!!

READ THIS BEFORE GOING ANY FURTHER!

How would you like to get your next eBook **FREE** <u>and</u> get new books for **FREE** too before they are publicly released?

Join our Self Empowerment Team today and receive your next (and future) books for **FREE**! Signing up is easy and completely free!!

Check out this page for more info!

www.SelfEmpowermentTeam.com/SignUp

Just a Friendly Reminder...

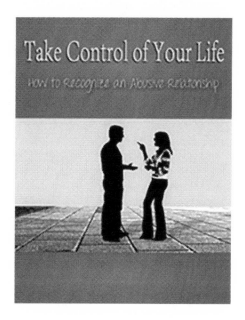

I'd like to offer you this amazing resource which my clients pay for. It is a report I written when I first began my journey.

Click on the picture above or navigate to the website below to join my exclusive email list. Upon joining, you will receive this incredible report on how to recognize an abusive relationship.

If you ask most people on the street what an abusive relationship is, chances are you'd get a description of physical abuse. And yes, that is most certainly an abusive relationship. However, abuse comes in many forms. The actual meaning of abuse is when someone exerts control over another person.

Find out more about recognizing an abusive relationship and learn how to take control over your life by clicking on the book above or by going to this link:

http://tinyurl.com/RecognizeAbusiveRelationship

CHAPTER 4

They're Not All the Same

Gaslighting and manipulative techniques are one thing, and the types of manipulators is another thing. Each person has a predominant technique that he or she uses on their victims, and the choice is dependent on multiple factors including the purpose for controlling the victim, the personalities of the manipulator and/or the target, the situation, and many more. Let us look at the different types of manipulators you are likely to encounter.

The Manipulator Who Uses Guilt

The manipulator who makes you take a guilt trip is, perhaps, one of the most dangerous gaslighting practitioners in the world. Here are some classic statements the 'guilt builders' employ on their victims:

- If you were a good child, you would listen to your mama.

- If you truly loved me, you would not say no.

- If you really understood what I have gone through, you would not speak to me like this.

- If you were a good husband, you would never refuse my request.

They fill the victims' minds with self-guilt and make them pliable. Then, such guilt builders enforce their main ideas and thoughts on the highly vulnerable victim. Nothing works like guilt to turn on a repenting attitude, and manipulators want their victims to show repentance so that they can use it to their advantage.

What happens when you repent? It means you are sorry and are prepared for punishment, which is a perfect situation for them to start controlling you and your mind. Such manipulators blame you for all the wrong things, including their own behavior. For example, 'If you hadn't said that nasty thing, I would not have behaved as badly as I did.' So, their bad behavior becomes your problem.

The ones who cannot take responsibility for anything in their lives are the ones who typically use guilt building tactic to control others. This kind of manipulative behavior is based primarily on emotionally weak people who are ready to take responsibility for real and imagined faults to be accepted by the manipulator.

Manipulators who use guilt tend to carry their emotional scars like a badge showing it off to everyone so that they can control the people around them. Here are some common words or situations used by this type of manipulator to make you guilty:

- I have had such a bad childhood.

- You don't know the amount of pain I went through looking after my sick father.

- I have had to put up with your horrible father, and you simply don't know what I have sacrificed for your sake.

- You are angry because I am not ready for commitment. But, you don't know how difficult it is for me considering that I suffered loneliness after my father abandoned me.

The Aggressive Manipulator or 'Threatener'

The most common forms of abuse perpetrated by the aggressive or threatening kind of manipulator is domestic abuse. Here are some classic lines that this kind of manipulator will spew from his or her mouth:

- I will beat you black and blue if you don't give me the money.

- I will kill you if you don't listen to me.

- I will throw you onto the streets if you don't heed my words.

- I will not give you food if you don't complete your homework on time.

People who have a lot of physical and mental strength generally tend to use this kind of manipulation tactic. They are confident of the fear they can instill in the victim using whichever method they can to get their work done. The 'threatener' will threaten to destroy your career, family, relationships, and more.

'Threateners' are great blackmailers who tend to take advantage of the secret information they have on others to control people. The thing about this type of manipulator is that they may be strong physically, and yet, they lack the courage to do things in the open. They tend to hide their aggressive behavior and will display it only in front of their victims and no one else.

The deep sense of fear created by 'threateners' can be powerful enough to drive victims to do their bidding,the including getting gaslighted. 'Threateners' also tend to isolate their victims from supportive family and friends. Being isolated like this makes victims surrender themselves entirely to the mercy of 'threateners.'

The most evident sense of fear is rooted in being physically abused by this type of manipulator. It is imperative that you do everything in your power to steer clear of such manipulators as their aggression can lead to fatality too.

While the physical threat is one way to manipulate, subtle forms of threats are also employed by manipulators. For example, a wife who wants to control her husband's diet might say, 'If you continue to eat this way, you can rest assured that in less than six months, you will look at a huge drum.' Here, the wife wants to control the eating habits of her husband. She uses this threat as a way of controlling one aspect of her husband's life. It's likely that the wife hates to see her husband's happy face when he eats and wants to wipe that pleasure from his life.

The Manipulator Who Uses the Silent Treatment

The ones who are not smart enough to get you on a guilt trip or be aggressive tend to use the silent treatment to manipulate. This type of manipulation is most effective when you, as the victim, desperately need the help of the manipulator. Such manipulative techniques withdraw all kinds of communication and contact with the victim until their desires are achieved.

When it comes to romantically involved partners, then this type of manipulator will withdraw even sex from the equation. In fact, women manipulators tend to play this card to control their male partners knowing full well that some men need sex like food and water!

A silent treatment manipulation is a powerful form of emotional abuse as it negatively affects the very basic need of human beings to be in touch with others. The silent treatment is meant to instill a fear of getting disconnected with the manipulator in the minds of the victims. It is also generally used by people in the initial stages of romantic relationships. The controlling partner would have used charm and fake compassion to build the necessary connection, and then turn on the silent treatment to start and deepen the controlling effect.

When faced with the silent treatment suddenly, the victim feels the fear of rejection and abandonment and will do anything to win back favor with the manipulator. The silent treatment giver can result in utterly frustrating the victim. There are many reasons why people use the silent treatment method, including:

- It makes them take the 'high moral road' giving them the upper hand in any relationship.

- Other methods of showing their displeasure have not produced their desired outcomes.

- It is easy to defend this kind of behavior later on. All that needs to be said is, 'I said nothing,' and wash off all blame and accountability in the relationship.

Examples, where silent treatment manipulators work effectively are:

- A mother ignoring her child

- Silent treatment on online platforms

- Nonverbal show of anger like throwing things randomly

- Keeping a colleague out of a collaborative project

The Manipulator Who Attacks Your Self-Esteem

This type of manipulator attacks your self-esteem by:

- Putting you down

- Labeling you

- Passing judgments

- Showing contempt

The self-esteem attackers do everything they can to criticize you and make you feel inferior. The worst thing is that these verbal attacks need not be direct. If someone tells you, ''Only working women wear lipstick during the day,' it translates to telling you that you are a whore, doesn't it?

It is extremely important to be very wary of such kinds of manipulators because they are highly skilled at discrediting you among you family and friends. This kind of manipulator expects you to surrender and give in to their control to avoid being belittled and shamed.

Here are some tell-tale signs to warn you if you are associated with a self-esteem attacker:

- You are always in a state of self-doubt, practically on a daily basis.

- You are always in comparison mode, comparing yourself and your capabilities with others and their achievements.

- You don't know how to take compliments and praise from others. Moreover, you don't appreciate your accomplishments and achievements. In fact, you minimize what you have achieved, even big achievements.

- You have no idea of your strengths and personality assets.

- You are scared to explore new possibilities and experiences. This fear is so deeply ingrained that you don't mind staying in a rut but will not attempt new ventures regardless of anything.

- You avoid attending social meetings and even keep interactions with your family and friends to a minimum.

All the signs mentioned above are directly connected to the fact that your self-esteem is under attack. Find out if these effects are the result of manipulators in your life. The self-esteem attacker uses this method because not only does he or she get to control victims but is also able to do it without physical violence and aggression.

The Manipulator Who Uses Competition

Can you recall the effects of the following statements?

- Let me see who will be the first to get ready for school?

- Whoever gets me the newspaper will become papa's favorite?

- Whoever finishes lunch first will get a surprise gift from mama?

Although they might seem innocuous, many parents use these competitive-driven statements to control their children. In fact, most of us were subjected to these competitions with our siblings during our childhood, right? Most parents, perhaps, don't even realize that they are using gaslighting techniques in such cases.

Most of them use this method simply because parenting becomes easy. They forget that if there is a winner, then there is a loser in the bargain, and being a winner or loser could result in long-term harmful consequences. Also, being in a competitive spirit at all times can cause a lot of psychological harm that will be carried forward into adulthood.

Even in other kinds of relationships, the competitive manipulator makes an appearance. For example, a manipulative husband might tell his wife that if she cooks her best meal for dinner for his friends, then he will buy her a nice piece of jewelry. A manipulative woman who knows that her boyfriend has self-confidence issues could say, 'I don't know if I want to spend this coming weekend with you or Jim. I think it depends on who will buy me the most beautiful pair of earrings.'

In an office environment too, these kinds of manipulators can be found. The boss will tell his team, 'The one who brings me the best presentation will be given a chance to travel with me to Paris for the upcoming business trip.' Yes, setting such competitions is a great way to get employees to give their best. However, if someone is doing it repeatedly, then it is likely to be a manipulative gesture to control his or team rather than to bring out the best in people.

Manipulators use the competition element not only because it is easy for them but also because they are obsessed with catfights. Even when there is no need for competition, such manipulators will bring it on just to satisfy their own cravings. Use these differences to help you discern between healthy competition and manipulation:

Manipulative people:

- Withhold critical information as collateral to achieve their desires
- Wield their power and control over others
- Twist the emotions and feelings of other people to achieve their own ends
- Want others to fail so that they come across as winners
- Use fear and guilt to motivate people to do their bidding

Competitive people:

- Use their power to empower others around them and help others achieve success
- Do not hold back information that can be used by everyone to achieve success
- Employ their own emotional intelligence to help others in need of emotional support
- Use positive reinforcement to motivate employees and team members
- Encourage a collaborative approach within their teams

The Manipulator Who Uses Criticism

This type of manipulator finds fault with everything you do. They use criticism and fault-finding mechanisms to wreck your confidence levels. When you continue to receive criticism from someone for everything you do, sooner rather than later, you are likely to lose your sense of self-reliance, which makes it easy for the manipulator to control you. You are repeatedly made to feel inferior.

And finally, it reaches such a stage that you are ready to surrender yourself to the manipulator in the hope that criticisms come to a halt. Psychology experts say that indulging in constant criticism is a deadly form of emotional abuse.

An indirect form of criticism that this type of manipulators uses is sarcasm. In fact, criticizing manipulator like all other types of manipulators prefers to work in an underhanded manner and avoid direct confrontation. Using sarcasm comes in very useful for such subtle occasions.

The criticizing manipulator becomes a self-proclaimed judge of your life and everything in it. Through repeated conversations, such people suddenly look like your 'spiritual guide' to you and to everyone around you. You don't take any decision in your life without running it through such manipulators. These people are skilled at telling you how you must lead your life.

In fact, criticizing manipulator uses a lot of philosophy to explain how you must lead your life. They will use reams of philosophical quotes and maxims and give your detailed step-by-step instructions on how to live your life. The worst part is that if things don't turn out as they 'promised' you, even then you will be blamed. They will find some tiny flaw in the way you handled the situation because of which the outcome was not as they predicted!

Sarcastic is a powerful weapon in the hands of criticizing manipulators. For example, they will not call you a dog, but they will offer you a bone! Criticizers use sarcasm to demean and devalue your thoughts, opinions, and all aspects of your life. For example, they could send you a message like, 'Maybe if you read a little more, you could have more distinguished friends.' In this case, the manipulator is finding fault with your friends indirectly. He or she wants you to disconnect with some or all of your friends in a bid to isolate you. This message could work for some of us who are very sensitive to criticism.

We are likely to look at our friends through new eyes and find the faults that the manipulator wants us to find. Consequently, we begin to think that the manipulator is right, and we are wrong. This way, criticizing manipulator controls who should be your friend and who should not.

Here is an illustration of how a manipulative husband who uses criticism to his advantage. Jane, the wife of the manipulative husband, Jim, has caught him cheating on her. She shows him the motel bill that she found in his wallet. Instead of focusing on his affair, he turns around and yells at her for going through his wallet. He raves and rants about the importance of trust in a marriage, and tells her that her act of searching his wallet undermines the trust he had in her. He criticizes her for her distrustful behavior.

Soon, poor Jane has become so caught up with his criticisms of her attitude that the affair is forgotten, and she starts to focus on her mistake. She begins to feel guilty about searching his wallet, and within a few minutes, starts to ask for forgiveness for her 'rash' behavior. The cheating ends up like a simple misunderstanding that she should never have brought to his attention at all.

The Manipulator Who Uses Charm

This type of manipulator starts with the act of charming you because they know that in order to ride a horse, the poor animal needs to be first stroked lovingly. Initially, the charmer manipulator lays on his or her charm nice and thickly through pleasant and disarming behavior.

These manipulators will flatter you and entertain you with their conversations and talk. They are invariably witty people who can make you laugh a lot. They pretend to be highly sensitive to your needs and expectations. All this charming attitude is the first stage of manipulation.

Once the charmer knows he or she has control over you, then the personality undergoes a drastic change. They start the manipulation process slowly and soon, thanks to their charm, you are in their complete control. The web of seduction that the charmers spin around you masks your objectivity, and you see everything through their eyes.

The charmer is not only witty but can be a great talker and conversationalist. They are great at changing topics too. For example, if they are talking to you about one topic and they get a whiff of the conversation not going their way, they will subtly and seamlessly change the topic to something else that is more suited to their needs. You won't even realize it until it's too late to do anything.

Here's an example. They will laugh at your attire and say, 'You look like a penguin in that dress.' When they see your hurt face, they will quickly say, 'Oh! I didn't realize you were becoming so sensitive these days.' The apology for hurting you is completely forgotten, and the topic has been changed from your 'penguin-looking' dress to your sensitivity which immediately puts you on the defensive, not to mention the fact that you might look at yourself in the mirror and actually find a penguin looking back at you!

Even if you had chosen to confront them with their insulting behavior, they are likely to change the topic to something else that has nothing to do with the insult. The apology didn't come at all, and you have also either forgotten it or simply taken it as a joke. That is the power of charmers. They will say nasty things to you and not just get away with it but also make you believe that they were right.

You see all the actions of the charmer as good because they show you what they want you to see. They conveniently and unobtrusively distract you so much that you cannot view them as being wrong and manipulative. You readily and wholeheartedly accept taking their side with regard to all your decisions and perspectives without realizing that you are being enslaved.

Whatever the type of manipulation used, the ultimate purpose of gaslighters is to control their victims so that they lose their sense of reality and life.

CHAPTER 5

Victim vs. Manipulator

An interesting fact is the manipulative tactics affect not only the victim but the manipulator too. Yes, the victim undergoes indescribable pain and agony and might even go crazy. However, the manipulator also feels the effects of his or her manipulative attitude. Knowing all sides of the manipulation cycle will help you deal with situations in a better way.

For example, if you realize that your husband is using manipulation to cover his sense of inferiority complex, it might be possible to help him overcome his problems, which, in turn, will help you become free of his nasty ways. So, read on and equip yourself with more knowledge to handle situations in an improved way.

Effects of Manipulation on the Victims

Manipulation can have short-term and long-term effects on the victim.

Short-term effects - In the initial days of being victims of manipulation, people feel confused, anxious, and uncertain. Here are some more details about the short-term effects of manipulation on the victims:

Confusion and surprise - Victims are confused as to what is happening with them, or in a particular relationship. They cannot understand what went wrong. The confounding thoughts that run through their minds are, 'What happened that made someone who was kind and warm with me turn against me? Why is he or she behaving like a total stranger?'

Self-questioning sets in - If you are the victim, you begin to question yourself a lot, right? Did you imagine what happened or is something wrong with you? Did you hear or see correctly, or were you dreaming? This self-questioning is a result of the manipulator's behavior that is telling you that you are wrong, and he or she is right.

Anxious and vigilant - Victims feel anxious and extra vigilant as to what is happening with them in the hope of preventing unpleasant situations arising in their lives. They are scared of making the slightest mistake, which might rock the boat in any way whatsoever. Also, they scan for behavioral signs in their manipulator's actions and words to try and gauge if an outburst is about to take place. Victims feel they are walking on eggshells at all times because they have to be extra careful of what they say and how they behave as they don't want to trigger nastiness in the manipulator.

Guilt and shame - Victims start feeling guilty and are ashamed that they are responsible for the presence of manipulation in their lives. Moreover, the manipulator starts using blame to enhance control over victims, which only increases the sense of guilt and shame in the minds of victims.

Passivity sets in - Victims notice that any action from their end leads to added emotional and psychological pain. Therefore, they prefer to be quiet which slowly but steadily leads to passivity in all aspects of their lives. Becoming passive and accepting the pain without reaction or response becomes the norm. Additionally, victims tend to make themselves smaller or invisible by avoiding eye contact with people they meet or even avoiding social contact altogether.

Long-term effects - As victims continue in a manipulative relationship, the effects change and harden over time, and some of them undergo such huge personality changes that friends from their earlier social circles (before being subjected to manipulation) can hardly even recognize them. Here are some of the long-term effects of manipulation that can cause utter devastation in the lives of hapless victims:

You feel utterly lonely and desolate - Over time, you can become numb to everything that is happening around you. Even in the most joyful moments, you lose the connection with your own emotions. Slowly, you only end up observing what is happening in your life rather than living it. You feel utterly lonely, hopeless, and desolate.

You always need approval before doing anything - The manipulator has controlled your mind so much that it is not your own anymore. Therefore, you lose the ability to make decisions for yourself. You always look out for an approval from the manipulator (or someone else, if he or she has dumped you and moved on) to decide even on simple things like what to wear, eat, etc.

Another manifestation of this dire need for outside approval is that you end up being a people pleaser. You are always looking for ways to keep people happy, even if you have to suffer a lot into the bargain. You could be a person who wants to look the best and want everyone to appreciate your appearance. In fact, dressing up becomes an obsession to the point that you refuse to go out if you don't have anything nice to wear. It is a clear sign of being controlled by a manipulator who kept telling you about your inadequacies. Consequently, you are always working to appear perfect in front of other people.

You could have depressive and anxiety disorders - Your nervous system has been under the constant strain of stress and anxiety. In the long run, this is most likely to have a drastic effect on your mind. Depression and anxiety disorders are common mental ailments in long-term victims of manipulation.

You become highly judgmental - You learn from and copy your manipulator's behavior and attitude. So, if you have been under the influence of a manipulator who had a judgmental attitude, then you are likely to become one yourself. Always being seen through a colored lens makes you believe that it is the only way to see things in the world.

Moreover, your manipulator's expectations from you were always sky high. In turn, you expect the same from others too, and look deep and long to find faults in the people in your life. Being judgmental becomes a form of control for you.

You become resentful - Resentfulness becomes a buzzword in your life in the long-term. After being treated badly by the manipulator for a long time, you end up focusing only on the bad behavior of everyone in your life. You find it difficult to let go of resentful feelings such as frustrations and anger from continuous exposure to manipulation, and this builds deep inside your system.

And finally, Stockholm syndrome can be triggered when the victim sympathizes with the manipulator and defends his or her way of thinking. The victims give in heartily to the fact that they need to be victims for the good of the manipulator. This is, perhaps, the deepest level of change in thinking and state of mind that a manipulator can cause.

Effects of Manipulation on the Manipulator

The effects of manipulation on victims is a well-known element in the equation, and most of us will agree that such effects are possible. Additionally, multiple scientific studies done by various authorized entities have proven the existence of the harmful effects of manipulation on the victims. Some of them have been discussed in the earlier section of this chapter. Now, it is time to discuss the manipulation from the manipulator perspective.

Why do people use manipulation? - All of us at some points in time, end up unwittingly or wittingly using manipulation to achieve our ends. Parents use it on their children in the name of parenting care, and partners use it on each other in the name of love, bosses use it on employees in the name of challenging them to bigger roles, and so forth. And moreover, it is not as if the manipulators don't feel the pain of using subversive tactics. Most of them also undergo the pain of using manipulation repeatedly to keep what they believe is 'happiness and love' in their lives. So, why do these people continue to use manipulation despite knowing about its harmful effects?

Also, it is important to remember that manipulation by itself is not a bad thing. Only when it gets uncontrollable, and people use manipulation as the primary and the only tool to achieve results, then it is a cause for concern. We are going to look at the manipulation of the second kind; the kind in which it is used to control the lives of other people. So, why do people get manipulative in their lives? Here are some reasons:

Manipulators are driven by a sense of fear, unworthiness, hopelessness, and helplessness - Manipulators hold a very deep fear that they will not get the desired outcomes from life without manipulation. This fear is grounded in their lack of self-worth and self-confidence. They feel so unworthy of themselves that they start to believe that the only way they can ever achieve their desired results is by manipulating and controlling other people to achieve their ends. Here is a small list of fears that manipulators with the lack of self-worth and self-confidence have:

- Fear of not getting what they want on their own merits

- Fear that life and the other people surrounding them will not favor them

- Fear that everything in their life is positioned against them

- Fear that they will not get what they want; but, others will get their desires fulfilled

- Fear of abandonment

- Fear that this is a 'dog-eat-dog' world with regard to emotions, money, and relationships

- Fear that resources are highly limited and nothing can be achieved without manipulation and control

Manipulators feel that they are not worthy of having good things happening to them. They feel they are unworthy of having joy and happiness. Consequently, they try to get these elements through manipulation and control. Therefore, the fears mentioned above are all based on one belief that they are not worthy.

Manipulators lack consciousness - Manipulators do not recognize or accept the fact that each of us is responsible for our own lives. Such people do not recognize the connection between their inner selves and external circumstances. They cannot correlate between the two. They don't realize that what is within us is what is represented or manifested in the outside world.

Manipulators disbelieve in the existence of this connection so deeply that they refuse to learn from their repeated mistakes and painful episodes from enduring manipulative behaviors that tell them the truth of connecting the internal and external worlds. It looks as if these people don't want to learn and evolve. They refuse to accept the truth that our actions and external manifestations are outcomes of our internal thoughts and beliefs.

This lack of consciousness makes manipulators perceive the world as 'unsafe.' Consequently, they think that using manipulation in this 'unsafe' world is the only way to get what they want even if it means pain, agony, and suffering that comes along with manipulative tactics. So, when they realize that one manipulation has achieved its end, then they automatically move onto the next manipulation. They keep moving from one manipulation to another because deep down they know that this kind of living will never give them an authentic life. They do it to hide their sense of unworthiness and the fear derived from this feeling.

The ultimate purpose of manipulation is to derive a sense of self-worth and to overcome this lack of consciousness and connection to the world.

Manipulators are low on self-esteem - There are two ways people handle low self-esteem. One is for them to become victims of unscrupulous manipulators, and another one is to become the manipulator themselves.

People with low levels of self-esteem are always looking for ways to build their facade of control. As they lack the necessary skills and the right kind of attitude to build the necessary skills to develop self-esteem, they turn to manipulation to achieve this end. Manipulating people weaker than themselves is, perhaps, the first and simplest way to build self-esteem, even if it is only as a facade to hide their own weaknesses and problems that go deeper than the surface. Such people use manipulation for self-enhancement and self-protection.

One of the most common forms of manipulation used by people with low self-esteem is to charm women into liking them. Once the women fall into the 'charm' trap, then the manipulators' real personality comes forward, and the process of controlling the hapless woman is complete.

What Goes On In the Minds of Manipulators?

Before that, do you know that manipulators can be helped out of their manipulative behaviors? Yes, they can be, and that is one of the primary reasons why we must learn to understand what goes on in their minds.

It is common to find a lot of information about how to identify manipulators, label them, and either ignore or judge them for what they are. While this is a good thing to keep innocent people from getting hurt, it is equally important for us to try and dig deeper into the minds of the manipulators and try to help them instead of outrightly painting them as the demons they are made out to be.

And yet, it is vital to remember that there is no need to condone or validate the actions of manipulators. Instead, it is only by learning to try to understand them better than they can be helped in facing up to and overcoming the challenges that lie deep in their psyche. So, what goes on in the minds of manipulators?

Manipulators and communication skills - First, most of the manipulators have a huge problem with their communication skills. We all learn how to communicate from the interactions we have with the people around us. We watch, observe, and ape the behavior and attitude of the influencers in our lives. So, if you choose a dysfunctional person to learn your communication skills, you are likely to pick up their dysfunctional habits without realizing your mistake.

In fact, most manipulators are puzzled by the fact that most people find their behavior and attitude strange. They are of the belief that they are doing things correctly, and that you are wrong. One of the main reasons why manipulators come off as authentic is because they deeply believe in their own reality. They just don't understand their way of behaving and communicating is different and that they have to change to adapt to the accepted ways of society.

Many manipulators have learned to ask for things in the wrong way. For example, they may have learned that saying yes is easier than saying no and prefer to do so, and then find ways to defend their stance through manipulation. Conversely, they find it difficult to interpret the responses of other people too. So, a 'yes' is misinterpreted as maybe or a 'no' as a 'yes.' This misunderstanding comes from their own learning from the wrong kinds of people.

They could have learned to say no to something when they actually want it, a strange behavior that evolved from being brought up by overly strict, or even abusive, parents. So, if you suspect that you are in a relationship with a manipulative person, then it might make sense for you first to accept that his or her 'yes' could just be a 'maybe.' This kind of forewarning regarding the uncertainty in the responses of manipulators helps you handle the relationship in a more productive and less harmful manner than before.

A manipulator could be telling you to leave him alone when he actually wants your company. When you do as he says, then he will get angry at you because you were not there for him. You see the conflicts going on in his mind. So, every level of manipulation entails a need, and if you can gauge that underlying need, you can choose to either fulfill it or find ways to deflect the situation effectively, causing little or no pain both for you and the manipulator.

Some psychological experts believe that the biggest problem with manipulators is that they have not evolved into adulthood and the accompanying behavioral changes. A manipulator is a small child who has refused to grow up. Sometimes, this refusal is unintentional because they believe they are doing the right thing because this is what was taught to them.

Therefore, most of us make the mistake of thinking that all acts of manipulators, including scheming, plotting, etc. are actually natural behavior from their perspective.

Goals of Manipulation

Regardless of the type of manipulation used, all manipulators want the same things from life as another average, normal human beings. Manipulators desire materialistic well-being, sex, strong relationships, and above all, want love and understanding from the people in their lives. The only difference between manipulators and normal people is that the former believe that manipulation is the only way they can get these desires. They think 'normal people' are actually abnormal.

A shift in perspective is all that is needed to bring manipulators to their senses, though it is easier said than done, especially if you are the victims bearing the brunt of their abominable behavior. Sadly, manipulators don't see the fact that manipulation only gets them hatred, ignorance, or worse still, pity.

Finally, imagine yourself in the position of the manipulator. Imagine a world in which you are trying to say 'yes' in your language, and the entire universe is reading it as 'no.' Imagine being misunderstood at every stage of your life, and it has so often now that you feel detached from the world around you.

On some rare occasions, you find someone who learns to love and understand you. Wouldn't you do everything you could to keep that person in your life? Does it not seem natural that this manipulator does not want to let go of the one breath of fresh air that he has been able to access in a world filled with people unwilling to listen or understand him? Well, that is what most manipulators go through, and maybe, sometimes, it is possible to help such people help themselves.

At this stage, it is important to repeat the fact this 'understanding' perspective towards manipulators does not condone or validate manipulative. It is only an attempt to try and understand the working of their minds so that we can help them overcome their problems, which is a good thing for the manipulators as well as the victims.

It is a pointer to a possible fact that the person whose manipulative control you are under could be hiding a highly vulnerable, hurt individual deep down, and you could help in bringing out that person who could have the power to love and show affection without malice. Manipulators are invariably cowards who try to hide their cowardice in an outward pretense of bravado. If you can teach such people that being scared is not a sign of weakness, then they are more willing to expose their hurt than before giving them the opportunity to get rid of old hurts and pains.

Failures Commonly Encountered by Manipulators

Although manipulators try to control other people through nasty and unpleasant means, they rarely get the satisfaction of being happy in their lives. Here are some common failures that nearly all manipulators encounter in their lives:

- They face numerous relationship and communication issues considering that they never learn to be honest and open with people.

- They get alienated from all the people whom they have cheated, harmed, or caused pain to in any way. Also, these stories go around in their social circle, and even those who were victimized by the manipulator keep away from him or her, thanks to the warnings given by earlier victims.

- Their professional and personal reputation takes a big hit, and they become known as unreliable, untrustworthy, and inauthentic.

- As they lose credibility, they end up losing a lot of good opportunities in their professional and personal lives.

- Manipulators also suffer from low self-esteem because deep down, they know they are 'frauds.' They can hardly be taken in by their own fakeness.

- They never have truly wholesome relationships considering their high levels of self-absorption and self-interest.

- The manipulator experiences physical, emotional, mental, and spiritual distress driven by shame and a guilty conscience.

- And finally, most manipulators struggle to live with themselves as they are continually going through internal moral and ethical conflicts.

Manipulators Can Change

The heartening thing about all human behaviors is that they can be changed. In the same vein, manipulators, especially the unintentional ones, can be taught to change for the positive. All they need is a facilitator, and someone who can help them find help better in this regard but their own victims (invariably loved ones who still care for them) who are likely to know the manipulators' personalities inside out, and they can reach out to professionals who can make a big difference.

Facilitators can help manipulators unlearn bad behavior and teach new behaviors that are acceptable to society. When you, a person who cares for and wants to help the manipulator, reaches deep down and touches his or her core being, then you are doing the person a big favor. Do it if you can. Before that, you must learn to understand the child within the manipulator, and his inability to break out from the shackles of thoughts and ideas carried forward from his childhood.

It is very important to remember that a manipulator can change for the positive only if he or she wants to. You cannot change them if they don't want to. That is a vital warning sign to look out for if you intend to help someone like this in your life. Moreover, remember that helping manipulators is not your obligation.

CHAPTER 6

Standing Up For Yourself

While there is no doubt that the manipulators have their own set of problems to deal with, you as a victim have every right to stand up and fight for yourself in the face of intense and uncontrollable manipulation. Yes, you must try and help the manipulator too.

But, not before you have helped yourself to overcome the dark effects of sustained exposure to dangerous and harmful gaslighting and manipulative behaviors. Standing up for yourself is the first thing you do, and when you are free, then you can go back and help the manipulator solve his or her underlying problems. So, let's jump right in.

Before giving you certain tips for countering manipulative techniques specifically in certain situations like in romantic relationships, at the workplace, in the family, etc. let us look at some learning tips that help you build your ability to recognize and manage manipulation in your life. These tips, when mastered, will help you handle manipulation and stand up strongly for yourself.

Common Tips to Help Counter Manipulation

Build Self-Awareness

One of the most significant reasons for many of us to become a victim of manipulation is that we cannot identify with ourselves. We have little or no idea about what is going on in our lives. We don't know what we want and simply drift along without a purpose.

Then, someone walks into our life, and inexplicably we take on their purpose as ours. If the person genuinely cares for us, then he or she will help us understand ourselves better. However, if the person is looking for a victim to manipulate and control, then we get stuck in the mire. Here are some reasons as to why building self-awareness is a critical tool to avoid being gaslighted:

Self-awareness develops your emotional intelligence - The more aware you are of yourself, your emotions, and how you react to them, the easier it is for you to preempt negative situations and work out ways to either avoid them or fight them. With a well-developed emotional setup, it becomes easy to identify manipulators and signs of manipulative tactics. In fact, with repeated practice, the power of your gut instincts improve considerably helping you recognize negative vibes that you might be getting from pretending charmers.

Self-awareness builds consciousness - You can act consciously and take intentional and informed decisions regarding all aspects of your life. You will be able to look at everything happening in your life objectively and rationally empowering you to see things lying underneath the facades that people are putting up to fool you.

Interestingly, despite knowing the importance of self-awareness, most of us find it difficult to become self-aware. The reason for that is that we are not taught to be present 'in the moment' and observe everything around us and within us, objectively and without judgment. We are all trained to react and respond to situations quickly (as it is considered efficient to act quickly), and therefore, we end up doing things impulsively. We don't give ourselves time to observe and imbibe the events and feelings in our lives and end up living like an automaton.

In fact, manipulators are more self-aware than the average person on the street because he or she needs it to survive and thrive in the world through control and manipulation. Therefore, building self-awareness helps you counter manipulators in a better way than otherwise.

Tips to build self-awareness - So, how does one increase self-awareness? Here are some suggestions that you can use. Practice if you want to get the full benefits of self-awareness.

Create some space and time for yourself - Regardless of how busy you are, you must make it mandatory to find some space and time when you can be with no one but yourself. Keep away from devices and their interrupting notifications. Just start with five minutes each day, and do nothing but sit quietly and observe your thoughts. Don't react or respond to them. Simply watch your thoughts and follow them one at a time. You will notice that each thought increases intensity, reaches a peak, and slowly fades away to give way to the next thought, which goes through the same routine.

Every thought brings feelings too. Connect with the emotions of each thought. If your mind is on last year's family holiday, you could feel happy remembering it. Again, don't react. Simply watch your emotions, which also follow the path of the thought. They increase in intensity in proportion to the thought and ebb away as the thought fades.

Do this exercise on a daily basis. Initially, it is going to be frustrating because our thoughts are quite random. However, if you focus and practice every day, you will find it increasingly easy to hold a thought and stay with it until it fades away into oblivion.

Practice mindfulness - Mindfulness is the art of being 'at the moment' fully and completely engaged with your current activity. Mindfulness calls for complete immersion in the task you are doing. Do you think you are mindful? Here is an example of telling you that mindfulness has to be practiced and does not come naturally until you make it a habit in your life.

Suppose you are peeling potatoes. What happens? Your hands are busy peeling potatoes. Your mind is somewhere else lost in some random thoughts, or even, on one thing that is central to your life at that moment in time. Your mind is totally disconnected from your physical self, which is caught up in peeling potatoes. This is the opposite of mindfulness.

Here is what mindfulness will be like in the same situation. Your hands are peeling potatoes, and your mind is also following the movement of your hands in the peeling action. You are aware of how you are standing or sitting while you are peeling the potatoes. You can feel the stress of standing in the same position for a long time, and yet, you continue to peel potatoes.

You know that when you pick up a potato, you are breathing in, and when you are putting down the peeled potato, you are breathing out. It could be the reverse for you. The thing is that you are aware of how you are breathing even as you peel potatoes. You know exactly how many potatoes you have peeled until now, and how many more are left over. You are not working in an automatic mode but are keenly conscious of every element of the action associated with peeling potatoes.

So, being mindfulness is putting your body, heart, and mind into the current task. When you do this, you feel focused and do not lose out to distractions around you. You not only increase your productivity, but you find yourself feeling refreshed and energized at the end of the task.

Moreover, you are building your self-awareness through mindfulness. You are not caught up with idle thoughts that create needless panic in your head. You are immersed and completely engaged in peeling potatoes, and you enjoy every moment of your life.

So, practice mindfulness in every action of your life, and build self-awareness even as you find the power to discern between useful and useless thoughts and emotions that come to disrupt your life. Knowledge is power, and with this power, you can keep manipulators at bay.

Keep a journal - Writing down your thoughts is one of the best ways to know what you are thinking and feeling. In a manipulative state, the more you write down your ideas and beliefs, the easier it gets to differentiate between imagination and reality. This power to differentiate gives you the strength to handle manipulation and use measures to counter it.

Build Self-Confidence

What is self-confidence? It is the ability to know your strengths and weaknesses with regard to the environment you are in so that you can leverage the advantages available to you at that point in time. Self-confidence is founded on self-belief, where you believe in your strength to do the things that are best for you. So, the more self-confident you are, the less likely you will be to fall prey to a manipulator's whims. Here are some recommendations you can use to build self-confidence:

Visualize yourself as being confident - Your mind is a powerful tool that can help you achieve your dreams. When you visualize yourself as being confident and strong, then your subconscious mind drives your body to achieve what you have dreamed. Low confidence is rooted in our belief that we are worthless and useless. Change this idea in your mind and gather the courage to convert it into reality.

Use confidence-building affirmations - Affirmations are excellent to 'install' thoughts into your heart and mind. When you say you are no good, then you begin to believe in your words. When you repeatedly say that you are good enough for yourself, then you begin to believe in these words. Therefore, use positive words about your self-image and repeat them as often as you can. Here are a few examples:

- I am confident and strong.

- I am capable.

- I am worthy of love and happiness.

Every day, do one thing that scares you - Fear plays a vital part in denting our confidence. A great way to overcome fear is to face it regularly so that you learn to deal with it. So, take one thing you are scared of doing, and do it at least once every day. For example, if you lack the courage to speak to strangers, make it a point to speak to one stranger a day. You don't have to start a conversation. A simple hello or even pretending to ask for directions is fine. The trick is to face the fear that comes with the act of talking to strangers. The more you do it, the more you will realize that your fear is unfounded, and it will become easy to overcome it.

Face your inner critic - We all have a voice in our head that keeps telling us that we should not get out of our comfort zone because we are not good enough. Face this critic in your head and argue your point fearlessly. Talk to it about the many strengths you have, and if need be, simply silence it.

Learn to accept rejections - Being rejected, failing, etc. are all part of human life. We cannot escape from it. And yet, we are so scared of rejections and failures that we don't want to try anything new. This kind of 'safe' attitude becomes an easy target for manipulators. They know that people who are scared of failures will do anything to prevent trying to get out of their comfort zones. Manipulators will use this against hapless people.

So, learn to face failures by accepting the fact that they come in your life to make you stronger than before. Manipulators will rarely seek out confident and strong people.

Enhance Your Friends' Circle

Human beings are social animals, and we need people to talk to and communicate with to survive. In times of need, it is people we reach out to, right? The larger your circle of friends, the more people you can seek help from. When you are under the mercy of a manipulator, you need multiple perspectives so that you can opt for the optimal solution. And for this, you need a lot of people who can give you numerous perspectives.

Additionally, a large circle of friends is a great deterrent to manipulators because they prefer to work on lonely people. Here are more advantages to having a healthy number of friends in your life:

- It gives you new and innovative perspectives on life and experiences.

- It helps you see both positives and negatives in any given solution, which, in turn, facilitates making informed choices.

- It helps you get out of your comfort zone, and consequently, build your self-confidence.

- It improves your knowledge levels and skills as people from varied backgrounds are likely to share their experiences and knowledge with you.

Take Time-Outs Regularly

If you don't take regular breaks from your hectic pace of life, you are likely to be filled with resentment which, in turn, will lead you to become depressed, anxious, and unhappy; a perfect target for manipulators. You must always strive to be happy and to do that; you must find ways to unwind regularly.

Do the things you love during these breaks. Stay away from electronic devices that keep disturbing you. Connect with yourself when you take your breaks. You will return refreshed and rejuvenated ready to take on the challenges of the world. Breaks give you the opportunity to reflect on your life and find gaps that need filling up.

Reach Out for Help

It is almost impossible to live alone in this world. Being social animals, we constantly need to connect with other people, which not only keep you happy and energized but also help to get a different perspective of your life. Additionally, there are people out there who are capable of helping you out in times of need. All that is needed is to ask for help. Don't hesitate to do so.

Seeking help when in trouble is the wisest thing you can do because being a victim of manipulation can take its toll on your ability to think straight, and you need a professional or a trusted person to help you see things in the right perspective.

Manipulation Countering Techniques in Relationships

Other than the above common elements that help in building a strong character, here are some tips that will help you manage manipulation in different aspects of your life. This section deals with manipulation counter techniques in relationships, at the workplace, and in the family. So, let's start with relationships.

Here are a few pointers to recall and summarize the tell-tale signs of being the victim in a manipulative relationship:

Your partner shifts between Dr. Jekyll and Mr. (or Ms.) Hyde - Manipulative partners typically have two faces; one of the soft-hearted, kind, and caring Dr. Jekyll, and another of the monstrous and controlling Mr. (or Ms. Hyde). If your partner is shifting between these two personalities, then he or she could be the manipulative partner.

Your partner presents passive-aggressive behaviors - They use underhanded means to hurt you. They are jealous of every other relationship you have in life, including those with your siblings and parents. They show you the silent treatment more often than you can handle. Such is a manipulative partner.

Your relationship could be stressing you out - Do you feel stressed whenever you spend time with your partner? If yes, then beware of manipulation and the effects it is having on your life. So, if any of the above signs exist in your life, then what can you do to help yourself? Here are a few suggestions:

Look at your relationship rationally - Be rational and get a good look at where and how your relationship is panning out. Take a pen and paper and write down notes. Recall the times when you felt happy with your partner, and delve deep into your mind, and see if you can pinpoint the time when the relationship began to sour. Leave out the emotions from your observation points. Read what you have written, and if you don't like it, then there is a problem.

Set clear boundaries and reiterate them as often as you can - Discuss with your partner and let him or her know where the line separating acceptable and unacceptable elements are drawn. Don't leave out opportunities to remind yourself and your partner about these boundaries.

Don't hold yourself responsible for your partner's behavior - Your partner cannot find an excuse and blame you for his or her bad behavior. Be firm and make sure your partner takes responsibility for his or her behavior and actions.

Do not accept any excuses for bad behavior - Bad behavior has to be kept in check, and no excuse regardless of how authentic it might seem should be used to substantiate the behavior. Right from the beginning, make sure you don't miss opportunities to correct irrational behavior of your partner without fear.

Take responsibility for your behavior too - Stand your ground and be prepared to accept the outcome of your own behavior. Suppose you ticked off your partner for something nasty he or she did, and you are likely to lose the relationship, then so be it. Prepare yourself to move on. The fear of losing out on things is one of the primary causes of becoming a victim to manipulation.

Reach out for help - Your partner's friends, family or your own friends and family are all standing by to help you. Learn to trust other people too, and reach out for help when you know that things are turning unpleasant. Asking for help is not a sign of weakness. It is a sign of strength and courage. An outside perspective is almost always unbiased, and therefore, seeking help from the people around you is also a way of helping you look at things objectively and rationally.

Let your partner know that the relationship is causing you pain and you are looking for a change - If things are not going well for you, then don't waste time sending clear messages to your partner that you are undergoing pain and are keen on seeing positive changes, failing which you are ready to face the consequences of a fallout.

And finally, if all else fails, do not hesitate to get out of the relationship. Nothing is more important than your life. In fact, if kids are involved in a relationship, you might have to take a stern decision sooner and faster than in the absence of kids.

No one deserves a stressful relationship, and yes, while the consequences of a failed relationship can be heartbreakingly painful, it is still better than to remain in the toxicity and live in lifelong agony. So, stand up for yourself, belief in the fact that you deserve better, and get a hold on your life.

Manipulation Countering Techniques at the Workplace

There are many ways you can counter manipulation techniques in your office; some of them are intense and some simplistic ones to manage your day-to-day problems arising out of manipulation at the workplace. Manipulation at the workplace usually takes place in disguised ways so that you think that they are working in your interests. In reality, these manipulators will have only their interests in mind, and everyone else can jump into a well, for all they care.

For example, they will act concerned, and tell you that everyone in the office thinks that you are useless and unworthy. They will say they want to help you change the way the office people look at and treat you. They will say they will teach you how to behave, improve your attitude, and much more. They will veil their threat to control you by saying that if you don't follow their ideas, your professional life will be ruined. This is what manipulators in the workplace want you to believe.

In truth, they don't care what happens to you. They want to control you so that they can validate their lives and use you to achieve their ends while you prevent yourself from growing and expanding your professional horizons. It is better to be wary of such individuals and not allow them to enter into your life because once they get control of you, then they will make false promises, slip away or hit back at you if you try to hold them accountable, and simply make your life miserable.

Ignore manipulators - Ignoring manipulators is one of the best ways to put them off in the first place. Moreover, studies have shown that ignoring offensive people and manipulators actually enhance your productivity and intelligence. The more you give in to the manipulator's gaslighting tactics, the more you will waste away your mind space and productivity.

If you choose to correct manipulators, you will only fall deeper into the trap, and getting out will get increasingly difficult. Therefore, ignoring manipulators at the workplace is a great way to counter their efforts to control you. Silence is truly golden in such circumstances.

However, it is not always possible to ignore and keep yourself safe from manipulative marauders. You must use more intense tactics to counter them. Here are a few of them to help you lead a more productive and manipulation-free life at your workplace.

Get offensive if you need to - Manipulators are continually finding ways to destabilize you. Sometimes, you can ignore them. But, sometimes, you cannot. In such situations, it is best to get on the offensive and destabilize them. Find what gives them the support needed to manipulate you. It could be a senior manager, a friend, or even a wily subordinate. Take your offensive to them and show them your professional tenacity. In the absence of any support, manipulators can back off.

Trust your judgment - Remember that no one knows your life purposes better than you. Don't depend on other people to define who you are or what you do. Taking feedback for self-improvement is good. However, don't take feedback so seriously that you alter your personality because you think you are not good enough to achieve your dreams.

Trust and define yourself based on your own experiences and belief system. When you stand strong on your own foundations, then the chances of falling for manipulators' traps are reduced drastically.

Don't try to fit into other people's lives - Many times, in our efforts to fit into the surrounding environment, we chose not to try new things. Avoid falling into this trap. Keep reinventing yourself, and find ways to indulge in new experiences and learning. The trick here is that most manipulators at the workplace use your sense of consistency to push their own agenda.

For example, a manipulative boss will demand punctuality from you while he or she chooses to come in late to work. And you will be manipulated into doing your boss's work instead of finishing up your own tasks so that you can leave early. To avoid this kind of a situation, it is best for you to keep reinventing yourself so that you can find a lot of opportunities outside the influence of this manipulative boss.

Moreover, your consistency and the lack of innovative attitude will help manipulative people box you into nothingness, leaving you little or no room for improvement. Push your learning and working boundaries and do your work in a way that makes you stand out, and people other than the manipulator will notice you and offer you new positions and responsibilities.

Don't compromise on your principles - Using guilt is a powerful tool that manipulators use to control you. Manipulators will continually remind you of your past mistakes and failures in an effort to dent your confidence and happiness. Manipulators are of the opinion that people should not be happy and satisfied, and this belief is rooted in their own unhappiness and lack of achievements.

When manipulators keep reminding you of your mistakes and failures, they are effectively working at enhancing your self-doubt. You slowly begin to doubt your abilities and sense of self-worth. One of the primary powers of manipulators is based on your level of uncertainty. The more uncertain you are, the more control they have over you and your activities. Therefore, stop doubting yourself and feeling guilty about past mistakes. Learn valuable lessons from your mistakes and failures and move on.

Don't always wait for permission - When there is no intention to make mistakes or errors from your end, you don't have to really ask for permission to do some things. Remember that it is easier to say sorry than to wait in line and ask for permission to initiate things.

Be confident and do what you want to do, and don't end up wasting your time waiting for permission for people. Unlearn what we as humans have been taught; that we have to wait in line to talk. No, many times, the line will not move. So, you make a move and say and do what you want to do, provided you know that you have no 'malicious' intent in your heart and mind.

In fact, manipulators use this 'asking for permission' against us. They tell us that if we keep quiet in meetings, then we will get a promotion by the end of the year. This makes us feel scared to raise our voices to explain our new and innovative ideas or even raise our hands to give an opinion. Manipulators talk of some vague rules regarding politeness and courtesy to prevent us from voicing our fears and concerns.

So, don't wait for permission. By doing so, you are only falling into the trap of control that manipulators are laying for you.

Take control of your professional life - Remember your life is your own, and no one can make it better or worse but you. This holds good for your career too. It is entirely up to you to take control of your professional life and take strides in your career that will help you achieve your goals and life purposes. The choice to take control is in your hands. Find the answer to the following question: Do I want to lead my life my way or the way of someone else?

Also, take responsibility for your career. Don't blame it on others around you. If your career is not taking off and you are constantly in a state of stagnation, then you are as responsible for the state as your manipulator, perhaps, more so, considering that you are the driver of your life. It is not only naive but also an escapist attitude if you just float around in your life, finding multiple people to blame for your mistakes and failures. Stop complaining, take responsibility, and get ahead.

Find your purpose in life - One of the main reasons why manipulators are able to manipulate others is because most of us have no idea what our life purpose is. What do you want to achieve in your career? What are your professional goals? In the absence of these gaps in self-awareness, manipulators are able to sow the seeds of their own goals and purposes and use you to achieve their desired results. When you feel out of control, take a day off, sit quietly in your room, and reflect on the purpose of your career. What do you want to do in your profession, and why?

Once these questions are answered, then the how to achieve the purpose falls into place automatically. Manipulators are left with no room in your heart and mind space to put in their ideas and thoughts.

Take time to reflect on your work and on yourself regularly. If you are continuously busy and have no time for your heart and mind, then too, manipulators will find their gaps and get into your life. The lack of time spent with yourself leads you to distraction because you tend to lose focus on things. Moving from one task to another, and then to a third leaves you with no time and energy to focus on yourself. The more distracted you are in life, the easier it is to fall into the trap of manipulation.

And finally, remember that no one can manipulate you without your permission. Take accountability for your life events and do the things you need to do to turn around your profession.

Manipulation Countering Techniques in the Family

When it comes to dealing with manipulative partners, bosses, and coworkers, at least you know that they are not family, and can bring in a little bit of objectivity in your interactions with them. Dealing with manipulators within a family is far, far more stressful than this. Family members are the ones we trust the most, right? And if such people manipulate you for their ends, then it is almost as if you lose trust in the world. Well, sadly, gaslighting happens in family environments too, and it is imperative that you stand up and fight for yourself before it is too late.

Identify other victims of the manipulative family member - In a family setup, manipulators are likely to have more than one victim. For example, if one of the parents is the manipulator, then the victims would be all the children, and maybe even the spouse. Get the victims together and discuss concerns in a group.

Focus on your state of mind - What is going on in your head? Are you doing things you want to do or are you blindly following the manipulator's lead? Get objective with your life and think for yourself. Learn to be independent and build the necessary skills for it.

Set clear boundaries - Once you are clear that you are being manipulated, start acting immediately. First, set clear boundaries with your manipulator. These boundaries are better managed if they are physical in nature. For example, if you have a separate room at home, then get yourself a new set of locks for your door, and keep it locked always. Don't give the key to anyone else, including the people you trust because they could also be victims of the same manipulator who could use this trusted person to get your room keys.

Identify intangible boundaries and areas where the manipulator is influencing your thoughts. Ensure you stay clear away from these areas so that you minimize contact with him or her. Also, engage with the manipulator only in a safe and open environment. Avoid staying alone with him or her. If you have no choice but to be alone, then make sure you put as much distance as you can between you and him or her.

Manipulation Countering Techniques When Dealing with Adult Children

Victimized parents can use the following suggestions and recommendations when dealing with manipulative adult children. The trick in this situation is that you are dealing with your child, and subjectivity comes into play far more than you can imagine as compared to other situations. So, beware of this element and be calm during your interactions with your child. However, don't be scared of displaying a firm attitude as you set forth the following guiding principles on which you expect your child to behave.

Set clear time limits - Let your child know how long you intend to help him or her. Let your child know that he or she has to find his own ways of dealing with life problems. Ask gently probing questions like what are your plans? By when do you hope to get out of this issue?

If your child comes back with some evasive answer, then offer solutions from your end, and take the discussion forward. End such conversations with confidence-building statements like, 'I believe in your capabilities and resourcefulness to solve your own problems. You will feel better if you spend some time and effort on the issue and write down your thoughts and solutions that come to your mind. I am sure you will come up with something good.'

Don't hesitate to tick off your child if you see excessive use of guilt-ridden manipulation - It is very easy to feel guilty when your child reminds you of past mistakes and failures and uses them against you today. While there may be some truth in what the child says, he or she has no right to hold you to ransom now. In fact, there could be numerous other ways in which you have already paid for and left behind those errors. So, if your child is repeatedly trying to get you on a guilt-trip, then stand your ground and don't hesitate to tick them off. Don't allow yourself to be manipulated by people who showed ideally show gratitude for many things you have done for them.

Encourage (you might have to insist on some cases) your working child to contribute to his or her room and boarding expenses - And there is nothing wrong with this attitude. The child is an adult who has to anyway take care of himself or herself. If the child is living with you for whatever reason, then he or she must not back away from contributing to the family expenses. Although this might come across as cruel, it works well to set clear boundaries between you and your adult children. The boundaries offer excellent protection from manipulative tactics of your adult child.

And if your adult child is yet to find gainful employment, make sure he or she helps out in the household chores like cleaning, cooking, gardening, etc. Not only are you setting boundaries with this attitude but also helping your child learn something useful. Don't think this approach represents a cruel attitude.

Control the money you dole out to your adult children - Don't give out money as and when they ask for it. Ask plenty of questions, put up blockages, give other options like taking a loan or waiting until they begin to earn before having desires to go on spending sprees, etc. Make sure you dole out money to adult children in proportion to their efforts in finding gainful employment.

Beware of getting caught off-guard - Manipulative adult children commonly try and catch their parents when they are off-guard to get their desires fulfilled. For example, you could suddenly get a message from your son with the money, 'I need money.' It is natural to feel scared that something bad has happened and you immediately and impulsively send the required amount. Now, remember to be wary of such off-guard requests.

Be prepared to answer without committing yourself to anything. For example, you could say, 'I don't know. I'll have to ask your mother (or father).' Alternately, you could say, 'I need more time. Let me see what I can do. I will get back to you by tomorrow afternoon' Take some time from your child, which will allow you to discuss some more and think and reconsider your decision if needed. Remember that manipulative people love to prey on people who act impulsively. Therefore, hold back your impulsive nature, or at least be wary of it.

Don't hesitate to change your mind - Yes, you did agree to something your child said. However, you are not obligated to follow through. You have every right to change your mind and not help out as you promised. Remember, the child is an adult, and his or her responsibilities are not yours. You have done what you could. Don't ruin your life (and that of your spouse or partner) by handing it over to the manipulations of irresponsible adult children. You are not in any popularity contest, and there is nothing left to prove to your child or to the world, at least in this regard.

Countering manipulative measure is not just difficult but also high energy and time-sapping. You have to be on your guard continually to prevent yourself from falling prey to expert manipulators because they always find a way to achieve their ends. So, if after a certain point in time, you feel tired, do not hesitate to ask for help from others, including professionals in the counseling field.

Yet, during your attempts to salvage a relationship, try and be the bigger person in the picture even if you are the child. Remember that the manipulator has a mind of his or her own, and needs some help to unlearn the wrong things. And yet, always remember that your safety comes first. It is all about balance.

Again, it is time to reiterate that the minute you think there could be in danger if you continued to live with the concerned person, don't hesitate to even report to the concerned regulatory authorities. Empower yourself using all of the above suggestions so that you are ready to face the challenges of being in a manipulative relationship. Stand strong and fight back with all your might. Sometimes, remember you might need to help the manipulator to help yourself. However, when you know that nothing is working, and things continue to be in the same horrible state or things just get worse, then it is time to get out and run for your life.

CHAPTER 7

Path to Recovery

So, now you have managed to escape from the clutches of a manipulator, it is time to recover and heal yourself and find a better life for yourself. It is imperative that you don't turn bitter after that nasty episode of manipulation. Remember, bitterness makes your life more difficult than it should be. Therefore, take an oath to heal yourself and recover from the trauma and become the positive person you once were.

How to Spot Manipulative Behavior and Stay Safe in the Future

Most manipulators have the following four characteristics that set them apart from normal, average human beings. Learn to identify and recognize them so that you can stay away as far away from such people as you can.

- Manipulators are highly skilled at detecting your weaknesses.

- When they find your weakness, they use it against you.

- They will then use one or many of the multiple methods described in the book to convince you to sacrifice a part of yourself so that they can use you to serve their ends.

- Regardless of the setting (whether at home, in a relationship, or at the workplace), once the manipulator has trapped you, then he or she will not stop manipulating you unless you choose to put a stop on it.

Here are some uncompromising principles you must adopt to prevent yourself from falling prey to manipulative tactics again.

Know and stand up for your fundamental human rights - Make sure the following human rights are uncompromised in any of the new relationships that you plan to get into:

- You have the right to expect respectful treatment from everyone.

- You have the right to express your opinions, feelings, and desires, and these can be different from those of others.

- You have the right to set your own priorities and are not obliged to follow those of anyone else.

- You can say 'no' without feeling guilty.

- You have the right to get what you paid for.

- You have the right to do everything in your power to protect yourself against emotional, mental, and physical harm.

You must build a new relationship on the basis of these fundamental human rights only. They also represent your boundaries beyond which no one is allowed to enter without your permission.

Maintain a dignified distance - Most manipulators have a way of dealing with different people differently. With some, they are highly polite and courteous, and with a few others, they are nasty and unpleasant. They can take on a groveling attitude with some people too. The shift in personalities is starkly discernible in manipulators. If you do see such a scene, remember to maintain a dignified distance from this person.

Stop blaming yourself for everything - When you are free from the clutches of your manipulator, look back at your own behavior and make necessary changes for positive outcomes. If you have been trained into taking blame and accountability for all the wrong things that happened in your relationship, then unlearn the lesson.

You are not accountable for anyone but yourself. Don't feel guilty and blame yourself for everything. If things go wrong in a new relationship, look at it objectively and find what can be corrected. Don't go about taking responsibility for the other person's behavior and attitudes. Ask yourself the following questions:

- Am I getting treated with respect?

- Are expectations being kept at reasonable levels?

- Is the relationship favoring only one person or are both being benefited?

- Most importantly, are you feeling good in the relationship?

The answers to these questions are critical pointers towards whether the relationship is worth your effort or not. Don't hesitate to step back if you are feeling uncomfortable. Don't allow yourself to fall too deeply in new relationships.

Ask a lot of questions and don't feel bad about it - An important reason you became a victim of manipulation earlier is that your questions were brushed under the carpet or you were made to feel silly for asking them. Don't repeat that mistake. Make sure you ask probing questions, and if you don't get satisfactory answers, maybe you must raise your radar.

Take time to respond to requests and queries - Most manipulators will want responses and reactions almost immediately leaving you very little time to think things through. This situation suits the manipulator because he or she does not want you to think independently.

Remember this lesson, and always take time to respond or react. Go home, reflect on what is being asked, see if there are options better suited to your needs, and then revert to the person. If the individual pushes you needlessly, step back, and don't give in. You have succeeded in avoiding falling into the manipulation trap.

Beware of the following terms and phrases that are deeply connected to gaslighting and manipulation tactics:

Monitoring - This phrase is a warning sign specifically in romantic relationships. In the initial stages of any romantic relationship, it is normal to wonder and know what your partner is doing all the time. However, if your boyfriend or girlfriend is monitoring you and your whereabouts excessively, then you should treat it as a warning sign and pay closer attention to the person's behavior before committing yourself.

Object Constancy - When normal people are angry at someone, they don't forget the love and affection they still feel for the other person. However, gaslighters and narcissists turn off all the positive feelings they had for the victim and the insults and abuses hurled can hurt the very core of your being. This phenomenon, called object constancy, is the reason why manipulators appear to have starkly different personalities at different times.

People with this problem tend to see things that don't really exist and believe things that are not true. In their minds, these things and beliefs exist, and then they go berserk when you try to counter their ideas. They can get highly violent and use multiple controlling methods to manipulate and control you so that their truth remains unchanged. Beware of people who exhibit this kind of behavior.

Attraction to your skills - While some manipulators prey on people weaker than themselves, there is a rare breed of manipulators who are attracted to you because you are highly skilled and stand out from the ordinary crowd. You are likely to encounter such people in the workplace.

Your co-workers or even your bosses want to manipulate and control you because they want to show that you are not as good as them. So, if you feel your skills and strengths are continually being faulted, then you could be dealing with this kind of a manipulator.

Beware of liars - Manipulators are excellent liars and can flip the script to suit their needs. If you have already been a victim once, it will be very easy to identify lies told by manipulators. If and when you encounter people who lie and try to alter what they meant, you know you have to be on your guard.

Trauma bonding - If you were to look back on your period as a victim to a malicious manipulator, you would have wondered how you managed to stay in such a toxic environment and what made you stick to him despite being aware of the danger. The answer lies in trauma bonding.

Manipulators are not always cruel. They choose suitable and convenient events and times when they will shower praise and love on their victim for a while. During this time, the victim feels deeply attached to his or her manipulator. When the situation changes for the worse, and the cruelty begins again, the victim yearns for that love.

Manipulators manage to keep their victims on tender hooks alternating between short periods of bonding and affection and long periods of manipulation and control. The poor, hapless victim gets so accustomed to this push and pulls that he or she forgets to get out, and instead, works towards getting more of the short periods of love and affection. This is called trauma bonding.

Remember that abuse need not be in the physical form - Manipulators need not use physical abuse to manipulate you. In fact, most of them prefer to use emotional abuse to control their victims. So, don't get into a complacent mode if you think that you cannot find fault with the manipulator because he or she has not physically hit you or caused you harm. Emotional abuse is one of the most powerful forms of gaslighting techniques.

Bargaining their way through your life is a common tactic - When you threaten to leave the relationship, does your manipulator bargain with you and beg you to give him or her another chance?

If it happens more than once, then you know you are dealing with a manipulator. Run from the person.

Don't forget to use the lessons you learned in the past to confirm and correct any potential mistakes you could repeat in the future. The traumatic pain of being in a manipulative relationship will, hopefully, be a thing of the past. However, don't forget the critical lessons learned.

How to Trust Yourself Again

An element that feels the impact of manipulation significantly is your intuition. After a bout of manipulative episodes, you are quite likely to lose trust in yourself. You find it exceedingly difficult to trust your instincts and treat everything and everyone around you with suspicion. In fact, the reasons why a manipulator was able to control you and your reality are:

- You were far too trusting and open than was good for you.

- The manipulator was successful in making you lose your trust in your gut instinct.

- He or she made you lose faith in your intuitive powers.

The manipulator was cunning and had got you tight in his or her hold. You are simply grateful for being out of the manipulator's clutches. All other good things, including learning to trust yourself, is put on the backburner. However, you must begin the process of trusting yourself and your intuition if you want to heal fully. Here are some pointers to get you going.

Remember that you never lost your intuition. Our intuitive powers are embedded in our psyche and can never be lost. It could have been muted or stilled for a while, thanks to the wily efforts of manipulators. But, you will never lose them. Therefore, take heart from this truth and work on recovering its power.

Start by going through how you are feeling presently. Are you happy, sad, depressed, or anxious? Then, ask yourself why you are feeling all these emotions. Think of a person and see if you can recognize your feelings for him or her. Do you enjoy thinking of the person, or do you think it is better to move on from thinking about the concerned individual?

Think of a food item and observe your feelings and thoughts about it. Are you salivating or feeling revulsion? If the feelings are vague or unclear, think of something else and repeat the exercise. In this way, you slowly start connecting with your intuition and setting the environment for its recovery.

Learning to trust yourself is going to take time. Your entire being has been assaulted multiple times and repeatedly. So, don't expect the ability to trust yourself come back to you overnight. It is a slow and hard process of self-healing. But, it will happen provided you don't hamper the process needlessly. Each time you find yourself being frustrated, tell yourself to be patient.

Breaking the bonds of trauma has to happen one at a time. Any activity or even a simple thought in your mind is likely to bring back horrific memories of the traumatic period. You must tackle each task with grit and determination until each painful memory is erased, or least soothed, in your mind. Repeat the process until you resemble your old self, the person you were before the manipulator came into your life.

And tell yourself this; if you can overcome this challenge in your life, you will be able to do anything else, and your future life is bound to be happy and joyful. So, until that time, hibernate into yourself and find ways to reconnect with your soul and become whole again. Take steps to cover up gaps that were created by the manipulator. Conserve your energy to be used for productive purposes only.

How to Prevent Yourself from Becoming Bitter and Begin the Healing Process

After a traumatic period of being under the control of ruthless, manipulative tactics, it is natural to feel bitter about everything in your life; the people, experiences, etc. In the initial periods after the break-off from the manipulator, you are likely to feel anger. Despite the negativity surrounding the feeling of anger, it can be a good thing because it can drive you to action so that you can make the best of whatever is left.

Bitterness is worse than anger because it leads you to a sense of utter helplessness. Bitterness comes from the belief that even anger is of no use because there is nothing left to do. Bitterness is something that leads to helpless inaction, which, in turn, could lead to a feeling of utter desolation and loneliness.

When you go through such deep emotion, remember one thing. Yes, you cannot undo what your manipulative partner, coworker, or family friend did to you. You cannot get back the lost time and energy. However, you can do a lot to put these bad experiences behind and move on with your life.

Bitterness and sustained resentment can lead to multiple problems including sleeplessness, loss of libido, and fatigue in the short term, and build-up of negative personality traits, low self-confidence, and a loss of purpose in the long term. While you can blame your manipulator for the problems created during the difficult times of being under his or her control, carrying forward the bitterness into your future life can be no one's fault but yours. Therefore, it is imperative that you make all efforts to let of the bitterness caused by the trauma of being in a manipulative relationship.

Re-evaluate your state of mind rationally - Sympathy from the people around us helps bitterness thrive in our lives. We keep repeating our story of trauma and agony to others, and thanks to their feelings of sympathy towards you, your bitterness continues to grow and expand. You begin to think that feeling bitter is your birthright and find comfort in it.

So, the first step to moving out of this comfort zone that you have found yourself is to do a serious re-evaluation of your status. Yes, you have gone through the trauma that few people would have had to bear. Yet, remember it is in the past, and holding on to the painful memories is only going to make your present and future horrible.

Dig deeper into your psyche and recall moments that you could have done better to prevent the condition. In such a case, aren't you partly responsible for what happened? What happened to make you so bitter? Are you feeling stupid for falling for the scam? Find the true answer within yourself. Take responsibility for the things you can. Use this lesson to wake up from your reverie and learn to let go of the past, including your mistakes and those of the perpetrator.

Stop telling your story of trauma to everyone - Put your story on hold. It is going to be difficult not to share your story with people, especially since you are not fully healed. But you can make a start. Begin by putting your story on hold for just one day. No matter who you meet on the chosen day, don't talk about your story. You will see that at the end of the day, even though some bit of emptiness from not sharing your story could be there, mostly there is an enormous relief, which comes from the fact that your mind did not feel compelled to feel sad today.

Push your boundaries and extend one day to two days to three days, and sooner than later, you will realize that even for you, the story has lost its charm. Consequently, sympathy will cease to flow, and your bitterness about life will slowly but surely begin to ebb.

Stop following your ex-manipulator - Thanks to the modern social media world, keeping track of people has become very easy. You are continually checking on the person's status updates, photos, social posts, etc. It is natural to follow the person who has created trauma in your life and see what he or she is up to. This natural need is based on the fact that you have not found the strength to let go.

The first thing you should do is to unfollow your ex-manipulator from every social media platform. Put the person out of all aspects of your life. Do this until you get back all the control over your life

- completely and unequivocally. When your bitterness has died down, then you can go back and thank him (sarcastically, of course) for helping you learn valuable life lessons!

Face your hidden fears - After a traumatic experience, fearing a repeat of the same and failing to stand up yet again is a big deterrent to the healing process. You feel so scared of trying to get into new relationships that you simply write off your life, which, in turn, only enhances your bitterness to life. Moreover, bitterness feeds that fear of repeated failure.

The best way to handle this is to take your fear head-on, and when you do so, bitterness also gets reduced in your life. Take small baby steps towards building relationships. Start with a simple exercise like going out on a double-date with a trusted friend. Relearn your communication and relationship skills. When you find yourself making progress with these small steps, your fears will recede slowly, and so will your bitterness.

Forgive the manipulator - The power of forgiveness should not be underestimated. Forgive the manipulator; but, only when you are truly ready to forgive. Fake and forced forgiveness only enhances your resentment and anger. Here are some powerful reasons why you must prepare yourself to forgive:

- When you forgive, you realize that you have set a prisoner free, and slowly you will also realize that the prisoner was no one else but you. Holding on to forgiveness not only keeps the pain of anger and hurt alive but also kindles it.

- Stop thinking that you were wronged not because you were not wronged but because it will help you to forgive. Remind yourself that forgiving the manipulator will do nothing for him or her. But, it will heal your pain and hurt.

- Forgiving your perpetrator also includes forgiving yourself for the parts you have taken responsibility for.

- Forgiveness translates to letting go of hatred, which has the power to slowly eat you up and rot your heart and mind inside-out.

So, don't hold on to hurt, pain, and resentment. Forgive your manipulator and set yourself free, and get rid of bitterness from your life. It is important to reiterate here that does not forgive until you are truly ready to do so. Do it at your pace. But do it.

Learn to live 'in the now' - Bitterness refuses to leave your life because you are caught up in the past and living there. Wake yourself up and live in the present moment. Engage with the present experience you are going through. Bring your entire being, including your heart, mind, and body into the 'now.' There is no bitterness in the present moment, and this exercise will help you disconnect with this debilitating emotion.

Go out and try new experiences - Bitterness fades away in the presence of joy and excitement. So, go out and try new experiences. Indulge in a new hobby. Learn to sing, dance, paint, or play a new instrument. Rediscover an old passion and reconnect with it. Attend some kind of creative classes or anything else that you always wanted to, and bring in sunshine into your life.

Take one day at a time - Set little goals for yourself on a daily basis and try to achieve them. Don't work at more than a couple initially until you feel ready to take on a heavier load.

Take those baby steps towards getting rid of bitterness and welcoming back the sunshine in your life. You will see that it does not take very long for those baby steps to become huge strides of happiness and joy.

When to Seek Professional Help and Other Useful Resources

You have been trying hard on your own or with the help of your loved ones to reconnect with your old self and try and find ways to overcome the trauma of being in a manipulative experience. You have tried all there is to try, and yet you find yourself faltering. Now, it is time to seek professional help.

In fact, it might make sense to seek professional help earlier on itself whenever you felt that things are not really going right. There are multiple trusted counseling groups and professionals available who can help you find solutions to your problems. Additionally, do not hesitate to seek help for the manipulator too, especially if he or she is a loved one.

Also, there are multiple online forums and groups that you can join and share your experiences and learn from those of the others in the group. The more you seek help, the better are your chances to get out of the pain and agony of being a victim of manipulation.

The trick is recognizing and accepting that you and/or your manipulator needs help as soon as possible. Considering that your manipulator will not seek help, it might make sense, if you can, to help the other person too. But it is very important to remember that you come first. First, take care and protect yourself, and then do something for the manipulator, if you want. You are not obligated to help the manipulator even if he or she is a loved one. YOU COME, FIRST!

WAIT!!!

READ THIS BEFORE GOING ANY FURTHER!

How would you like to get your next eBook **FREE** <u>and</u> get new books for **FREE** too before they are publicly released?

Join our Self Empowerment Team today and receive your next (and future) books for **FREE**! Signing up is easy and completely free!!

Check out this page for more info!

www.SelfEmpowermentTeam.com/SignUp

Thank you for reading my book...

Don't forget to
leave an honest review...

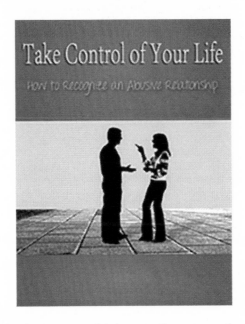

I'd like to offer you this amazing resource which my clients pay for. It is a report I written when I first began my journey.

Click on the picture above or navigate to the website below to join my exclusive email list. Upon joining, you will receive this incredible report on how to recognize an abusive relationship.

If you ask most people on the street what an abusive relationship is, chances are you'd get a description of physical abuse. And yes, that is most certainly an abusive relationship. However, abuse comes in many forms. The actual meaning of abuse is when someone exerts control over another person.

Find out more about recognizing an abusive relationship and learn how to take control over your life by clicking on the book above or by going to this link:

http://tinyurl.com/RecognizeAbusiveRelationship

CONCLUSION

So, summarily, the ideas, tips, and suggestions for recognizing and avoiding gaslighting can be briefly wrapped up.

Gaslighting is a form of manipulation that abusers use to control their victims. The most difficult aspect of identifying gaslighting behavior is that the manipulators skillfully and subtly convince their victims that they are going crazy. The victims believe that they are losing their sanity on their own. Victims get led to a distorted of reality.

Gaslighters are skilled at creating situations and taking advantage of vulnerabilities of victims to undermine them that seem innocuous to the innocent bystander. It takes a lot of practice and skill to identify gaslighting tactics.

Gaslighters use various techniques to achieve their end including withholding, countering, blocking or diverting, trivializing, denying or forgetting, and more to discredit the victims and make them feel that they are losing their minds.

Gaslighting can happen anywhere, including between parents and children, romantic partners, bosses and subordinates, and everywhere else where power dynamics come into play.

There are different kinds of manipulators and gaslighters, and each type uses different mechanisms depending on the need, state of mind of the victim, and other factors.

Manipulators use guilt, aggression, silent treatment, criticism, competition, attacking your self-esteem, and many more methods to control and manipulate you.

Ultimately, victims of gaslighting begin to doubt their own capabilities and realities and come completely under the influence of the manipulators to the extent that the latter control their minds.

Victims suffer from short-term and long-term effects of being in manipulative relationships. The effects on the victim range from sleeplessness, fatigue to chronic depression and even loss of sanity.

While victims feel a lot of pain and agony, manipulators also don't lead happy lives. They are also ridden by guilt, shame, alienation, and loss of love and affection right through their lives. They also need help, and it might make sense to help those who are genuinely looking to change their ways.

Telltale and warning signs of manipulators include:

- Lying and twisting facts

- Discernible shifting between two personality types

- Continually finding fault with you

- Withholding critical information and/or resources and the help of all kinds to weaken your stand

- Running away or blocking/diverting from discussing important topics

- Brushing your ideas and opinions under the carpet

- Trivializing your thoughts, ideas, and your entire life

- Pretending things happened or didn't happen depending on the need

- Suddenly changing the subject

- Shifting blame for all the wrong things on you

- Isolating you from all your loved ones and friends

It is extremely important to stand up for yourself and fight against manipulators and gaslighters so that you can free yourself from their deadly clutches and lead your life on your terms.

Some important lessons you must master in order to stand up against manipulation include building self-awareness, developing confidence, expanding your social and friends circle, taking regular breaks for self-reflection, and reaching out for help when things go out of your control.

When you have been able to get out of the clutches of a manipulator, remember to get back on the recovery track as fast as possible. Learn not to allow the pain and agony of that traumatic experience to eat into your mind so much that you become irrevocably bitter in life.

Instead, find the strength to walk the difficult but happy path of recovery by allowing yourself to heal. Learn to forgive your manipulator because in doing so, you are letting go of the horrible past. Only when you let go can you move forward. Use the lessons learned to spot and stay away from manipulators in the future.

Learn to trust yourself and your intuitive powers. Your intuition is your faithful friend and will never leave you because it is deeply embedded in your psyche. While the trauma of manipulation might have dulled the power of your intuition, it will always be a part of you. Rediscover your ability to connect with your instincts and learn to live a good life.

Remember that no one can manipulate you unless you give them permission. Therefore, know what you want from life and make sure no one else decides how to lead your life. You are the master of your destiny.

And finally, there is plenty of help available to you in the form of family, friends, support groups, and professional counselors. Do not hesitate to reach out and seek help. Remember you are not alone in this fight against gaslighting. So, go and find help and get your life back under your control.

Resources

http://gorovr.com/expanding-social-circle-can-positively-impact-life/

https://blog.melanietoniaevans.com/why-do-people-manipulate/

https://exploringyourmind.com/7-ways-identify-master-manipulator/

https://gaslightingbully.wordpress.com/tag/withholding/

https://journals.sagepub.com/doi/abs/10.1177/0265407512473006

https://liveboldandbloom.com/02/relationships/emotional-manipulation

https://lonerwolf.com/gaslighting/

https://medium.com/@SoulGPS/getting-your-intuition-self-trust-back-online-after-narcissistic-abuse-a5d6247b4bda

https://medium.com/moments-of-passion/why-manipulative-people-manipulate-us-the-child-within-and-how-to-deal-with-them-2d5966c0c400

https://medium.com/the-mission/how-the-power-of-forgiveness-will-set-you-free-8b3c95068bc2

https://peaksrecovery.com/blog/effects-of-psychological-emotional-manipulation

https://positivepsychology.com/self-awareness-matters-how-you-can-be-more-self-aware/

https://psycnet.apa.org/record/1995-05356-001

https://slate.com/human-interest/2016/04/the-history-of-gaslighting-from-films-to-psychoanalysis-to-politics.html

https://themindsjournal.com/gaslighting-signs-psychologically-manipulating/

https://thriveworks.com/blog/gaslighting-techniques-manipulators-undermine-contradict-victims/

https://today.yougov.com/topics/health/articles-reports/2017/06/27/it-could-be-happening-you-3-4-us-adults-dont-know-

https://wehavekids.com/family-relationships/Musts-When-Coping-With-Scheming-Family-Membets

https://workplaceinsight.net/gaslighting-widespread-in-the-uk-workplace/

https://www.aconsciousrethink.com/6766/gaslighting-examples/

https://www.bestofthislife.com/2018/04/boost-self-esteem.html

https://www.businessinsider.in/The-9-terms-and-phrases-you-need-to-know-if-you-think-youre-being-manipulated/2-Object-constancy/slideshow/65718317.cms

https://www.bustle.com/p/7-signs-your-parents-are-gaslighting-you-42457

https://www.entrepreneur.com/article/281874

https://www.goodtherapy.org/blog/psychpedia/gaslighting

https://www.goodtherapy.org/blog/psychpedia/silent-treatment

https://www.harleytherapy.co.uk/counselling/12-steps-to-overcoming-bitterness.htm

https://www.karen-keller.com/content/healthy-competition-vs-manipulation-how-tell-difference

https://www.learning-mind.com/attention-seeking-behavior/

https://www.learning-mind.com/gaslighting-techniques/

https://www.learning-mind.com/manipulation-techniques/ https://time.com/5411624/how-to-tell-if-being-manipulated/

https://www.linkedin.com/pulse/how-deal-sneaky-manipulative-people-dr-isaiah-hankel

https://www.nbcnews.com/better/health/what-gaslighting-how-do-you-know-if-it-s-happening-ncna890866

https://www.powerofpositivity.com/how-to-deal-with-a-manipulative-partner/

https://www.psychologytoday.com/ca/blog/communication-success/201805/12-failures-highly-manipulative-people

https://www.psychologytoday.com/intl/blog/communication-success/201406/how-spot-and-stop-manipulators

https://www.psychologytoday.com/intl/blog/liking-the-child-you-love/201707/5-ways-your-struggling-adult-child-may-be-manipulating-yo

https://www.psychologytoday.com/intl/blog/think-act-be/201811/when-is-it-gaslighting-and-when-is-it-not

https://www.psychologytoday.com/us/blog/enlightened-living/200805/understanding-constancy-in-relationship

https://www.psychologytoday.com/us/blog/here-there-and-everywhere/201701/11-warning-signs-gaslighting

https://www.psychologytoday.com/us/blog/in-flux/201610/9-classic-traits-manipulative-people

https://www.psychologytoday.com/us/blog/mind-in-the-machine/201808/trump-is-gaslighting-america-again-here-s-how-fight-it

https://www.verywellfamily.com/is-someone-gaslighting-you-4147470

https://www.yourtango.com/experts/zita-fekete/6-most-commonplace-tools-used-manipulation

Made in the USA
Middletown, DE
10 January 2020